Common Schools, Uncommon Futures

A WORKING CONSENSUS
FOR SCHOOL RENEWAL

Common Schools, Uncommon Futures

A WORKING CONSENSUS FOR SCHOOL RENEWAL

Edited by Barry S. Kogan

Teachers College, Columbia University
New York and London

Published by Teachers College Press, 1234 Amsterdam Avenue, New York, NY 10027

Copyright © 1997 by Teachers College, Columbia University

Library of Congress Cataloging-in-Publication Data

Common schools, uncommon futures : a working consensus for school
  renewal / edited by Barry S. Kogan.
      p.   cm.
    Papers from two programs on public education held during 1994.
    ISBN 0-8077-3655-4 (cloth : alk. paper).—ISBN 0-8077-3654-6
(pbk. : alk. paper)
      1. Educational change—United States—Congresses. 2. Education—
Aims and objectives—United States—Congresses.   I. Kogan, Barry S.
LA210.C5386   1997
370'.973—DC21   97-22041

ISBN 0-8077-3654-6 (paper)
ISBN 0-8077-3655-4 (cloth)

Printed on acid-free paper
Manufactured in the United States of America

04 03 02 01 00 99 98 97   8 7 6 5 4 3 2 1

If public education flounders, so
does governance in a democracy.
—From the Foreword

Contents

FOREWORD BY JOSEPH STEGER & ALFRED GOTTSCHALK   *ix*
ACKNOWLEDGMENTS   *xi*

Introduction   1

Barry S. Kogan

1   School Reform: The Riddle of Change and Stability   14

    Larry Cuban

2   What Are We Learning About Learning in Schools?   33

    Jerome Bruner

3   Learning, Teaching, and Existential Meaning   49

    Nel Noddings

4   Habits of Mind: Democratic Values and the Creation of
    Effective Learning Communities   60

    Deborah Meier

5   Mobilizing Schools and Communities to Develop Ethics
    and Social Responsibility   74

    Edward T. Joyner

6   Professional Development: Learning from Experience   89

    Lee S. Shulman

7   Preparing Teachers for Twenty-First-Century Schools:
    Teacher Learning in Global Perspective   107

    Albert Shanker

8   Bringing Success to Scale in Public Education: Strategy,
    Designs, and New American Schools   123

    John L. Anderson

9   Building Bridges: How to Make Business–Education
    Partnerships Work   132

    Robert L. Wehling

10 Equity and Liberty in Education Funding   139

    Kern Alexander

11 Equity, Adequacy, and Variable Spending in Public Education 166

    Richard A. Rossmiller

12 An American Primer: A Guide to Democratic School Reform 185

    Joseph Featherstone

ABOUT THE EDITOR AND THE CONTRIBUTORS   211
INDEX   215

Foreword

DEMOCRACY'S FOUNDING BELIEF affirms the value of each individual's participation in governance. The bedrock of that belief is education—especially public education. In order to realize successfully its premise of participation by the people at large, democracy requires broad-based access to learning and communication skills in many forms. If public education flounders, so does governance in a democracy.

Within the last 50 years, two major educational developments have occurred in the United States. The first has been the establishment of the best higher educational system in the world, led largely by the advent of public universities. The second has been the decline of the K–12 educational system, especially in urban areas. This second development has led to reforms, political action, unionization, and new solutions such as "the voucher system" of financing public education. It has not led, however, to any broad public consensus on what is needed to reverse the decline or what the goals of public education should be.

This volume deals with just such questions—what the agenda of public education (K–12) needs to be, what it is to be held accountable for, and whether it is in fact fulfilling its agenda. Certainly, we see evidence of education's failures readily enough in the media and also in our private lives each day. But we see wonderful successes each day as well. To make sense of both kinds of evidence in any effort to rethink and reform public education today, clarity and perspective are indispensable. In recognition of that need, the programs on public education sponsored by the Hebrew Union College–University of Cincinnati Ethics Center were designed to bring such clarity to our public discussion and to provide scope and perspective beyond the individual's experiential analysis.

This volume will help the reader to refocus on the basic issue of education for "what." How do we raise consciousness through the educational process not only to acquire knowledge of salient facts, but also to cultivate what Dr. Albert Schweitzer called "reverence for life."

As one reads this volume, one will certainly gain an appreciation for the complexities facing those who are engaged in turning around primary education's decline in this country. One will also gain both a historical perspective and a healthy respect for the complexity of the issues

facing all of us as citizens. Indeed, we believe that every thoughtful
reader will sense immediately the urgency of dealing with these issues.

Hebrew Union College and the University of Cincinnati are partners
in fostering public awareness and discussion of such issues through our
Ethics Center series. We hope that, in fact, a renewed and expanded public awareness will be the first step in creating solutions for a better
America.

Joseph Steger   Alfred Gottschalk
President   Chancellor
University of Cincinnati   Hebrew Union College–Jewish
                                            Institute of Religion

Acknowledgments

THIS BOOK and the programs on which it is based represent the collaborative efforts of many dedicated individuals. Their energy, ideas, assistance, and encouragement underlie all that follows, and I welcome this opportunity to acknowledge and thank them for helping to make the publication of COMMON SCHOOLS, UNCOMMON FUTURES possible.

Dr. Alfred Gottschalk, Chancellor of Hebrew Union College–Jewish Institute of Religion, and Dr. Joseph Steger, President of the University of Cincinnati, had both expressed strong interest in a program on ethics and education soon after they jointly founded the HUC–UC Ethics Center. After the failure of a major local school-funding levy, they urged the Center to begin planning a major conference on rethinking public education, and so we did. For their initiative in both establishing the Center and supporting this and other discussions of important public issues, I am deeply grateful.

Funding for the conference and various postconference activities was made possible by a generous grant from the Procter & Gamble Fund, with additional support provided by G. E. Aircraft Engines, the Mayerson Academy, and the E. W. Scripps Company. I would specifically like to thank Gerald Gendell, Robert Fitzpatrick, Robert Wehling, Jane Juracek, Larry Roewedder, William Burleigh, and Denise Kuprionis for their efforts on behalf of the Ethics Center.

Valuable suggestions regarding the content and format of the conference came from many individuals. While it is impossible to acknowledge all who offered their ideas, expertise, and advice, I would especially like to express my appreciation to Drs. Betty Steffy, Richard Friedman, Hendrik Gideonse, Nancy Hamant, Louis Castenell, Lois Miller, William Cutter, Michael Zeldin, Isa Aron, and Henry Winkler for their proposals and critical reflections. In addition, Sr. Jean Patrice Harrington, J. Michael Brandt, Monica Curtis, Rosa Blackwell, Raymond Brokamp, Jennifer Cottingham, William Friedlander, Rabbi Sam Joseph, Marvin Koenig, Judy Meiering, Ron Marec, Jack Moreland, Dean Joseph Tomain, Denise Hewitt, and Zakia McKinney contributed many useful ideas during various stages of planning; they also provided welcome feedback as the program took shape. Mr. William Burleigh, CEO of Scripps Howard, and Dr. Henry Winkler, President Emeritus of the University of Cincinnati, were instrumental in bringing William Bennett, former U.S. Secretary of Education, to Cincinnati to lead the opening symposium. The contribution of all these individuals to both the original programs and to the shape of this volume is very great.

Phyllis Binik-Thomas and Jenny Broh, my administrative assistants, have devoted remarkable energy, ingenuity, and care to helping organize the Ethics Center's programs on public education and to preparing the proceedings for publication. Together with Bernadette Fay and Pat Gibbons, who assisted with characteristic skill in scanning and proofreading, they have done an excellent job in bringing these discussions to a wide audience. Warm thanks are also due to Brian Ellerbeck, Sarah Biondello, and Lyn Grossman of Teachers College Press for all their efforts in seeing this volume through the publication process.

Above all others, I want to thank my wife, Steffi, for her steadfast love and encouragement. As always, she readily gave of her time, energy, and good judgment to help me complete various editorial tasks. In the process, she has been my best example of how collaborative learning can generate enthusiasm and sustain its own momentum. With my children, Avi and Elana, she also reintroduced me to the inner world of a public high school and reminded me of what wonderful things good schools can accomplish. Words cannot begin to express my appreciation for all that she has given; one can only give in return. Accordingly, I dedicate this volume to her.

Common Schools, Uncommon Futures

A WORKING CONSENSUS FOR SCHOOL RENEWAL

Introduction

BARRY S. KOGAN

OVER THE PAST HUNDRED years, there has been a remarkable increase in access to public education throughout the United States. This phenomenon was initially a response to the growing urbanization of American society and to successive waves of immigration to our shores. It also reflected the belief of progressive social visionaries that public education was an effective way to respond to the dislocations and excesses of industrialization. Following World War II, the baby boom, and the demise of legalized racial segregation, more egalitarian social and educational ideals, which make public schools the main focus of significant change, have also emerged. All of these factors underscore the importance of public education in our common life, and they have helped to generate successive calls for educational reform as well. While reform efforts have certainly brought many changes to our public schools with respect to goals, curricula, structure, and governance, the impact of these changes on teaching and learning is far less clear. Hence we regularly need to rethink what public education is meant to accomplish and what it is, in fact, accomplishing.

At the most fundamental level, such rethinking is concerned with how to accommodate and do justice to three traditional goals.[1] The first is to transmit the values and habits of mind that fashion character and sustain a common culture. The second is to teach those basic skills that enable a person to enter the world as a productive member of society. The third is to provide each individual with the opportunity to realize his or her full potential. Controversies over educational reform during the past two decades have centered largely on how to realize these educational goals, either individually or in combination. Thus, while advocates of increased federal aid to education held out the prospect of greater resources to accomplish all these goals, opponents expressed concern that such aid compromised state and local control in determining how those same goals should be met. When busing became the principal instrument for ending racial segregation and held out the promise of enabling all students to reach their highest potential, opponents rejected it as likely to compromise that very opportunity. More recently, debates over multicultural education and cultural literacy have raised the question of what constitutes the best means to sustain a common culture consistent with our highest values and traditions. Again, controversies about how to achieve equity in funding public education often turn on whether equity applies simply to providing education in basic skills or whether it also extends to realizing one's full potential.

In an effort to clarify the values at stake in current controversies over educational reform, and to find areas of common ground among diverse opinions, the HUC–UC Ethics Center sponsored two programs on public education during 1994. The first was a symposium, which took place on June 1, 1994, entitled "Funding and Fairness in Public Education." The symposium featured Kern Alexander (Professor of Education Finance, Virginia Polytechnic Institute) and Richard A. Rossmiller (Professor of Education Finance and Administration, University of Wisconsin). This in-depth discussion was convened for educational professionals and community leaders in the Cincinnati area.

The second program was a national conference on "Rethinking Public Education: Teaching and Learning for Life" held on November 6–8, 1994. Underscoring the importance of educational issues in the tristate region of Ohio, Indiana, and Kentucky, teachers and administrators from public, parochial, and private schools, school board members, parents, college educators, high school and college students preparing for careers in education, and community leaders attended this program. Those addressing the conference either as panelists on its opening night or featured speakers included: William J. Bennett (former U.S. Secretary of Education), John L. Anderson (President, New American Schools Development Corporation), Lynwood L. Battle (former President, Cincinnati Board of Education), Jerome Bruner (Research Professor of Psychology, New York University), Larry Cuban (Professor of Education, Stanford University), Joseph Featherstone (Professor of Education, Michigan State University), Sr. Jean Patrice Harrington (former President, College of Mount St. Joseph), Theresa Henderson (Director, Coalition of Innovative Schools), Edward T. Joyner (Director, Comer Project for Change in Education, Yale University), Deborah Meier (Co-Director, Central Park East Secondary Schools, New York City), Judith A. Meiering (Social Studies Chair, Walnut Hills High School, Cincinnati), Nel Noddings (Professor of Child

Education, Stanford University), Albert Shanker (President, American Federation of Teachers), Lee S. Shulman (Professor of Education and Director, Carnegie Project for the Advancement of Teaching, Stanford University), Joseph P. Tomain (Dean and Professor of Law, University of Cincinnati), and Robert L. Wehling (Senior Vice-President, Procter & Gamble Company). The topics they addressed included a progress report on public schools in America; the theory and practice of what we are learning about learning; how families, schools, and community support networks can foster educational success; the emergence of business–education partnerships; how to prepare teachers for twenty-first-century schools; the moral and practical problems of education finance; and, finally, the political dimension of school reform. Taken together, their presentations offered an unusually insightful and welcome overview of current thinking on educational reform in the United States.

This volume contains all of the formal presentations delivered at the symposium on educational finance and the conference on rethinking public education. In several cases the papers are significantly expanded beyond the oral presentation. The discussions and exchanges that took place in the opening symposium of the conference do not appear here but are available in an edited videotape format from the HUC–UC Ethics Center under the title "Education as a Public Good and as a Private Good." The highlights of the formal presentations are summarized briefly in what follows.

Larry Cuban illuminates the historical context of recent reform efforts by identifying a persistent paradox in the reform process and suggesting a solution to it. The paradox is that despite numerous changes in school and district organization, these changes have had little impact on actual teaching practices, especially in big-city and rural districts. He distinguishes among organizational-effectiveness reformers, who seek to bring coherence, clarity, and agreed-upon national standards into all levels of the educational process; pedagogical reformers, who want to change how teachers communicate content and skills to their students; and blended reformers, who are committed to bringing about fundamental changes in both areas. After tracing the impact of each of these reform programs on the three tiers of American public schools (affluent school districts, suburban and small school districts, big city and rural districts with large numbers of minority and/or poor children), Cuban proposes his own solution to the original puzzle. The reason schools so often seem both change-prone and change-resistant is that reformers and practitioners all too often inhabit different worlds and talk past one another. Organizational effectiveness and even pedagogical reformers typically focus on policies, programs, incentives, laws, and ideas. While they can succeed in creating a new prevailing wisdom, they have little impact upon actual classroom practice until the teachers' ideas and skills are brought into the equation. Thus real and lasting school reform either takes place in the classroom, and even then very slowly, or it does not take place at all. Accordingly, reformers of all kinds will want to pay much closer attention to classroom practice if the mistakes and disappointments associated with past reform efforts are to be overcome.

Jerome Bruner proceeds to map out what we have learned about learning in schools by identifying three antinomies, or paradoxes, that characterize our revolutionary times. They represent, in effect, the enduring but conflicting truths about education today. The first antinomy holds that the function of education is to enable people to achieve their fullest potential, and also that the function of education is to reproduce and carry forward the culture that supports it. The second antinomy maintains that learning is a process that unfolds within the individual mind so that learners must rely on their own intelligence and motivation in order to benefit from it, and also that learning is essentially a collective process, situated in and determined by one's environment, which either favors or discourages certain ways of thinking, knowing, and mastering skills. The third antinomy proposes that individual experience is ultimately self-validating and not to be reduced to some "higher," more authoritative, universal framework, while maintaining, by contrast, that individual experience ceases to be meaningful if it is not rooted in what is authoritative and universal in our culture. Bruner then traces the history of experiments showing the effects of deprivation on learning and cognitive development, which led to the creation of the Head Start program. In assessing its accomplishments and limitations as a microcosm of the learning process, his key conclusion is that learning is most effective when children and adults collaborate together in enabling communities. When everyone helps in the teaching process, children contribute to constructing knowledge rather than merely finding it and, in some cases, gain a much-needed sense of their own abilities. In addition, by treating learners as capable and responsible members of the collaborative community, we increase the possibility that more learners will enter it. Bruner concludes his essay with an analysis of how each of the opposing ideas in the three antinomies express themselves in our culture today. While noting the stresses, sacrifices, and trade-offs generated by these antinomies, he also points out that when learning is "participatory, proactive, communal, collaborative, and given over to constructing meanings," the interaction of teachers and students can create the scaffolding that builds cultural cohesion as well as individual development. Because teachers are uniquely situated to help create this collaborative culture, they should be given a far more prominent role in serious discussion of educational reform than they presently have.

Nel Noddings emphasizes that the link between effective teaching and the motivation to learn consists largely in a capacity to find existential meaning in what one is studying. The reason for this is that a sense of who we are naturally guides both what we are willing to learn and what we are willing to do. Beyond that, a learner's capacity to retain what has been learned depends on continually using it and/or finding personal significance in it. What we learn incidentally can be a very powerful factor both in opening up new vistas and perspectives on some aspect of the world and in establishing deep connections to our personal experience. Thus what a teacher says incidentally about the dignity of labor, for example, may change one's entire outlook on life and establish a bond of trust with the world. What the teacher communicates at this level, as Martin Buber suggested, is not content as much as the experience that meaninglessness cannot be the real truth, no matter how hard one is pressed by it. The student's dilemma is somehow to find an answer to the question: How can I know what I am supposed to do, when I do not know who I am? The teacher's task in turn is to acknowledge the student's dilemma, to sharpen it, and to share it. But ultimately it is to clarify which qualities in life are always highly valued, which are never valued, and which will keep many possibilities in all desirable directions open to a student. This is the kind of education that is capable of having the most enduring impact. It is not the result of artificially imposed outcomes in traditional disciplines but a matter of students recognizing what they are to do by first learning who they are and what is worth their aspiring to become.

In her essay, Deborah Meier identifies, as essential components of any functioning democratic society, five habits of mind that need to be cultivated in public schools.[2] These habits of mind call for supplying evidence to support one's claims; being able to identify the perspective from which a claim is made; making connections among ideas, events, and texts; being able to imagine what would happen if things were otherwise; and being able to show the importance of what is at issue. Even these five habits are reducible to two: skepticism and empathy. But, however they are enumerated, these habits of mind aim at fashioning thoughtful, informed, and active citizens who respect one another and can work together to resolve common problems. Meier argues that public schools are the most natural place in which to create communities of thoughtful students. For more than two decades, the Central Park East Secondary School, followed by several other small schools influenced by the work of Ted Sizer of Brown University, has enjoyed increasing success in devel-

oping these habits of mind in its students. As a requirement for graduation, the students must demonstrate their mastery of the five habits in
both traditional and interdisciplinary fields. What enables them to do so
is the safe, supportive environment and shared culture of the school. That
culture encourages close collegial interaction among the teachers as
thoughtful adults and close collaborative interactions between teachers
and students designed to develop the latter into thoughtful young
people. Both the small size of the school community and the provision of
sufficient time for members and stakeholders to meet together are essential to the success of this new structure. But most important of all are the
five habits of mind themselves, which allow for the development of the
school's shared culture. Exceptional schools like Central Park East Secondary School and its associated schools have proved that small, self-
governing communities of learning can really work. The next task is to
develop new ways to create a "system of exceptions" like them.

In attempting to identify what single factor contributes more than
any other to developing ethics and social responsibility in children, Edward Joyner contends that it is the norms and values of closely knit
groups of adults expressing approval and disapproval in appropriate situations. Today, however, the power of adults to shape behavior is significantly compromised by their failure to provide positive models worthy
of emulation and by the fragmentation of efforts by caregivers to create
standards that will foster socially acceptable behavior. Still, these problems can be overcome when schools, families, and community groups
collaborate with each other to create both a common set of values and
expectations for children and the kinds of programs and activities capable of realizing them. Building upon the work of James Comer and Eric
Schaps, he outlines six pathways that are needed to foster the optimal
development of the whole child. They are: the physical pathway, the cognitive pathway, the psycho-emotional pathway, the language pathway, the
social pathway, and the moral pathway. Taken together, these six pathways represent a framework for understanding and analyzing a student's
behavior. In addition, they can also serve as the foci of integrated pro-
gramming by schools and community groups that can best represent the
"conspiracy of adults" needed to nurture the moral development of children. Joyner devotes the remainder of his essay to clarifying the overlap-
ping processes developed by Comer and Schaps to create the necessary
synergy among parents, teachers, children, mental health professionals,
and community members.

Characterizing himself as a pedagogical reformer, Lee Shulman argues that the success of any reform program ultimately depends upon
the interaction between teachers and students. Based on his 30 years of

research in the area, he finds that what makes teaching so difficult is the extraordinary complexity of that interaction. It is chiefly the teacher's task to manage such complexity on an ongoing basis. When a teacher does this successfully and things work in practice, we should try to clarify and learn from what David Hawkins calls "the wisdom of practice." Typically, such wisdom is isolated and unarticulated. Nevertheless, it certainly exists and constitutes the real basis for learning from experience.

To illustrate, Shulman reflects upon the work of Mary Budd Rowe in showing the positive correlation between teachers allowing a longer interval, or wait-time, between their questions and the student's response and the likelihood that more thoughtful, higher-order answers to such questions will be given. Yet even after teachers had been trained to provide longer wait-times between their questions and student responses, there was relatively little change in actual classroom practice. After considering several possible reasons for this, Shulman concludes that increasing the wait-time would also have the effect of turning safe, manageable classrooms into "intellectual minefields" that would severely challenge any teacher's knowledge, organizational skills, and patience. The work of Deborah Ball in teaching mathematics for deep understanding reveals the same negative possibilities but also shows how the unpredictability of higher-order answers can be successfully nurtured to enhance the learning process. The indispensable requirement for such nurturing is that teachers be continuous learners themselves. Shulman then elaborates on the principles that make this possible for all learners and the specific contexts and communal settings that make learning for deep understanding possible for teachers. In essence, collaborative groups of teachers, who talk with each other about their work within both school and out-of-school networks, make the decisive difference. Thus, if school reform is to be successful, it will have to support teacher learning no less than student learning and create the kinds of structures that will enable teachers to cope with the risks of learning for deep understanding.

Albert Shanker expresses skepticism about several of the key assumptions underlying calls for radical reform in education today. One assumption is that the traditional model of education, which stresses the centrality of the teacher in conveying information to students, simply does not work, even though there is much evidence, especially from abroad, that it does. A second assumption is that the current system is rigidly focused on academic mastery, when in fact the values of socialization, inclusion, and nonrigidity outweigh academic emphasis. Another assumption is that frequent testing makes our public schools high-stakes institutions, even though schools and students can fail on nearly every indicator without suffering consequences in terms of promotion, college admission, and other measures of advancement. Increasingly, colleges and universities have accommodated themselves to this development by providing remediation within their own programs. Shanker also compares the results of American public education with those of England, France, Germany, and Japan, and notes that these nations produce far higher proportions of well-trained students with less testing than do our own programs. He attributes their success to reliance on explicit standards of what students should know at various junctures, judicious use of testing with real stakes, and tracking at crucial junctures in the educational process. Once real standards and stakes become part of the culture, this fact works to reinforce those standards and empower both parents and teachers in helping students to achieve them. The additional advantage is that teachers know exactly what they need to teach at any given level of the curriculum.

Accordingly, Shanker stresses that successful teaching requires solid mastery of subject matter and real opportunities for teacher learning, particularly within collaborative frameworks. He notes that teachers in China plan lessons jointly, then go off and teach, and finally return to discuss the results and how they can be improved. They see themselves as artists working together to polish a gem. By contrast, most American teachers prepare, teach, and reflect on the results as individuals. While they also regard themselves as artists, their artistry is more like that of writing a concerto and playing it at the same time. This approach may provide teachers with maximum flexibility, but it works against having common objectives, a shared curriculum, clear standards of achievement, and solid mastery of all the subjects taught. Thus he concludes that we need a system of assessment to test teachers' knowledge of subject matter before they go out to teach, just as we have for physicians, accountants, and lawyers about to enter their professions. Continuing education should aim at bringing teachers out of isolated teaching situations and self-contained classrooms in order to jointly develop their skills, refine their knowledge, discuss their goals, and review their techniques. Teachers will also need to be given opportunities to experience new models of teaching with clear incentives to take advantage of those opportunities.

John Anderson devotes his essay to describing New American Schools (NAS), an initiative undertaken by corporation and foundation leaders to create systems of high-performance schools for all students. The mission of NAS is to design, test, integrate, and disseminate new and creative approaches to school management, governance, and structure. Its overall plan reflects the work of seven design teams comprised of creative thinkers in business, education, science, and the humanities; their aims, in turn, embrace both school-based and systemic reforms. The work of these teams involves designing interdisciplinary curricula, models for project-based instruction, consensus-building forms of governance to reduce excessive bureaucracy, new ways of integrating computer and communications technology into the learning process, and, finally, building alliances and networks among stakeholders to provide resources and professional support for positive change. The success of the plan depends upon creating a critical mass of schools within a jurisdiction that are prepared to implement the work of NAS's design teams and lead the way in extending improvements outward into the system. The environment needed to foster such change is one that gives individual schools a high degree of autonomy. This would include control over internal spending; the power to hire, train, and release staff; local control over curriculum and instructional strategies; freedom to raise performance standards; and opportunities for students and parents to choose to attend or leave a particular school. By focusing in this way on both individual school improvement and systemwide transformation, Anderson and his colleagues hope to be able to produce not only change but also a self-sustaining process that will endure.

In his essay, Robert Wehling underscores the fact that business–education partnerships can help to create strategic alliances among schools, communities, and government that can contribute significantly to making educational reforms work. While many business leaders have volunteered their services and expertise in such efforts, enduring partnerships have nevertheless proved difficult to forge and sustain. After analyzing the reasons why this is the case, Wehling identifies a series of models in which such partnerships have proved to be successful and produced impressive results over time.

One such partnership is the Cincinnati Youth Collaborative, which has helped to build bridges between youth culture and adult culture, and between school and the workplace, while also providing disadvantaged students with new opportunities for mentoring, guidance, and support in planning for their future. A second model is the Ohio Education Improvement Consortium, which represents a statewide partnership of businesses, teachers' unions, school administrators, PTAs, chambers of commerce, business roundtables, the NAACP, the Council of Churches, and the Inter-University Council of Ohio. Through the consortium, all the key players in supporting educational success can jointly work out a coherent agenda for meaningful reforms on all levels. Wehling describes several of the tasks that such alliances have successfully addressed and the ways in which a combination of mandates, support, and extended autonomy help to bring about positive change. He concludes by noting that there are three common denominators for genuine success in business–education partnerships: finding people who will take personal and passionate responsibility for producing successful results over the long haul, involving all stakeholders in the process, and staying in communication with them through good times and bad.

Kern Alexander addresses the question of whether, under a republican form of government, citizens in one school district can legitimately claim that they have no moral or legal obligation to educate children in other school districts on a level equal to the education of their own children. Based on his analysis of cases such as *DeRolph v. Ohio* (1994), in which lower courts have found wide disparities in state education funding per pupil to be unacceptable, he provides a comprehensive overview of the principles and arguments underlying this litigation.

Precisely because education is essential to self-government and the exercise of liberty, Alexander maintains that equity in funding is the fundamental obligation of both the citizenry and the states. When republican forms of government function as they should, they are dedicated to promoting the public interest above self-interest. Providing the widest possible access to education comes naturally under that public interest. After tracing the origins of the case for equity in both funding and access to education back to Rousseau, Kant, and ultimately the Golden Rule, Alexander explores in detail the various types of inequality that affect public education today. State-created inequality through the malapportionment of revenues for education turns out to be the most egregious kind of inequality. The remainder of the essay examines closely the grounds that warrant deviation from absolute equality in funding, such as those that address different educational needs, and criticizes the reasons most commonly offered to justify state-created inequality, which include the availability of adequate funding and the need for local control. The thread that underlies Alexander's argument throughout is that the foundation of liberty is a social contract that aims at the common good. Liberty, in turn, is construed not as the absence of constraint but as the result of adhering to just and equitable laws. It is when legislatures fail to establish such laws that those who are disadvantaged by unjust ones naturally turn to the courts for redress.

Richard Rossmiller responds to Alexander's moral and political defense of funding equity with a historical analysis of how our conception of fairness in providing educational opportunity has changed over the last 200 years. His analysis culminates in a series of suggestions on how to ensure improved fairness and adequacy in funding without sacrificing local control. Rossmiller contends that concepts of equal educational opportunity have evolved from having common schools to teach reading in early colonial New England, to having schools able to provide a basic education for those entering the work force in the late eighteenth to the early twentieth centuries, to providing equal spending per pupil in the first half of the twentieth century, to providing variable spending suited to each pupil's needs in the 1960s to the present, to ensuring equal outcomes in educational attainment today. Litigation over the past 30 years has focused primarily on the constitutionality of state funding arrangements that permit wide disparities in per-pupil expenditures. However, because there is no agreement on what standards to apply in determining how much disparity in funding is permissible, only about half of the suits lodged by plaintiffs have been successful. Even in these cases, as Rossmiller points out, the courts have not in any way endorsed the principle of equal spending per pupil. If they were to do so, funding would be equalized at levels far below what is adequate to educate students to reach their full potential. Accordingly, Rossmiller argues that states should aim at funding an adequate basic education for every child within the state, following models developed by Cubberly, Updegraf, Strayer, and Haig. Assuming that the minimum level of adequacy is met, local school districts should have the authority to tax themselves above that minimum up to a fixed limit (175%), since local school districts represent the most effective means of generating school improvement. Even here, the state should maintain a level playing field by recourse to "power equalizing," that is, allotting a portion of state tax revenues to equalize funding in all districts within the state that are at or below a specific level of per-pupil expenditure.

Finally, Joseph Featherstone's guidelines for democratic school reform highlight many of the themes discussed at the conference and outline both their political and educational ramifications. He contends that school reform is inevitably part of a political process in which different values about what is required to prepare students to participate in the life of the community are at odds. Acknowledging this political dimension can help make the debates about school reform both more civil and more fruitful. It would teach us, for example, to appreciate the antinomies described by Jerome Bruner and to learn to live with complexity and ambiguity, since certain tensions are never finally resolved. Within our polity, it could foster a vision of schools and even classrooms as embryonic democracies that place a premium on participation by all stakeholders, like those developed by Deborah Meier. Such an acknowledgment would also suggest important standards of evaluation by identifying groups excluded from the process, such as teachers and poor kids, as noted by Larry Cuban, and distinguishing between substantive and symbolic reforms such as funded and unfunded mandates.

Seeing school reform as a form of tug-of-war between competing interests and visions of society, Featherstone stresses the importance of identifying the point of view from which questions about educational reform are asked. Consequently, his primer emphasizes the need to understand who is reforming whom and who sets the standards of what counts as success or failure in educational reform. The goal in raising these questions is to gain a long-term perspective on the reform process rather than to merely follow a succession of educational fads. Building on the work of Berliner and Biddle, he examines in succession unfounded claims about American public schools, the real problems that beset them, and the issues that most need to be addressed in connection with school reform. Featherstone readily acknowledges that reform as such is not always positive and that often good practice is impaired by reform. As illustrations, he contrasts administrative progressives during the past century, who advocated a "one best system" approach, with contemporary proponents of the local, "hybridized" democratic community approach. The former generally advocated large-scale change in schools, introduced from the outside by reformers, while the latter generally support site-based, incremental change initiated by parents, teachers, and community members working from the inside outward. It is also this latter tradition that makes equality central to its purposes in an effort to reestablish a sense of mutuality and shared meaning within the learning process. By favoring reforms that support the development of teachers and pedagogy, build upon the wisdom of practice, and give the poor an equal opportunity for educational advancement, Featherstone identifies the ultimate goal of educational reform as one of encouraging the widest possible participation in the adult activities of work, culture, and politics.

We may say, in conclusion, that despite the diverse perspectives and periodic disagreements revealed in these essays, their authors clearly share a growing, albeit cautious, confidence that public schools can change and make significant improvements in the education students receive. It is a confidence rooted in numerous examples of successful reform, from the Comer Project for a Change in Education to Central Park East Secondary School, that emphasize continuous collaboration among stakeholders in the educational process, shared reflection on what is being done and what needs to be done, and the creation of networks and communities capable of supporting these reforms. Whether the focus of such efforts is on the individual classroom, a school system, or national structures, there is definitely a renewed concern in these discussions with attaining mastery of traditional areas such as mathematics, science, and the humanities. Such mastery, however, is no longer defined primarily by test scores. It is also measured by the integration and display of what is learned in relation to real-life situations that the students can expect to experience for themselves. Thus projects and portfolios tell a fuller and more nuanced story about a student's level of achievement than grades and test scores alone. Yet even here, intellectual achievement is recognized as only one aspect of an educator's concern in teaching. Cultivating critical habits of mind and heart that encourage sharing responsibility in solving common problems and developing all available pathways by which to educate the whole child are equally important concerns. The vision of successful learning articulated in this volume is thus a holistic one. It is an ongoing process that is active and collaborative in character, rooted in the learner's affects and aspirations, designed to construct both knowledge and meaning, and sustained by a community committed to the learning process itself. It is a vision that is applicable in principle to teachers and students alike, since it reflects "the wisdom of practice" when learning is optimal for both groups. As a product of continuous reflection, this vision will certainly be reformulated and refined further. Still, its overall shape is increasingly clear. The question that remains largely unanswered is how such a vision of successful learning can be extended as equitably as possible throughout our educational system. To answer it, the work of rethinking public education will have to be as continuous and collaborative as the vision of learning that nurtures it.

NOTES

1. I would like to thank Dr. Michael Zeldin, Professor of Education at Hebrew Union College–Jewish Institute of Religion, Los Angeles, for describing to me these three goals of education and clarifying their relationship to one another.

2. I would like to thank Dr. Nancy Hamant, Associate Professor of Education and Co-ordinator of Field Experiences at the University of Cincinnati College of Education, for her helpful summary comments on the presentations made by Deborah Meier and John Anderson.

School Reform: The Riddle of Change and Stability

LARRY CUBAN

EXACTLY TWO DECADES ago, I became superintendent of the Arlington, Virginia, public schools. Shrinking enrollments and increasing numbers of minority students had set off tremors in the community over falling test scores and a perceived decline in the schools' academic quality. Mainstream wisdom among federal officials then was that schools do not make much of a difference in children's lives. Policy makers cited major research studies that supposedly proved that spending money on schools failed to yield returns in students' test scores (Coleman et al. 1966; Jencks et al. 1972).

Just as other school boards around the country did, the Arlington School Board resisted that gloomy "wisdom" and made changes. All courses of study, texts, tests, and staff evaluations were aligned with the school board's instructional goals. Teachers and principals worked together in drawing up plans for their school's improvement. To be accountable to parents and taxpayers, each school published information about its enrollment and performance annually (Cuban 1988).

What occurred in Arlington in the mid-1970s was a brief preview of coming attractions for the Effective Schools movement that swept across the nation in the following decade and continues today in many districts. The central beliefs fueling the Effective Schools movement became a national agenda for change: All children can learn; schools must have high academic standards; for a school to succeed, its goals, texts, tests, and the curriculum must be tightly coupled; and, finally, published test scores will prove to a skeptical public that schools are accountable. That should sound familiar to ears attuned to the policy talk about schools in the mid-1990s (Cuban 1993).

For those who appreciate irony, consider that within two decades policy-maker "wisdom" on schooling has flip-flopped from schools not making much difference in children's lives to the school being the single most important instrument in securing equity and excellence for all children. But that 180-degree change in mainstream policy wisdom is not the only change that has occurred. In Arlington, as elsewhere in the country, there have been in the last two decades many changes in school governance, organization, and curriculum.

Those who scold schools for being highly resistant to planned changes, impervious to reform, and led by individuals who dig in their heels at the slightest hint of change are ignorant of the history of school reform. Changes in mainstream policy wisdom, governance, organization, and curriculum have occurred repeatedly throughout the last century and a half of American schooling.

It is precisely this puzzle that appeals to the practitioner and historian parts of me. Although school boards, administrators, and teachers pursue planned changes often, they have the reputation among state and national policy makers, foundation officials, corporate leaders, and academic experts of stubbornly resisting reformers' 24-carat-gold ideas that will, according to their advocates, improve the conduct of schooling. This gap between reality and reputation needs to be explored because such confusion over whether schools are, indeed, change-prone or change-resistant institutions (or some combination of both) makes a considerable difference in what strategies current reformers choose to pursue.

To explore this gap, I will examine the origins of the last decade of school reform, the second longest uninterrupted period of such activity since the turn of the twentieth century, and point out which changes have been adopted and implemented and which ones have not. I begin by asking: Why has there been more than a decade of school reform?

REFORM SINCE THE EARLY 1980s

For well over 10 years, U.S. presidents, corporate leaders, and critics have blamed public schools for contributing to a globally less competitive economy, sinking productivity, and the exodus of jobs overseas. The United States, as the highly popular *Nation at Risk* report put it in 1983, had educationally disarmed itself in a hostile economic war. "If only to keep and improve on the slim competitive edge we still retain in world markets," the report said, "we must dedicate ourselves to the reform of our educational system" (National Commission on Excellence in Education 1983, 7).

Since then, most states have legislated higher graduation requirements, a longer school year, new curricula, and more tests. In the late 1980s, another surge of reform began delegating to teachers more professional authority in making schoolwide decisions. Reformers argued that unless teachers were deeply involved in making school-site changes, little could happen in their classrooms to increase student academic achievement. Other reformers desired student-centered classrooms, seeking to change how teachers customarily taught. In the early 1990s, another wave of national reformers seeking better schools as an engine for a better economy crowned their efforts with strong bipartisan support for President Clinton's educational bill, which set eight national goals while establishing curricular standards and tests that would prod 15,000 school districts to reach those goals (Murphy 1989; Smith and O'Day 1991b, 233–267).

Thus over the last decade diverse groups of reformers have advocated changes in school governance, organization, curriculum, and classroom teaching. Some reformers were far more interested in reorganizing the system of schooling; others were far more interested in altering how teachers taught content and skills. Still others shared a mix of these agendas. To keep track of these diverse reformers, I will call those interested in reshaping schools to make them work better "organizational-effectiveness reformers." These reformers were largely national and state policy makers, corporate leaders, foundation officials, occasional academic experts, and a smattering of school district administrators. They enjoyed access to media and drafted legislation.

I call those interested in getting teachers to create student-centered, reasoning-driven classrooms "pedagogical reformers." These reformers were largely academic entrepreneurs and researchers and groups of practitioners funded by sympathetic corporate and foundation officials. Lacking the access to the media that organizational-effectiveness reformers had, these pedagogical reformers nonetheless wrote for academic journals and practitioner magazines. They occasionally appeared on national news shows or testified before state and federal committees considering school reforms. But they lacked political clout and access to media to either mobilize coalitions or draft legislation.

Finally, there were those reformers who were eager for both the organizational-effectiveness and pedagogical agendas. They not only sought improved classroom practices but also wanted to make teaching a stronger profession through involving practitioners in school-site decision making. I label this group "blended reformers."

The organizational-effectiveness reformers dominated the political agendas for school reform in the 1980s and 1990s. They mobilized state and national coalitions, bringing together corporate leaders, foundation officials, union officers, and educators from both political parties. They drafted bipartisan legislation and lobbied for swift implementation of their reforms. What brought them together was a consensus over the goals of improving students' academic achievement, enhancing teacher professionalism, and making schools accountable—all to be achieved as cheaply as possible in an era of huge federal budget deficits (Cuban 1993; Elmore 1990).

But what was the fundamental problem that these organizational-effectiveness reformers said had to be solved in order for these goals to be met? They saw the central problem of American schooling as a fragmented policy system with too much dispersed power and little alignment between goals and actions. Such splintered decentralization prevented gains in academic achievement, teacher professionalism, and school accountability. Thus an organizational solution to the problems of schooling was constructed and eventually named "systemic reform." It became mainstream policy wisdom in the mid-1990s and was embedded in the Goals 2000 legislation (Cohen and Spillane 1991; Smith and O'Day 1991b, 233–267).

The assumptions and logic of systemic reform went like this: For the United States to regain economic competitiveness, every isolated fragment of what we know as public schooling—its diverse goals, 50 different state curricula, varied texts and tests, uncoordinated teacher education—must be aligned to work in concert, as they do in many European nations. Professional groups must agree on curricular standards. Policy makers must figure out how to assess the achievement of those standards because once students clearly see the link between their school performance and getting jobs or being admitted to colleges, they will work harder.

But with a large, bottom-heavy system of public schooling—comprised of 42 million students, more than 2 million teachers, well over 100,000 schools, and 15,000 districts in 50 states—how do you move this unwieldy, fragmented system toward some uniformity? Among mainstream policy makers of both political parties, the answer was clear: Set national goals and then forge curricular standards and tests built upon the work of many pace-setting states during the 1980s.

So a more aggressive federal role in education called for setting national goals, curricular standards, and tests that were tied to a "voluntary" national curriculum created by professional groups. Moreover, the federal government established incentives to spur state and local improvement and penalties to prod laggards. What states, districts, and local schools were to do, as in the corporate world, was to figure out how best to reach those goals and then find out through national tests how they had done.

Since the early 1980s, many states led by organizational-effectiveness reformers have increasingly come to align their goals, curricula, texts, and tests. Districts and schools across the nation have changed their governance, organization, and curriculum in the last decade. Goals 2000 legislation established agencies to monitor and assess national standards. Although it is premature to assess the effects of systemic reform, some researchers have argued that the earlier surges of reform in the 1980s have already had the desired effects (Kirst and Kelley 1993; Murphy 1989).

Regarding courses taken, for example, they point out that more students—male and female, minority and majority—now take academic subjects than in the 1970s. More students take tough Advanced Placement (AP) courses. In 1991, more than one out of four students taking AP courses were from minority groups, double the rate of a decade earlier. More and more states have adopted curricular frameworks in math, science, and other subjects and either have aligned their state tests to these curricula or are now doing so (Kirst and Kelley 1993).

Insofar as test scores are concerned, reading proficiency has remained fairly constant in these years, but test score results in math and science on the National Assessment of Educational Progress (NAEP) have shown gains for younger students throughout the 1980s. These gains occurred most often among the lowest-scoring students. Minority students began to close the gap in scores between themselves and white students, although the gap remains quite large. Even SAT (formerly the Scholastic Aptitude Test and now renamed the Scholastic Assessment Test) scores no longer declined during the 1980s. They remained stable, with slight gains in average math scores. Finally, overall dropout rates declined during the 1980s. Among blacks, 78% of 19- and 20-year-olds had completed high school or received the General Equivalency Diploma (GED). Organizational effectiveness reformers point to such figures as evidence of their success (Kirst and Kelley 1993).

They are also interested in accountability and point to the spread of public reporting of information on school and individual student performance. Moreover, the application of business methods to enhance efficiency in schools through eliminating middle-management positions, introducing pay-for-performance clauses in administrator contracts, and privatizing certain school operations has become common across the country (Bradley 1993; Capper and Jamison 1993; Harp 1992; Rothman 1993).

For pedagogical reformers deeply interested in reshaping both content and practice in classrooms, the focus on establishing curricular standards in different subjects over the last decade in math, science, history, and other disciplines has been a decided plus. These new curricula have embedded within them the recent findings of cognitive psychologists about children's learning and the heartfelt dreams of those practitioners who have sought student-centered pedagogies. The math standards created by the National Council of Teachers of Mathematics (NCTM), for example, aimed at increasing student understanding of concepts using real-world problems, have been adopted by almost all states. So, too, have some of these reformers embraced interactive computer software as a direction that will shift the teacher's role from that of chief of class operations to that of coach (Cohen and McLaughlin 1993; Gardner 1991; NCTM 1989).

Insofar as measuring actual shifts toward student-centered instruction is concerned, however, no recent national studies on classroom practices have been yet undertaken. While magazine and televised stories do profile unusual classrooms where teachers use the new pedagogies, different studies of how teachers are teaching the new math and other subjects have revealed, if anything, stubborn problems of implementation and varied classroom results. The picture, then, is decidedly blurred when it comes to determining how many teachers have embraced the beliefs and materials embedded in the new curricula and altered their routine classroom practices (Cohen and Ball 1990; Darling-Hammond 1990; Elmore and McLaughlin 1988; Peterson et al. 1993).

The blended reformers, deeply interested in empowering teachers, have pointed to the growth of shared decision making in schools and the rapid spread of site-based management teams as signs of success. Strong linkages between teacher decision making and pedagogical changes, however, are still beyond the reach of researchers' studies. No such connections have yet emerged (Malen et al. 1990, 289–342).

So after a decade of sustained and determined school reform aimed at building a better economy, many changes in school governance, organization, and curriculum have been adopted and implemented. There is evidence of gains in academic achievement, spreading teacher involvement in school-site decision making, and accountability. Furthermore, the framework of systemic reform is now law and in place, although a Republican-dominated Congress since 1994 has considerably slowed its implementation. If achieving reform is measured by the number of changes that have been put into practice, organizational effectiveness and blended reformers have been strikingly successful. It is, however, still unclear whether the pedagogical reformers have succeeded in having their ideas alter existing classroom practices.

There is, however, another system out there beyond the fragmented,

multilayered political system of federal, state, and local districts that reformers have targeted. I speak of a three-tiered social system of schooling
and inequalities in funding and student outcomes that have hardly
changed in the last few decades of intense national, state, and local school
reform. Substantial portions of that three-tiered social system of public
schooling have so far escaped the effects of the politically driven systemic
reform. In describing this three-tiered social system, I will connect reformers' work to each of these tiers.

THE LIMITS OF SYSTEMIC REFORM: THE SOCIAL SYSTEM OF SCHOOLING

The top tier of American schools, serving less than 10% of all students,
work with mostly affluent, white communities and send four out of five
of their graduates to higher education. These schools in the Palo Altos
(California), Beachwoods (Ohio), Princetons (New Jersey), and Great
Necks (New York) of the country already meet or exceed the national
goals, and their students do very well on state and national tests. Recent
reforms have had little influence on their organization, governance, curriculum, and pedagogy, since most parents, teachers, and administrators
are largely satisfied with what the districts offer to their children and seek
no major changes in existing practices (Coleman et al. 1966; Wise 1968).

The second tier is the largest, comprising about half of all American
schools. These suburban and small school districts have decent test scores
on national standardized tests; about half or more of their graduates go
on to college, and they are able to secure adequate community resources
to fund a range of school services. Second-tier schools have responded
vigorously to the organizational-effectiveness, pedagogical, and blended
reformers in recent decades. New curricula have been added; multicultural programs for the gifted, "at-risk," and disabled have been
adopted; computers have been purchased. Site-based management teams
have been organized. Teachers have been retrained in the newest ways of
getting students to learn. National goals, curricula, and tests will continue to spur these schools to work harder (National Assessment of Chapter 1 Independent Review Panel 1993; Tyree 1993; U.S. General Accounting Office 1989).

In the bottom tier, consisting of more than one-third of all schools,
are schools in mainly big-city districts with large percentages of minority
and poor children.[1] They, too, have been the target of reformers' passion
for national goals, standards, tests, enhanced professional power, and
student-centered classrooms, but these schools have largely fallen beyond

the reach of these well-publicized national reforms (Kantor and Brenzel 1992; Kozol 1991; Orfield and Ashkinaze 1991).

Their stories seldom make the newspaper's front page or lead the 6:00 P.M. TV news anymore except when an honor-roll student is slain or guns are found in a school. The high percentages of dropouts and teenage pregnancies that make up the topography of these urban schools are often met with shrugs of helplessness. Inside many of these schools, there is less drama and far more tedium. By the end of the third grade, a pattern of academic failure for large numbers of children begins to emerge, and by the middle and upper grades the pattern of failure and low academic expectations is marked clearly. High school becomes a salvage operation to rescue a small and lonely contingent of survivors who have displayed academic and vocational promise (Fine 1991; Rist 1973; Smith and O'Day 1991a; Spindler 1974, 69–81).

Many resilient youth do overcome obstacles in the harsh Darwinian world that would shock even Darwin. Within the same family, one brother goes to jail while another goes to college. Such grinding-poverty-to-academic-success stories only underscore the loss of the many, who end up wasting their talents. Similarly, there are stirring examples of school principals and teachers who defy the norm and achieve unusual success with their students. Such islands of achievement make feature stories in magazines and become televised documentaries. They, too, only underscore how few big-city schools serve their children well (Anderson 1990; Clark 1983; Mathews 1988; Olson 1993).

Has systemic reform through national goals, content standards, curriculum-based tests, and new pedagogies been embraced by bottom-tier schools? In the 1980s, California, Texas, New Jersey, New York, Kentucky, and other states raised their academic standards, installed new curricula, mandated tests, and decentralized district authority to local school sites; in short, they did what the organizational-effectiveness, blended, and pedagogical reformers—including the president, both political parties, and Congress—wanted to be done. Since then, other states have done the same or even gone further. In Illinois, for example, to reform the governance of Chicago schools, the state mandated in 1988 that every single one of the district's almost 600 schools have a local site council composed of parents and teachers that hires and fires principals and makes curricular and instructional decisions (Bryk and Rollow 1992; Fuhrman et al. 1988; Massell et al. 1994).

Yet the results of these changes in pace-setting states during the 1980s and early 1990s have been disappointing for bottom-tier schools. Big-city schools in these states continue to have a sorry record. These districts continue to struggle with high dropout rates, spotty attendance, and dismal academic performance, especially in secondary schools. Teachers continue to teach in traditional ways. Jonathan Kozol (1991) and others have documented these persisting issues.

In recent years I have returned to those big-city high schools in which I taught decades ago and listened to their teachers and principals speak about what they face. The literal sameness of what I experienced years ago quickly became apparent in their descriptions. What I have seen firsthand, then, and what is available in the research and popular reform literature convince me that these persisting problems in bottom-tier schools are resistant to such organizational solutions as raising graduation requirements, changing state curricular frameworks, providing incentives and sanctions, sharing decision making, establishing new curricula, and publishing school-by-school tests scores in local newspapers.

As you can see, the historian and practitioner sides of me converge in my skepticism regarding both the agendas and direction that the organizational-effectiveness, blended, and pedagogical reformers have used to prod the multitiered social system of American schools to move in the last decade. Yes, organizational, governance, and curricular changes have occurred in response to state and federal initiatives in second-tier schools—but not necessarily in bottom-tier schools or in the arena where all of these changes are supposed to pay off: classroom teaching practices.

This presents a puzzle to me as both a historian and a practitioner. *Although many changes have occurred in school and district organization, governance, and curriculum over the last decade—even the last 150 years of public schooling—these changes have not fundamentally altered a core of teaching practices that have been frequently a target for reformers.*

I will elaborate on this apparent paradox more fully because I believe it is at the heart of repeated efforts to improve schooling among reformers who are often confused or unconcerned (or both) about whether schools are change-prone or change-resistant institutions.

CHANGES IN GOVERNANCE

By governance, I mean centralizing and decentralizing decision-making authority. Over a century ago, there were more than 100,000 school districts in the nation. In big cities, school boards with 50 or more members often doled out teaching jobs to their constituents. Untrained principals and superintendents were hired for their loyalty to a political party rather than for their administrative and leadership skills. Supporters saw this decentralized system as democratic and responsive to voters. But to critics—the good-government reformers called progressives—the system was inefficient and even corrupt (Tyack and Hansot 1982).

By the 1920s, progressive school reformers had won. They consolidated many tiny rural districts into larger ones. They centralized big-city districts' decision-making power into the hands of smaller, more efficient school boards that hired college-educated and trained administrators to run their schools. Centralizing decision making at the top of school systems, creating efficient bureaucracies, and hiring professional administrators had become, by the 1950s, mainstream policy wisdom (Peterson 1985; Raftery 1992).

By the early 1960s, the wisdom of these solutions for governing schools had come under attack. Civil rights activists questioned the legitimacy of small school boards in big cities where officials were distant from the lives of poor minority children. Calls for educators to be more responsive to their communities swelled into proposals for local control and administrative decentralization. Philadelphia, New York, Detroit, Los Angeles, Washington, D. C., and other cities subdivided their school systems into smaller districts. However, by the mid-1970s, the surge of interest in decentralization had spent itself (Mirel 1993; Ravitch 1983; Tyack and Hansot 1982).

In the 1980s, again, centralizing authority gained support from state policy makers who concentrated funding and decision making at the state level to improve schooling. By the late 1980s, however, a slow recognition grew that state-driven reforms were not penetrating individual schools. New reform proposals to decentralize decision making to the school site were heavily influenced by the Effective Schools research literature on the individual school as the unit of change, by a Carnegie Commission report urging a more salient role for teachers in school-based reform, and, finally, by corporate executives who pointed to their success in delegating decision making to the sites where products were made or services delivered (Carnegie Forum on Education and the Economy 1986; Elmore 1990; Murphy 1989).

What happened to centralizing authority? It still exists side-by-side with the insistent pulse of school-site decision making. In the last few years, federal policy makers have established national goals, advocated curricular standards, and sought national tests. Although the trend of centralizing authority at state and federal levels is clear, cyclical changes have occurred over centralizing and decentralizing authority (Cohen 1990; Cuban 1990).

CURRICULAR CHANGES

In the 1990s, we are still in the full flush of state-driven reforms that aim for a common core of academic knowledge. We hear that 17-year-olds cannot solve math problems, locate Siberia, or tell the difference between the Bill of Rights and a bill of sale. Higher graduation requirements now mandate that all students take more academic subjects. Yet this passion for a core of subject matter shared by all students would be familiar to Harvard University President Charles Eliot, who chaired the Committee of Ten in 1893. That committee urged that every high school student, regardless of future destination in the labor market, take four years of English and three years of history, science, math, and a foreign language. Yet having all students take the same academic subjects posed serious issues for educators at the turn of the century as they saw urban classrooms flooded with immigrants from eastern and southern Europe and black and white migrants from rural America (Cremin 1961; Kliebard 1986; Ravitch and Finn 1987).

In the decades before and after World War I, progressive educators challenged this idea of one best academic curriculum. They saw huge numbers of students leaving school at ages 12 and 13. They wanted to fit the formal curriculum to the student rather than the other way around. By the 1920s, they had created their crowning achievement and their solution to the problem that a one-size curriculum did not fit all students. It was the comprehensive high school and its cousin the junior high school, where administrators using newly invented tests placed students into academic and vocational curricula and created schools geared to students' future occupations. The academic and practical were now open to all (Krug 1964; Tyack and Hansot 1982).

Severe criticism of these reforms, however, came in the 1950s, when another generation of reformers attacked a flabby high school academic curriculum and the excessive number of practical courses that seldom stretched students' minds. The National Science Foundation launched major innovations in science and math curricula. James Conant's studies of secondary schools underscored the necessity for rigorous academic content for able, college-bound students. Advanced Placement courses were established in 1960 (Ravitch 1983).

By the mid-1960s, however, broad political and social movements aimed at freeing the individual from bureaucratic constraints and helping ethnic and racial minorities end their second-class status had swept across the schools. If desegregation, compensatory education, magnet schools, and community control became familiar phrases, so did free schools, open classrooms, flexible scheduling, and middle schools. Reformers redoubled their efforts to create different courses and schools for low-income, minority children. Alternative schools, broadened vocational programs, and new curricula blended academic and practical subjects to recapture the interest of disengaged students. By the late 1970s and early

1980s, reformers, spurred by economic fears, renewed a call for traditional academic curricula in high schools. Demands for academic excellence translated into more required subjects, a longer school year, more homework, and a fevered quest for higher test scores (Kozol 1972; Murphy 1989; Rogers 1968).

For almost a century, this enduring curricular tension between academic and practical subjects has ebbed and flowed among reformers just as much as the tensions between the different kinds of classroom instruction that are embedded within these curricular choices have.

CHANGES IN TEACHING

For many centuries there have been two major traditions in teaching. One is teacher-centered instruction, which positions the teacher as the central authority in matters of knowledge, behavior, and values. In public schools for the last century, this tradition has translated into teaching the whole group at the same time mainly through lecturing, explaining the textbook, and asking questions of students. Marks and grades are used to determine who will pass and who will fail. In this tradition of teaching, the class is often arranged in rows facing the chalkboard and teacher's desk (Jackson 1986).

Another tradition of teaching, also centuries old, is student-centered instruction. Authority here still rests with the teacher, but the student's relationship to that authority differs markedly. Core teaching practices in this tradition include a mix of grouping techniques. Students meet as a whole group, work together in small groups, and do independent study. Talk in classrooms is split between students and teacher. Students ask questions of one another and of the teacher. Teachers do lecture, explain, and ask questions, but only as such activities are appropriate. Subject matter comes from many books, including the text, but it also comes from experiences in the classroom, the home, the meadow, the store, and the community. In these classrooms, clusters of desks, rows facing one another, or similar patterns permit students to work together (Jackson 1986).[2]

Although the dominant tradition in public school classrooms has been teacher-centered, challenges to it have occurred continually. In the 1840s and 1850s, for example, in the debate over how teachers should teach, pedagogical reformers introduced the idea of the whole child. Innovative educators introduced animals, flowers, and photographs into classrooms. The German import of the kindergarten, with its heavy emphasis on play, expression, and the emotional development of the child, was established. These attempts at introducing student-centered instruction before the Civil War, however, hardly altered what most teachers did in their classrooms (Cuban 1990).

By the early 1900s, another generation of pedagogical reformers was determined to make schools into child-centered places and end the regimented forms of teacher-centered instruction. They introduced innovations such as using small groups, projects, combining English and social studies, joint teacher–student planning, and bringing into classrooms newly developed technologies such as film and radio. By the 1950s, researchers did find some changes in elementary school classrooms in grouping practices and growing informal relationships between teachers and students, but in secondary school academic subjects, the dominant practice remained formal and teacher-centered (Cuban 1993; Zilversmit 1993).

In the mid-1960s to early 1970s, a subsequent generation of pedagogical reformers tried to make classrooms student-centered. Open classrooms and open-space buildings popped up across the country. Different-aged students were placed in the same classroom and moved from one learning center to another. New science and math materials that children could physically handle became available. Small-group work on projects and individualized learning were reintroduced. By the late 1970s, however, when researchers went into classrooms to see how teachers taught, teacher-centered instruction was still evident in most classrooms, especially in high schools. And now in the 1990s, another generation of pedagogical reformers fight for cooperative learning, active student involvement, and the virtues of desktop computers that will link students with many worlds (Brown 1994; Cuban 1993; Goodlad 1984).

BACK TO THE ORIGINAL PUZZLE

Here we should recall the puzzle that I offered earlier: Many changes have occurred in school and district organization, governance, and curriculum in the last 150 years of public schooling. Yet these changes have not fundamentally altered a core of teaching practices that has frequently been a target for reformers.

How can schools be change-prone and classrooms seemingly change-resistant? Let me offer a tentative explanation that tries to make sense of frequent organizational, governance, and curricular changes that coexist with a durable, yet slowly changing, teacher-centered classroom practice.

What I argue is that organizational-effectiveness reformers, past and present, basically talk, trade ideas, and latch on to what they believe will fly politically every election year. That is their job. This rhetoric of reform and ideas matters because both often get translated into laws and turn into newly funded programs. The policy talk, ideas, laws, and programs become a prevailing wisdom, driven by an electoral clock. And, as conditions change, as elections tick-tock by, the reformer-driven policy talk, ideas, and programs turn into yet another prevailing wisdom (Tyack and Cuban 1995).

But these organizational-effectiveness reformers, past and present, who traffic in talk and ideas, who frame problems and design solutions, who mobilize resources and adopt programs, do not teach in classrooms or run schools. Implementation, the putting of ideas into practice, is not their bailiwick. That is for practitioners. And for most practitioners, policy talk about ideas and policy action in adopting programs seldom shape their daily routines. Teachers measure time not by a clock that rings every election year but by personal and institutional clocks that chime far more slowly (Elmore and McLaughlin 1988).

For teachers to alter their practices, there must be changes in the actual materials they use, changes in their beliefs, and changes in how they teach. All of these interacting layers of a teacher's work shift very slowly over time as one tradition of teaching eventually gives way to another. Such changes occur slowly because classroom change is multi-layered; changes in one dimension may or may not necessarily mean changes in the others (Fullan 1982).

Most organizational-effectiveness and pedagogical reformers ignore or are misinformed about classroom change. They still believe that schoolwide and classroom changes can be manipulated by policy talk, mandates, incentives, and penalties. Yet, where classroom and school changes have occurred, invariably they have been in places where policy makers and administrators have invested in developing teacher ideas and skills. In the past decade, academic and nonacademic entrepreneurs such as Ann Brown, James Comer, Ron Edmonds, Howard Gardner, Henry Levin, Eric Shaps, Ted Sizer, and Robert Slavin, to name only a few, joined by practitioner reformers such as Deborah Meier and scores of other principals and superintendents, have led local and even national efforts to change schools, one by one. These reformers have learned that what counts in classrooms is what happens between teachers and students, and what happens there cannot be ordered or coerced; you cannot mandate what matters, as Milbrey McLaughlin and Richard Elmore have put it. In the bottom-heavy system of governing American schools, leadership, more often than not, springs from local schools and districts rather than from state and national officials.

The central point of this explanation for the initial puzzle is that there are two very different worlds that policy makers and practitioners inhabit. Both may use the same vocabulary, yet they talk past one another. But the primary responsibility for understanding the machinery and process of school change does not rest upon the shoulders of practitioners; it rests on policy makers. Why?

First, because policy makers have the power and legitimacy to adopt new ideas and to mobilize resources for their implementation. Practitioners lack both. This is especially true for the inequities and entangled problems embedded in big-city schools. In the last decade, reformers' talk and action have hardly touched these schools and classrooms. Policy makers need to reframe the problem of poor schooling from one of a lack of national academic standards, inadequate curriculum, and poorly designed tests to one that simply asks why the tradition of teacher-centered practices remains dominant in these and most other schools.

Second, policy makers need to think through which of these teaching traditions and blends of the two traditions they want to encourage as dominant practice in classrooms. Such decisions are seldom research-based, although cognitive psychologists may make such a case; more often, they are value-driven. Each tradition of teaching contains within it a view of the nature of children, what learning is, what knowledge is important, and how teaching should occur. These views are hardly technical or expert-derived questions answered by a convincing array of evidence. In fact, there is conflicting evidence on student outcomes for each tradition because the goals for each differ. Presently many pedagogical reformers are passionate about the superiority of the student-centered tradition. Yet many parents and practitioners reared in a teacher-centered tradition are also true believers. Policy makers seldom recognize the value conflicts embedded in their proposals or even bring parents and practitioners into open debate over which teaching traditions should be used in classrooms.

Third, policy makers need to understand the hidden conflicts embedded in their organizational, curricular, and pedagogical reform agendas. Strong national pressure for higher scores on standardized achievement tests by the year 2000 and other organizational-effectiveness reform initiatives, for example, simply run counter to the impulse for student-centered learning embedded in curricular frameworks and pedagogical reformers' agendas. Policy talk cannot easily paper over the inherent conflict between such programs.

This, then, is my assessment of change in the immediate and distant past. I offered a conundrum of reform again, again, and again in governance, organization, and curriculum, but much less so in the classroom because I am convinced that frequent shifts in mainstream policy talk have coaxed both policy makers and practitioners into plunging head-first into school reform without regard to the underlying three-tiered social system of schooling. Too often, they try to apply technical solutions to value-based problems. Such head-first plunges have produced changes in some aspects of schooling without clarifying why other reforms, such as ones in the classroom, are much harder to secure. Schools are, indeed, change-prone, shifting in organization, governance, and curriculum over the last century. While there have been modest changes in classroom teaching over the decades, such changes have occurred very slowly, responding to a different clock. Some have survived when leadership was school-based and focused on the classroom. Cycles of policy wisdom and a lack of understanding or outright ignorance among reformers, particularly policy makers, about the world of school and classroom practices have often left a corrosive residue of disappointment among practitioners and parents. It is now time to say "enough."

NOTES

1. I also include in the bottom tier, schools in poor rural areas. Such schools in Appalachia, the South, Southwest, and other parts of the nation are less noted by analysts but clearly belong in this category. See U.S. Congress, House Committee on Education and Labor, Sub-Committee on Elementary, Secondary, and Vocational Education. 1992. *Hearing on the Challenges Facing Urban and Rural Schools.* Washington, DC: U.S. Government Printing Office.

2. Philip Jackson is deeply concerned over the meaninglessness of the common words to describe these traditions, such as subject-centered versus child-centered and traditional versus progressive. He uses the word "mimetic" to describe what I call a teacher-centered instructional tradition and "transformational" to capture what I call the student-centered tradition.

REFERENCES

Anderson, E. 1990. *Streetwise: Race, class, and change in an urban community.* Chicago: University of Chicago Press.

Bradley, A. 1993. The business of reforming Cincinnati's schools. *Education Week,* 19 May, 12(34): 1, 16–17.

Brown, A. L. 1994. The advancement of learning. *Educational Researcher,* November, 23(8): 4–12.

Bryk, A., and S. Rollow. 1992. The Chicago experiment: Enhanced democratic participation as a lever for school improvement. *Issues in Restructuring Schools,* Fall, 3: 3–8.

Capper, C. A., and M. T. Jamison. 1993. Let the buyer beware: Total quality management and educational research and practice. *Educational Researcher,* November, 22(8): 25–30.

Carnegie Forum on Education and the Economy, Task Force on Teaching as a Profession. 1986. *A nation prepared: Teachers for the 21st century.* Washington, DC: Carnegie Forum on Education and the Economy.

Clark, R. 1983. *Family life and school achievement: Why poor black children succeed or fail.* Chicago: University of Chicago Press.

Cohen, D. 1990. Governance and instruction: The promise of decentralization and choice. In *Choice and control in American education.* Vol. 2, *The practice of choice, decentralization, and school restructuring,* ed. W. Clune and J. Witte. New York: Falmer.

Cohen, D., and D. Ball. 1990. Relations between policy and practice: A commentary. *Educational Evaluation and Policy Analysis,* Fall, 12(3): 249–256.

Cohen, D., and M. McLaughlin. 1993. *Teaching for understanding: Challenges for policy and practice.* San Francisco: Jossey-Bass.

Cohen, D., and J. Spillane. 1991. Policy and practice: The relations between governance and instruction. Position Paper. Clearing House. EA 023384. Database ERIC ED 337865.

Coleman, J., E. Campbell, C. Hobson, J. McPartland, A. Mood, F. Weinfeld, and R. York. 1966. *Equality of educational opportunity.* Washington, DC: U.S. Government Printing Office.

Cremin, L. A. 1961. *The transformation of the school: Progressivism in American education, 1876–1957.* New York: Vintage.

Cuban, L. 1988. *The managerial imperative and the practice of leadership in schools.* Albany: State University of New York Press.

Cuban, L. 1990. Reforming again, again, and again. *Educational Researcher,* January–February, 19(1):3–13.

Cuban, L. 1993. *How teachers taught: Constancy and change in American classrooms, 1890–1990.* 2d ed. New York: Teachers College Press.

Darling-Hammond, L. 1990. Instructional policy into practice: The power of the bottom and the top. *Educational Evaluation and Policy Analysis* 12(3): 233–241.

Elmore, R. F. 1990. *Restructuring schools: The next generation of educational reform.* San Francisco: Jossey-Bass.

Elmore, R. F., and M. McLaughlin. 1988. *Steady work: Policy, practice, and reform in American education.* Santa Monica, CA: Rand Corporation.

Fine, M. 1991. *Framing dropouts: Notes on the politics of an urban public high school.* Albany: State University of New York Press.

Fuhrman, S., W. Clune, and R. Elmore. 1988. Research on education reform: Lessons on the implementation of policy. *Teachers College Record,* Winter, 90(2): 237–257.

Fullan, M. 1982. *The meaning of educational change.* New York: Teachers College Press.

Gardner, H. 1991. *The unschooled mind: How children think and how schools should teach.* New York: Basic Books.

Goodlad, J. L. 1984. *A place called school: Prospects for the future.* New York: McGraw-Hill.

Harp, L. 1992. Group dissects education "industry" with eye to improving productivity. *Education Week,* 18 November, 12(11): 1, 13.

Jackson, P. W. 1986. *The practice of teaching.* New York: Teachers College Press.

Jencks, C., et al. 1972. *Inequality: A reassessment of the effects of family and schooling in America.* New York: Basic Books.

Kantor, H., and B. Brenzel. 1992. Urban education and the "truly disadvantaged": The historical roots of the contemporary crisis, 1945–1990. *Teachers College Record,* Winter, 94(2): 278–314.

Kirst, M., and C. Kelley. 1993. Positive impacts of reform efforts in the 1980s. Paper prepared for symposium at University of California, Berkeley, 8 April.

Kliebard, H. M. 1986. *The struggle for the American curriculum, 1893–1958.* London: Routledge & Kegan Paul.

Kozol, J. 1972. *Free schools.* New York: Bantam.

Kozol, J. 1991. *Savage inequalities: Children in America's schools.* New York: Harper-Collins.

Krug, E. 1964. *The shaping of the American high school.* Vol. 1. New York: Harper & Row.

Malen, B., R. Ogawa, and J. Kranz. 1990. What do we know about school-based management? In *Choice and control in American education.* Vol. 2, *The practice of choice, decentralization and school restructuring,* ed. W. Clune and J. Witte. New York: Falmer.

Massell, D., et al. 1994. Ten years of state education reform, 1983–1993: Overview with four case studies. *Center for Policy Research in Education (CPRE) Research Report Series RR-028,* January. New Brunswick, NJ: Rutgers University.

Mathews, J. 1988. *Escalante: The best teacher in America.* New York: Holt.

Mirel, J. 1993. *The rise and fall of an urban school system: Detroit, 1907–1981.* Ann Arbor: University of Michigan Press.

Murphy, J. 1989. Educational reform in the 1980s: Explaining some surprising success. *Educational Evaluation and Policy Analysis,* Fall, 11(3): 209–221.

National Assessment of Chapter 1 Independent Review Panel. 1993. *Reinventing Chapter 1: The current Chapter 1 program and new directions; Final report of the national assessment of the Chapter 1 program.* Washington, DC: U.S. Department of Education, Office of Policy and Planning, Planning and Evaluation Service.

National Commission on Excellence in Education. 1983. *A nation at risk: The imperative for educational reform.* Washington, DC: U.S. Department of Education.

National Council of Teachers of Mathematics (NCTM). 1989. *Curriculum and evaluation standards for school mathematics.* Reston, VA: National Council of Teachers of Mathematics.

Olson, L. 1993. The future of school. *Education Week,* 10 February, 12(20): 14–18.

Orfield, G., and C. Ashkinaze. 1991. *The closing door: Conservative policy and black opportunity.* Chicago: University of Chicago Press.

Peterson, P. 1985. *The politics of school reform, 1870–1940.* Chicago: University of Chicago Press.

Peterson, P., R. Putnam, J. Vredevoogd, and J. Reineke. 1993. Elementary teachers' reports of their goals and instructional practices in six school subjects. *Elementary Subjects Center Series,* No. 103, March. East Lansing, MI: Center for the Learning and Teaching of Elementary Subjects, Institute for Research on Teaching, Michigan State University.

Raftery, J. R. 1992. *Land of fair promise: Politics and reform in Los Angeles schools, 1885–1941.* Stanford, CA: Stanford University Press.

Ravitch, D. 1983. *The troubled crusade: American education, 1945–1980.* New York: Basic Books.

Ravitch, D., and C. Finn. 1987. *What do our 17-year-olds know? A report on the first national assessment of history and literature.* New York: Harper & Row.

Rist, R. C. 1973. *The urban school: A factory for failure; a study of education in American society.* Cambridge, MA: MIT Press.

Rogers, D. 1968. *110 Livingston street: Politics and bureaucracy in the New York City schools.* New York: Random House.

Rothman, R. 1993. Taking account: States move from "inputs" to "outcomes" in effort to regulate schools. *Education Week,* 17 March, 12(25): 9–13.

Smith, M., and J. O'Day. 1991a. Educational equality: 1966 and now. In *Spheres of justice in education: The 1990 American Education Finance Association yearbook,* ed. D. A. Verstegen and J. G. Ward. New York: Harper Business.

Smith, M., and J. O'Day. 1991b. Systemic school reform. In *The politics of curriculum and testing,* ed. S. Fuhrman and B. Malen. New York: Falmer.

Spindler, G. D. 1974. Why have minority groups been disadvantaged by their schools? In *Education and cultural process: Towards an anthropology of education,* ed. G. D. Spindler. New York: Holt, Rinehart & Winston.

Tyack, D., and L. Cuban. 1995. *Tinkering toward utopia: A century of public school reform.* Cambridge, MA: Harvard University Press.

Tyack, D., and E. Hansot. 1982. *Managers of virtue: Public school leadership in America, 1820–1980.* New York: Basic Books.

Tyree, A. K., Jr. 1993. Examining the evidence: Have states reduced local control of curriculum? *Educational Evaluation and Policy Analysis,* Spring, 15(1): 34–50.

U. S. General Accounting Office. 1989. *Education reform: Initial effects in four school districts.* Report No. GAO/PEMD-89–28 B-2344358. Washington, DC: U.S. General Accounting Office.

Wise, A. E. 1968. *Rich schools, poor schools: The promise of equal educational opportunity.* Chicago: University of Chicago Press.

Zilversmit, A. 1993. *Changing schools: Progressive education theory and practice.* Chicago: University of Chicago Press.

What Are We Learning About Learning in Schools?

JEROME BRUNER

MY PURPOSE in this chapter is to provide a working map of what we know about learning, particularly about the kind of learning that occurs or *should* occur in schools, and whether, altogether, our knowledge of these matters can guide us in improving the conduct and quality of education and, eventually, the quality of our lives. These are deep matters, and very troubling ones as well, for we are living in revolutionary times whose uncertainties push us either toward retrogressive despair or progressive euphoria, neither of which is a useful stance in times of swift change. Alas, the collision of the two extremes leads to a good deal of over-heated rhetoric.

ANTINOMIES OF A REVOLUTIONARY TIME

Like most revolutionary times, ours is caught up in contradictions, indeed, in genuine antinomies: reasoned pairs of large truths, which, though both may be true, nonetheless contradict each other. Antinomies, though real enough, provide fruitful grounds for confusion. So let me begin by briefly setting out three of the most baffling of these antinomies. They provide us with themes upon which to play out variations later— variations because antinomies do not permit of logical but only of pragmatic resolution. As Niels Bohr liked to remark, the opposite of little truths are false; the opposite of big ones may also be true. So let us dive right in.

The first antinomy is this: On the one hand, it is unquestionably the function of education to enable people to operate at their fullest potential by equipping them with the tools and the sense of opportunity to use their wits, skills, and passions to the full. That the practice of this truism is always faulted probably inheres in the other horn of the antinomy, which goes somewhat as follows: The function of education is to reproduce the culture that supports it. It should not only reproduce it but also further its economic, political, and cultural aims. For example, the educational system of an industrial society should produce a willing and compliant labor force to keep it going: unskilled and semiskilled workers, clerical workers, middle managers, risk-sensitive entrepreneurs—all of whom are convinced that such an industrial society constitutes the right, valid, and only way of living.

Can schooling be construed both as the agency of individual realization and as a reproductive technique for maintaining or furthering a culture? Here the answer is "not quite yes"—an inevitably flawed "not quite yes," for the unfettered ideal of individual realization through education inevitably risks cultural and social unpredictability and, even further, the disruption of legitimate order. The second horn, education as cultural reproduction, risks stagnation, hegemony, and conventionalism, even if it holds out the promise of reducing uncertainty. Finding a way within this antinomic pair does not come easily, particularly not in times of rapid change. Indeed, it could never have come easily at any time. But if one does not face it, one risks failing both ideals.

The second antinomy reflects two contrastive views about the nature and uses of mind, again both meritorious. One side proclaims that learning is, as it were, inside the head, intrapsychic. Solo learners must, in the end, rely on their own intelligence and their own motivation to benefit from what school has to offer. Education provides the means for strengthening and enabling our mental powers for dealing with the "real world." In this view, education raises everybody's level of functioning, the more so the greater their inherent endowment or energy; but please do not equate these with IQ. It is more complicated than that.

The contrastive view to the solo learner in this second antinomy is that all mental activity is "situated" in and supported by a more or a less enabling social setting. We are not just an isolated mind with skills added. How well the student does in mastering and using skills, knowledge, and ways of thinking will depend upon how favoring or enabling a cultural context the teacher creates for the learner. Favoring contexts—opportunities for cultural interaction—matter at every level, and even determine whether or not one's underlying capacities become actualized. Favoring contexts are principally and inevitably interpersonal: collaborative settings involving joint enterprises with peers, parents, and teachers. It is through such collaboration that the developing child gains access to the resources and technology of the culture. But even more benefits accrue from interaction, for there is now good reason to believe that it is through joining in collaborative effort that one forms a self and comes to a sense of one's own agency (Meltzoff and Gopnik 1993, 335–366).

The risks (and the benefits) inherent in pushing either side of this antinomy to the exclusion of the other are so critical that their discussion is better postponed until we can look at them in context, which we will do shortly. Otherwise, we might get stuck in the nature–nurture controversy, for the "inside-out/outside-in" antinomy is too easily converted into Herrnstein–Murray rhetoric (Herrnstein and Murray 1994).

The third and final antinomy is one that is too rarely made explicit in educational debate. It is about how the meanings of everyday experience are to be construed and by whom. That sounds remotely abstract—until you encounter it face-to-face. Let me outline it bluntly and with some needed exaggeration. One side of the antinomy holds that human experience, "local knowledge" as it were, is legitimate in its own right; it cannot be reduced to some "higher," more authoritative universalistic construal (Geertz 1995). All efforts to impose more authoritative meanings upon local experience are suspect as hegemonic, serving the ends of power and domination, whether so intended or not. This, of course, is a caricature of the kind of antifoundationalism sometimes referred to as "postmodernism" (Derrida 1978). It is not only an epistemological stance but also a political one. The claim of nonreductiveness and untranslatability often appears in radical feminism, in radical ethnic and anti-imperialist movements, and even in critical legal studies. In education, it undoubtedly fueled the "deschooling" movement and its kin. But even in its extreme versions, it cannot be dismissed out of hand. It expresses something deep about the dilemmas of living in contemporary bureaucratized society.

The contrastive side of this third antinomy—the search for an authoritatively universal voice—is also likely to get puffed by self-righteousness. But ignore for a moment the pomposity of the self-appointed spokespersons for undisputable universal truths, for there is a compelling claim on this side, too. It inheres in the deep integrity, for good or evil, with which any culture's way of life expresses its historically rooted aspirations for grace, order, well-being, and justice. Human plights, though they may always express themselves locally in time, place, and circumstance and be linked uniquely to the local context, are nonetheless universally rooted in history. While history may be an interpretation of the past, it is not an arbitrary interpretation. To ignore a culture's best historical efforts to cope with its encounters with the universal human condition on the grounds that such efforts fail to capture the political immediacy of the local here-and-now or that they undermine identification with a more local ethnic, gender, or class history is to risk parochialism. Cultural pluralism does not have to prove its virtue by ignoring or vilifying the integrity (and the inevitable transition pains) of its host culture. For all that experience and knowledge may be local and particular, it is still part of a larger continent (Geertz 1995).

Those are the three antinomies: the idiosyncratic/conventional, the individual inside-out/cultural outside-in, and the particular/universal. Without keeping them in mind, it would be impossible to evaluate what we have learned about school learning, for they help keep the issues in balance. There is only one way to have both sides of the three antinomies. As I shall argue now, that way is to take seriously the individual as both an expression of and as an agent of human culture. And this must begin with teachers and pupils in the setting of the school. Let me turn to this now.

HEAD START AS A MICROCOSM

I begin with Head Start, a revealing microcosm. Though it had many incipient precursors, all rather ideological and utopian, it is unique for having been fueled or ignited by a series of scientific discoveries about the nature of early development. Like most important facts about the human condition, these were quickly converted from facts to metaphors. First, the bare facts insofar as one can strip them down. Animals reared in impoverished environments were later found to be deficient when tested on standard learning and problem-solving tasks (Hunt 1961). Not only that, but their brains seemed to be underdeveloped as well, if I may be permitted to condense a great many, very complicated particulars (Calvin 1983) into an overly simple summary. Some of these findings, by the way, were literally inadvertent by-products of other concerns, as when white rats were reared in "germ-free" environments to see whether they would develop normal antibodies. They did not; but more interesting still, the germ-free environments, being mighty pallid places, made the rats raised in them exceptionally backward in their learning activities in comparison with their more friskily and unhygienically raised littermates (Calvin 1983).

From these meager beginnings, the so-called deprivation hypothesis was born. But education was not an issue; neglected newborns in respirators were the first source of alarm (Ribble 1944). Very soon afterward, however, new research began appearing showing that kids from poverty backgrounds fell progressively further behind once they started school (Bloom 1964 and 1976). This work alerted a much wider community to the possibility that the lack of a "good start" might lock a kid into later failure. The deprivation hypothesis had found a human locus. Though it was an exceedingly crude formulation, it had the moral force behind it of saying that poor kids were being deprived of a key growth vitamin or some vital immunization shot. That was a powerful start.

Soon after, a spate of direct, controlled studies of real (rather than retrospective) infants began in earnest: their perception, memory, attention, imitation, and action. Such work had been rare. Why it began at just that time and with that much vigor I will leave for historians to decide (Mussen 1970, ch. 5–7). Had there been an implicit taboo on studying little babies in laboratories—a collision between the ethics of tenderness and the cool detachment of research? Or was it just the transistor recording with its miniaturizing possibilities that made it possible to let babies suck pictures into focus or to control what came into view by a slight head turn or flick of the leg (Kalnins and Bruner 1973; Papousek 1979)? Imagine the excitement of finding that the older the infant, the more complicated the checkerboard the infant chose to look at (Salapatek 1975), or that an infant's eye movements were not that different from an adult's when scanning familiar figures (Mackworth and Bruner 1970).

Not surprisingly, these findings quickly caught the public's imagination, and even the august *Times* of London carried a series of articles in praise of the new work. The equally august British historian Lord Bullock was soon quoted to the effect that we were entering a new era in our conception of humans. Infants, it turned out, were much smarter, much more cognitively proactive rather than reactive, much more attentive to the immediate social world around them, and so on than had previously been suspected. And they emphatically did *not* inhabit a world of buzzing, blooming confusion; they were after stability from the start. At least this suggested what the deprivation might be all about.

The burden of these studies pointed to something more active than gross sensorimotor deprivation. One kind of "deprivation" was social or interactive. Infants sought out and were rewarded by interaction with others; they went out of their way to establish joint attention with others by following their line of vision to discover what they were looking at; infants sought and were calmed by eye-to-eye contact with their caregivers, and so on (Scaife and Bruner 1975; Stechler and Latz 1966). Withholding these opportunities, it was shown by the few studies that undertook to do so (for infancy researchers hate tormenting their subjects), distressed and upset the infants. So the first thing was human interaction.

The second thing infants needed was self-initiated activity. In a nutshell, what infants *did* to their mundane environments seemed to have more lasting effects on them than what the environment did to *them*. And what, in fact, they did in their visual search and awkward groping was far more systematic and varied than had been suspected—at least by researchers (Meltzoff and Gopnik 1993, 335–366).

Out of these considerations grew a rather weird and ethnocentric notion of "cultural deprivation." "Culture" somehow got equated with an idealized middle-class version of childrearing in which mother and child interacted with each other in an attuned way, and in which the child was given ample opportunity to initiate things within this interaction. Being deprived of this idealized opportunity was translated as "cultural deprivation." There were soon new projects to teach mothers in poverty how to talk more and play more with their infants and how to hand over agency to the child. These projects produced real results. Head Start's curriculum rapidly moved in that same direction. However, one should note something ominous: "Cultural deprivation" as a term had the effect of blaming the victim—or at least the victim's mother (Cole and Bruner 1971). Since in America, the mothers in question were predominantly black or Hispanic, the implication was that these cultures were at fault, rather than poverty or its despair.

All this was taking place in the decade after *Brown v. Board of Education* (1954), when affirmative action programs were still new and highly disputable. Head Start was seen as the other side of the coin of affirmative action. It was seen as dedicated to stopping the culture from reproducing itself yet again, particularly its system of racial discrimination that had assured a supply of cheap, unskilled, exploitable labor. Besides, we did not need that kind of labor any more. It looked as if a new consciousness had come to replace the old culture-reproducing inertia.

But never underrate the power of antinomies. By the early 1970s, research began "proving" that IQ gains from Head Start disappeared within a few years. Ghetto children seemed unable to sustain the gains they made from the initial Head Start boost once they got further into school. There were Jensens and Herrnsteins around to reassert the old inside-out view: Poor kids, particularly black kids, just did not have the endowment—the IQ—to benefit from Head Start (Herrnstein 1982; Jensen 1969). This was not unwelcome music to political tax-cutters playing to an increasingly squeezed middle class who, in any case, had fled to the suburbs to put big cities, high taxes, and poverty problems behind them. So big cities lost not only their manufacturing industries but also their middle class and grew poorer and poorer. Head Start did not disappear, but neither did it grow as much as it might have. Ironically, when the 25-year results on Head Start began coming in, even by itself it had made an astonishing difference. Kids who had been through it were, by comparison to "controls," more likely to stay longer and do better in school, to get and to hold jobs longer, to stay out of jail, to commit fewer crimes, and the rest. In fact, it "paid." The cost per pupil, even in fancier Head Start programs, far offset economic losses from unemployment, cost of imprisonment, and welfare payments, even leaving aside the moral issues involved (Abt Associates 1979; Barnett 1993; Clarke-Stewart 1982; Schweinhart and Weikart 1980; Zigler and Valentine 1979).

Plainly, Head Start is not a magic bullet, but not because it is not always up to standard; that is easily fixed. It is not enough because, on its own, merely as a starting subculture for young kids, it cannot counteract the social alienation of poor black and Hispanic kids and their mothers, or their mothers and fathers where the family is intact. There is too much in the society working against it. School after Head Start is rarely geared to getting inner-city kids to see schoolwork as a viable option for getting out of poverty. After all, even when one holds IQ constant, the percentage of black youth who are unemployed is twice as high as the rate for the IQ-matched whites. So, as drug peddling and turf wars increase as one of the few viable lines of activity for blacks, homicide becomes the chief threat to life among black inner-city kids, and prison a residence for more than a third of them at some point between ages 16 and 25.

Nevertheless, what we have learned about learning in all this discouraging morass is anything but trivial. It is this, and let nobody overlook it: Even under the least favorable conditions—psychologically, fiscally, educationally—we still succeed in giving some children a sense of their own possibilities. We do it by getting them, and sometimes their parents, to collaborate in an enabling community. My own view is that experiments such as Head Start give kids, and perhaps their mothers, a sense of a possible way through a poverty culture even when it seems to them to be blindly reproducing itself. But its key idea needs to be extended upward to older kids as well.

Let me describe what I mean through a case history, using a school that picks up ghetto kids at around 10 or 11 years of age. Some of them had the benefit of Head Start; most did not. This is a school that is part of the Oakland school system, and it is part of a program financed by both federal and foundation funding, although the greater part of the costs are met by Oakland. It vividly illustrates what we have come to recognize as crucial for enabling children not just to build their skills but also to develop an effective sense of participating in an enabling community.

The project is directed by Ann Brown of the School of Education at the University of California at Berkeley, and it is now becoming the hub of a consortium of schools spread all around the country (Brown 1994; Brown and Palincsar 1989, 393–449). It easily achieves the usual: raising reading levels, raising test scores, and all the other standard end-result things that school reform is supposed to do. Much more to the point, however, is the kind of collaborative school culture it creates for its participating students and teachers alike.

The Oakland project follows a very few but very powerful principles. The first is that it is a learning community, a collaborative community. This means everybody is learning, everybody is helping in the teaching, and everybody is sharing the labor; they are into it as a group. When I was visiting, the class was involved in studying the *Exxon Valdez* oil spill in Alaska, its causes and consequences, and what it could tell us about how to manage an environment. The kids were *not* at the receiving end of an educational transmission belt, nor were the teachers at the sending end. They were all in the business of *constructing* knowledge. Answers were not in books or teachers' heads. They were something you had to construct, and constructing was the real business. The kinds of questions you asked mattered. So did your guesses. Hunches could be checked against information and others' opinions. But you could also reason out answers, either by yourself or with somebody else. That is number two on the list of fundamentals: *knowledge is made, not found.* There are lots of places to get information—these kids had access to some Apple II computers plus the usual dictionaries, clippings, and so on—but knowledge is made from organizing and discussing these things.

How you organize things—for example, how you put things into the computer's memory or, for that matter, into your own—makes a great deal of difference in what you come to know from it when you use it later. So it is very important to discuss how you are going about organizing things, "you" individually or "you" working in pairs or small groups, or "you" at the Apple II. So there is a lot of encouragement, as we say these days, for "going meta" on what you are doing. That is the third fundamental. Indeed, one teaching assistant served as class ethnographer, and her feedback to the teachers and students about how they did that week was discussed with real reflectiveness the week I was there.

If students have "hot ideas" during class—like one kid who thought about getting oil off birds by using peanut butter as an "oil blotter"—they are encouraged to present them either to the class or to the small group they are working with. Children learn how to receive these ideas respectfully. Even if the idea is a little wacky, somebody may come up with a better version. That peanut butter idea led to an interesting discussion of what makes a "blotter." And everybody gets a turn at teaching what they have learned, even the hangers-back. They very quickly learn a practical version of "no man is an island entire unto himself." The deep lesson, of course, is that thinking and learning are functions of discourse, no matter what your endowment. These kids are enormously stimulating to talk to. Or to use that dreary banality, they are way above average. What?

It is really old stuff. We have known for years now that if you treat people, kids included, as bright, responsible, and part of the group, they will grow into it—some better than others, obviously. Even old people in nursing homes, if treated as responsible members of the community, live longer, get sick less often, and keep their mental powers brisker and longer. I can assure you at firsthand that a good part of the success of Kanzi, that chimpanzee who is mastering language so remarkably at the Yerkes Lab, is that he is being treated by that group of researchers as if, well, he were nearly human. Korean immigrants in America score 15 points higher in IQ than Korean immigrants in Japan, where they are detested, segregated, and treated as if "inferior." We desperately need to have a closer look at what we mean by an "enabling" culture, particularly the enabling culture of a school (Stevenson and Stigler 1992).

Perhaps the successful school cultures—the Oaklands and good Head Starts and many others—are only countercultures for raising consciousness. That would be a real boon, if the little counterculture of a good school produced reflections about other possible worlds. I think there is more to it than that, however. I spoke to some people at the Ministry of Education in Norway who had been involved in a new program to reduce school bullying in that compassionate country. Just raising the topic had had an electric effect on the kids. It obviously had been in the closet waiting for a passport into open discussion, but consciousness raising was not enough. It needed some way of finding its way into the routines of mundane daily actions. It was the very same lesson that Vivian Paley learned in her stunning study of nursery school kids excluding other kids from their little cliques—her wonderfully titled *You Can't Say You Can't Play* (Paley 1992).

The heart of the matter seems to be praxis: how one conducts life in ordinary, everyday, expectable, banal cultural settings. School, too, is ordinary cultural praxis. It is so crucial to the idea of how a culture enables mind that I want to pause over it for a moment. Let me discuss it in the unusual language of a distinguished friend of mine, the French social theorist Pierre Bourdieu (1991). Praxis takes place in any and all settings that provide a "market in distinctions," to use his terms. A market in distinctions is anywhere where one "trades" some form of capital—

economic, cultural, or symbolic—in return for some culturally bestowed distinction: profit, approval, identity, respect, collegial support, favors, or recognition. These markets in distinction are ubiquitous: They are in conversation, on the trading floor of the stock exchange, in politics, in school, and around the dinner table. They are ubiquitous, too, in the collaborative exchanges of a classroom. Growing up, and throughout life, we develop mental and bodily orientations toward the world that guide us in the markets where we trade our capital for distinctions—particularly our capital in the form of knowledge, beliefs, values, services, allegiances, and the like. It provides the unremarkable stuff of daily life, and it forms our characters and predispositions. In a word, we act our way into thinking more readily than we think our way into acting.

BUILDING A COLLABORATIVE CULTURE

It is now time we returned to our three antinomies for a coda. Should education reproduce the culture, or should it enrich and cultivate human potential? The standard double-talk is that, of course, it should do both as best it can. But if we leave it unexamined at that, we have a recipe for mindlessness. I suppose we could do better than that by thinking it through further. So when we proclaim that we will be first in science, math, and languages by the end of the decade to compete in world markets, we ought also (if we are true to the ideal of developing human potential as well) proclaim that when we get there, we will reward everyone by redistributing the wealth, by creating a new GI Bill, or whatever. This might assure the poor and the alienated that working hard in school will not just make the rich richer and the poor poorer. Perhaps if the rules of the game would stay still, and change would stop its tumultuous course, we could approach our compromises in that way. The idiosyncratic would simply provide entry into the reproductively conventional.

I doubt whether we are willing enough, united enough, or courageous enough to face up to the revolution we are living through. If we were, would there really be an issue about *reproducing* the culture? The real issue is trying to get some sense of what we are changing into. I think that we have little better sense of where the culture is moving than did the French in 1789. Was it any better understood by activist Jacobins than by Girondists or the hold-back peasants of the Vendee or the crusty gentry of the ancien régime? Even America's demographic changes are too mind-boggling to grasp firmly. For example, there was a larger proportion of parents who had achieved high school educations in 1980 than there was of parents with grade school educations a half-century before—

more than eight in ten. We do not even live where we used to. At the turn of the century, nearly half of America's families lived on farms, with all hands pitching in. That proportion had dropped to less than 5% by 1980. And the number of siblings in the median American family had dropped to less than two per family in 1993, down from nearly four in 1920. Perhaps the swiftest change of all was that the number of children with mothers at work outside the home rose from one in ten in 1940 to six in ten in 1990. In that same short period, the divorce rate increased tenfold— from roughly two per thousand marriages to about twenty-one per thousand. In consequence, during that same period, the percentage of kids living in mother-only households swelled threefold from 6.7% to 20%. Indeed, the number of kids born into "Ozzie and Harriet" families—as a recent Russell Sage Foundation report (Hernandez 1993) calls families in a first marriage with father working and mother at home—dropped to about a quarter of live births. This is *smaller* than the proportion of our children born into families living at or below the official poverty level, which amounts today to nearly a third. Immigrant and black children, as has traditionally been the case, fare far worse on all the indices linked with economic well-being.

We seem to be creating two population streams, each with a different culture: the highly urban and increasingly disorganized poor, mostly black or recent immigrant; and the suburban/small-city, mostly white or recent immigrant-descended middle class. While the representation of blacks in this middle class has increased, it is still notably in the minority. Obviously there are other smaller groupings as well, posing problems of their own: the rural poor; isolated and dwindling small-town dwellers; the emerging professional, highly educated upper-middle class, whose chief legacy to their children is an up-scale education rather than inherited wealth; and so on. Let me concentrate on the two main streams: the urban poor and the suburbanized middle class. Nobody planned it that way. Nobody planned it *any* way. And grand aspirations about training up a competitive labor force for the next generation do not touch the intimate issue of how we conduct our schools either in our increasingly poor and disorganized cities or in our lawn-manicured, increasingly self-contained, yet uneasy suburbs. What I am left with is the conviction that the ambitious Charlottesville science–math–language goals set forth in 1989[1] will get their due attention because of the sheer economic vitality of this nation, but that in the process we may lose the sense of community and civility and collaboration that constitutes American grace.

So let me turn back to the issue of school as a collaborative culture, a medium for community rather than a repository of skills for converting inner endowment to real-world savvy (our second antinomy). The difficulty with that isolated solo approach in such times as ours is that competitive skill pickup cannot be counted on. Inner-city poor kids are too apt to believe the skill endowment game is a con game, and suburban kids are too apt to find it boring. On the basis of what we have learned about human learning—that it is best when it is participatory, proactive, communal, collaborative, and given over to constructing meanings rather than receiving them—we would do better to renew our schools along these lines even if only to meet the Charlottesville goals better (National Education Goals Panel, 1991).

There are deeper reasons why we need something like the Oakland/ Ann Brown model to cope with the third antinomy, the particular–universalistic one. We know that, given the appropriate collaborative community, children come quickly and easily to taking particulars as tropes or metaphors of something more general circulating in the group. They learn, too, how to negotiate these matters with others. This is surely one wise way to grow in and benefit from revolutionary times. But there are many ways to proceed. Oakland is only one among many. Building to the strengths and interests expressed in different forms of intelligence, along Howard Gardner's (1983) lines, is another. Ted Sizer's Coalition of Essential Schools, financed by the Annenberg Foundation, has its virtues. There is never just one formula for so deep and pervasive a problem. There are even bad errors with good motives from which we can learn. Teaching black history to black children by the old and stunted methods of history teaching in the interest of creating ethnic pride is probably no more successful than teaching pride in America by teaching about George Washington and Parson Weems's apple tree.

What I do know on the basis of the centrality of interpersonal interaction in human development is that whatever the innovation, it cannot get off the ground without an adult actively present—where school is concerned, a teacher willing and prepared to give aid, comfort, scaffolding, and cultural cohesion. You cannot carry on with just the good intentions of governors meeting in Charlottesville; you cannot do it with a bank of the best-programmed computers; and you cannot do it with the best-intended ideology, be it inspired by multiculturalism and bilingual education, by feminist pride, or by scornfully creating lists of great books written by "dead white males" (like Dante, Locke, and Melville!). Learning in its full complexity involves the creation and negotiation of meaning with others in a culture, and the agent, or the vicar, of that process is a teacher. You cannot teacher-proof a curriculum any more than you can parent-proof a family. So I believe we must begin our refreshment and renewal of American schooling with a new and radical reconsideration of how we recruit, educate, and help our teachers in achieving the kinds of goals I have been discussing. I am not talking about "teacher training" on the cheap, but the formation and enablement of teachers. This is a serious undertaking. Remember that it was a dedicated teacher corps that finally created the French Republic nearly a century after the Revolution (Judge 1994).

There is a deep puzzle in what I am saying. In the years since *A Nation at Risk* was published (National Commission on Excellence in Education 1983), when our national debate on education became a "public" media event, we have virtually closed our eyes to the nature, uses, and role of teaching. We have sourly damned the teaching profession as unqualified and concentrated on raising their licensing qualifications. Teaching has been treated as a necessary evil; would that we had computers that could do it. In the process, we have probably alienated our most important ally in renewal: the teacher.

There is nobody in America today who knows better the temper of the American teacher than Ernest Boyer. He conducted a study of their views in the five years following the 1983 publication of *A Nation at Risk*. This is what he reported in his 1988 Annual Report of the Carnegie Endowment for the Advancement of Teaching:

> We are troubled that the nation's teachers remain so skeptical. Why is it that teachers, of all people, are demoralized and largely unimpressed by the reform actions taken [thus far]? . . . The reform movement has been driven largely by legislative and administrative intervention. The push has been concerned more with regulation than renewal. Reforms typically have focused on graduation requirements, student achievement, teacher preparation and testing, and monitoring activities. But in all these matters, important as they are, teachers have been largely uninvolved. . . . Indeed, the most disturbing finding in our study is this: Over half the teachers [surveyed] believe that, overall, morale within the profession has substantially declined since 1983. . . . What is urgently needed—in the next phase of school reform—is a deep commitment to make teachers partners in renewal at all levels. . . . The challenge now is to move beyond regulations, focus on renewal, and make teachers full participants in the process. (Boyer 1988, 13–21)

Let us remember the picture I drew of the American family earlier in this essay—whether in the inner city or the rimming suburbs. It can be condensed into one focal image. Children, through a variety of circumstances, have been put on increasingly short rations where *live* interaction with grown-ups is concerned. Working mothers, absent fathers, television isolation, and the rest leave kids peculiarly cut off from a sense of how you enter and cope with the adult world. I am not proposing that schools and teachers stand in for the family. My proposal is more radical than that. Teachers can create the sense of a collaborative culture as no other group in our society can. There are teachers around the country who are doing it now. We must bring them back into the discussion, into the shaping of both ends and means. Everything we know about school learning tells us that teachers are not messengers carrying the word, but a crucial ingredient of the message itself.

NOTES

I am grateful to the Spencer Foundation for their grant in support of the work reported in these pages.

1. The Charlottesville goals are a set of six national goals to be met by the year 2000. They were formulated and agreed upon by the president and the nation's governors in Charlottesville, Virginia, in September 1989. At the same meeting, the National Education Goals Panel was set up to establish means of assessment for measuring progress and reporting results. The panel consists of six governors, four members of Congress, and four members of the administration. The six goals are as follows: By the year 2000, all American children will start school ready to learn; the high school graduation rate will increase to at least 90%; American students will leave grades 4, 8, and 12 demonstrating competency in challenging subject matter, such as history, math, science, and geography; American students will be first in the world of science and math achievement; every adult American will be literate and possess the knowledge and skills necessary to compete in a global economy and exercise the rights and responsibilities of citizenship; and every school in the United States will be free of drugs and violence and offer a disciplined environment conducive to learning.

REFERENCES

Abt Associates. 1979. *Final report of the national day care study.* Vols. 1–5. Cambridge, MA: Abt Books, and Washington, DC: Day Care Division, Administration for Children, Youth and Families (DHHS).

Barnett, W. S. 1993. Benefit-cost analysis of preschool education: Findings from a 25-year follow-up. *American Journal of Orthopsychiatry* 63(4): 500–508.

Bloom, B. S. 1964. *Stability and change in human characteristics.* New York: Wiley.

Bloom, B. S. 1976. *Human characteristics and school learning.* Chicago: University of Chicago Press.

Bourdieu, P. 1991. *Language and symbolic power.* Cambridge, MA: Harvard University Press.

Boyer, E. 1988. *Report of the President.* In *The Carnegie Foundation for the Advancement* of Teaching: The eighty-third annual report. Princeton, NJ: The Carnegie Foundation for the Advancement of Teaching.

Brown, A. L. 1994. The Advancement of Learning. *Educational Researcher* 23(8): 4–12.

Brown, A. L., and A. S. Palincsar. 1989. Guided, cooperative learning and individual knowledge acquisition. In *Knowing, learning, and instruction: Essays in honor of Robert Glaser,* ed. L. B. Resnick. Hillsdale, NJ: Erlbaum.

Brown v. Board of Education of Topeka, Kansas, 347 U.S. 483 (1954).

Calvin, W. H. 1983. From nervous cells to hominid brains. In Calvin, *The throwing madonna: Essays on the brain.* New York: McGraw-Hill.

Clarke-Stewart, A. 1982. *Day care.* Cambridge, MA: Harvard University Press.

Cole, M., and J. S. Bruner. 1971. Cultural differences and inferences about psychological processes. *American Psychologist* 26(10): 867–876.

Derrida, J. 1978. *Writing and difference.* Chicago: University of Chicago Press.

Gardner, H. 1983. *Frames of mind: The theory of multiple intelligences.* New York: Basic Books.

Geertz, C. 1995. *After the fact: Two countries, four decades, one anthropologist.* Cambridge, MA: Harvard University Press.

Hernandez, D. J. 1993. *America's children: Resources from family, government, and the economy.* New York: Russell Sage Foundation.

Herrnstein, R. J. 1982. IQ testing and the media. *The Atlantic Monthly,* August, 250(2): 68–74.

Herrnstein, R. J., and C. Murray. 1994. *The bell curve: Intelligence and class structure in American life.* New York: Free Press.

Hunt, J. M. 1961. *Intelligence and experience.* New York: Ronald Press.

Jensen, A. R. 1969. How much can we boost IQ and scholastic achievement? *Harvard Educational Review,* Winter, 39(1): 1–123.

Judge, H. G. 1994. *The university and the teachers: France, the United States, England.* Wallingford, England: Triangle Books.

Kalnins, I., and J. S. Bruner. 1973. The coordination of visual observation and instrumental behavior in early infancy. *Perception* 2: 307–314.

Mackworth, N. H., and J. S. Bruner. 1970. How adults and children search and recognize pictures. *Human Development* 13(3): 149–177.

Meltzoff, A. N., and A. Gopnik. 1993. The role of imitation in understanding persons and developing a theory of mind. In *Understanding other minds: Perspectives from autism,* ed. S. Baron-Cohen, H. Tager-Flusberg, and D. J. Cohen. Oxford: Oxford University Press.

Mussen, P. H., ed. 1970. *Carmichael's manual of child psychology.* 3rd ed. New York: Wiley.

National Commission on Excellence in Education. 1983. *A nation at risk: The imperative for educational reform.* Washington, DC: U.S. Department of Education.

National Education Goals Panel. 1991. *The national education goals report: Building a nation of learners.* Washington, DC: U.S. Government Printing Office.

Paley, V. G. 1992. *You can't say you can't play.* Cambridge, MA: Harvard University Press.

Papousek, H. 1979. From adaptive responses to social cognition: The learning view of development. In *Psychological development from infancy: Image to intention*, ed. M. H. Bornstein and W. Kessen. Hillsdale, NJ: Erlbaum.

Ribble, M. A. 1944. Infantile experience in relation to personality development. In *Personality and the behavior disorders: A handbook based on experimental and clinical research.* ed. J. M. Hunt. New York: Ronald Press.

Salapatek, P. 1975. Pattern perception in early infancy. In *Infant perception: From sensation to cognition*, ed. L. B. Cohen and P. Salapatek. Vol. 1. New York: Academic Press.

Scaife, M., and J. S. Bruner. 1975. The capacity for joint visual attention in the infant. *Nature* 253: 265–266.

Schweinhart, L. J., and D. P. Weikart. 1980. *Young children grow up: The effects of the Perry preschool program on youths through age 15.* Monographs of the High/Scope Educational Research Foundation, no. 7. Ypsilanti, MI: High/Scope Press.

Stechler, G., and E. Latz. 1966. Some observations on attention and arousal in the human infant. *Journal of the American Academy of Child Psychiatry* 5: 517–525.

Stevenson, H. W., and J. W. Stigler. 1992. *The learning gap: Why our schools are failing and what we can learn from Japanese and Chinese education.* New York: Summit.

Zigler, E., and J. Valentine, eds. 1979. *Project Head Start: A legacy of the war on poverty.* New York: Free Press.

Learning, Teaching, and Existential Meaning

NEL NODDINGS

BOTH EDUCATORS AND the general public express great concern about what children are learning (or failing to learn) in today's public schools. Is the central problem to be found in a "dumbed-down" curriculum? In teacher incompetence? In faulty pedagogical strategies? In the collapse of family life? In lack of standards? Armies of experts raise, study, and report on such possibilities. I will suggest an approach that is at once deeper and more direct. As a philosopher, former mathematics teacher, mother of a large and heterogeneous family, and teacher educator, I want to raise some questions about learning, teaching, and existential meaning.

At the center of my exploration will be the connection between two questions: "What am I to do?" and "Who am I?" The scope of the first question ranges from one that is at the very core of moral life (What *ought* I to do?) to the more mundane questions of everyday life (What am I to do with the next hours?). Whenever we ask the first question—"What am I to do?"—the most natural responses emerge from answers to the second question—"Who am I?" This is the question largely ignored in our schools. I want to ask why it is ignored and whether, as educators, we have a responsibility to be sure that it is not.

I will start the discussion with a brief account of some things that we have known about learning for a long time. Then, with this material as background, I will discuss the student's dilemma—how to answer the question "What am I to do?" without a clear answer to the existential question "Who am I?" Finally, I will use the initial material to suggest ways in which we might share and, perhaps, help to resolve the student's dilemma.

One thing we have known for a long time was described by John Dewey as a "permanent frame of reference" amidst "all uncertainties"—"namely, the organic connection between education and personal experience" (Dewey 1938, 25). All sorts of slogans and strategies for curriculum and instruction have sprouted from this basic frame of reference. "Start where the kids are," we tell new teachers. "Make your lessons relevant." In curriculum, the present movement in math education toward heavy use of "real-world" problems is tied to this longstanding belief that there is a vital connection between what people learn and the experiences they have had and hope to have in the future.

Still, for all our apparent attention to the connection, we have rarely explored it deeply and reflectively. We are too easily persuaded to settle for a measure of cognitive readiness or relevance as it is seen by workers in the adult world. We fail to acknowledge what I will call "the student's dilemma"—namely, that, cognitively ready or not, students may not want to do what the teacher suggests; it just does not fit with their life stories, with who they are. We fail to see that when we present math problems that are real to engineers, biologists, or salespersons, they may still bear no resemblance to reality as it is construed by the student.

One aspect of the organic connection identified by Dewey is the well-known link between motivation and learning. Teachers are forever being urged to motivate their students. But how is this to be done? At a broad policy level, we assume that everyone is motivated by a desire for material goods; that is, everyone wants a reasonable level of material comfort. This seems right, but what comes next does not. Educators and policy makers leap to the conclusion that the desire for material comfort should motivate learning. If students want decent jobs, they should get an education. However, students need more than a motive. They also need *reasons* for supposing that this choice (education) is rationally connected to the motive—and not just to this one motive but to the whole network of motives embedded in their life narratives. After all, if material comfort can be acquired without learning algebra, why learn algebra? For that matter, if material comfort does not ensure happiness, why bother with anything directed so obviously at material comfort? At bottom, if the things students are asked to do just do not fit with their construal of who they are, they will answer the question "What am I to do?" with "Well, I ain't doing *this* stuff."

A second thing we have known for a long time is that the retention of learning depends heavily on purpose, regular use, and personal significance. Set aside personal significance for a moment and consider purpose. When we look up a telephone number or park our car at the airport's long-term lot, we remember the number and location just long enough to make our call or retrieve our car. Indeed, anyone who remembered all of these numbers for longer than was necessary would be considered very odd—a curiosity of sorts. In schools, we see the telephone-number phenomenon over and over again. Students learn the material for a test and promptly forget it. Even high school competency tests, strongly touted as a solution to the problem of falling standards, too often produce this effect. The kids pass the competency tests—frequently given to them by considerate educators in segmented parts—but they do not perform any better on wide-ranging tests of achievement. They learn and, when the need has been met, they forget.

One block against this natural and healthy tendency to cleanse the mind of details no longer needed is long-term or continuing use. It may not matter a bit whether we learn arithmetic processes by rote or by understanding. If we have to use those processes daily for years and years, we remember them. Here we educators are up against a tough problem. Much of what we teach is *not* embedded in what comes next. There is no provision for continuous use. Recognizing this, astute thinkers have advised us to concentrate on the large concepts and intellectual skills that appear over and over again and are used repeatedly (Bruner 1960). We have been urged to think in terms of a spiral curriculum—a lovely and powerful idea that has been pushed aside by atomistic curricula and bit-by-bit competencies.

But surely, some might object, if all that stuff about structure and spiral curricula *worked,* would we have abandoned it? It did not work! Again, I think we have not reflected deeply enough. Bruner in *"The Process of Education* Reconsidered," an address I found both wise and enormously touching, admitted that, for all the effort and promise, curriculum is not the answer to the problems we face (Bruner 1971, 19–32). However, that admission does not imply that the view of learning described in *Process* was itself wrong or that curriculum is not part of the answer. Rather, it suggests that a wider analysis is needed. For students who could answer the question "Who am I?" in a certain way, the curricula of the 1960s were exciting and effective. We *do* know that continual use and individual purpose are vitally connected to learning and its retention, but we have not analyzed the connection at the level of existential meaning.

Consider the learning of mathematics. The meaning of mathematics is, in one sense, certainly embedded in its structure, but, in an existential sense, its meaning lies in the connections students can make with the problems of lived experience. At this level—the existential level—we educators have thought too narrowly in terms of material well-being. We argue for including mathematics in the curriculum almost solely on the basis of its power to get better jobs for those who master it. Our lack of imagination is staggering. Has the study of mathematics nothing to do with self-awareness, eternity, gods, creation, politics, beauty, and reality? If it does not, then I agree with the kids: If my proposed occupation does not require it, why study it? In response to this sensible question, we propagandize. We tell them that all occupations do now or will in the future require mathematics. But the life stories of the adults they know contradict this message, and so again there is a gap between what they are asked to do and how they identify themselves.

A third thing we know is directly connected to the second—to the matter of personal significance that we temporarily set aside in the discussion of retention. This is that incidental learning can be enormously powerful. Many of the things we remember stick with us not because we use them daily but because they catch us "where we live." They motivate us to further study or just tickle our fancy. We pick up all sorts of information while reading for pleasure, in conversation, and while engaged in seemingly unrelated tasks.

Almost all of us remember more vividly what Philip Jackson calls "untaught lessons" than we do the specific objectives of our teachers' carefully planned lessons (Jackson 1992). It is as though our antennae are always tuned toward personal meaning. I remember, for example, a brief speech my high school history teacher made about the dignity of labor. I do not recall what triggered it; it had nothing to do with the history we were studying. But I left the classroom that day with a better feeling about my father, whose occupation was at that time "laborer." The teacher's comments were not part of a planned lesson, and my newfound respect for the dignity of labor did not emerge from any project I was pursuing. What happened came as a result of the teacher's generosity of spirit in sharing his convictions and my need for a special form of meaning.

Powerful as it is, incidental learning is incomplete. Students who plan to enter occupations that require the extensive use of mathematics need more and better-organized mathematics than they can get incidentally. But why should we think that any powerful method has to be used exclusively on everything? We make that mistake again and again. "Drill and practice" seems to be a poor method for inducing understanding. Does that mean that it has no place at all in instruction? Group work has powerful social and intellectual effects. Does that mean it should be used for every academic task? Educators too often take an all-or-nothing, "whole-hog," approach. Those of us who have been around long enough remember that there were even people who actually suggested that kids, in an introduction to astronomy, should "discover" the names of the constellations!

Besides being guilty of the "whole-hog" approach, some movements have wanted to limit what is taught in order to fit the hog. For example, many advocates of behavioral objectives recommended eliminating or minimizing material that would not fit the pattern of behavioral objectives. The longing for existential meaning that manifests itself in open conversation, digressions, and stories shared out of love and concern was squelched. Today there is an attempt to restore affect, attitudes, and values in so-called outcomes. This may be as wrongheaded as leaving them out entirely. There simply is no objectives-like prescription for responding to existential longing. It has to be done personally, incidentally, with great care and intelligence.

An important source of incidental learning is the teacher as person. Martin Buber put it this way:

> Trust, trust in the world, because this human being exists—that is the most inward achievement of the relation in education. Because this human being exists, meaninglessness, however hard pressed you are by it, cannot be the real truth. Because this human being exists, in the darkness the light lies hidden, in fear salvation, and in the callousness of one's fellow-man the great love. (Buber [1947] 1965, 98)

Somehow, without measuring it and without organizing the whole curriculum around it, time has to be allowed to develop relations of care and trust and to widen opportunities for other forms of incidental learning.

In this opening discussion, I have drawn attention to three things we know about learning. First, motivation to learn depends heavily on existential meaning; a sense of who we are guides what we will try to learn. Second, the retention of what is learned depends on continual use and/or personal significance. Third, incidental learning, although incomplete, is powerful in opening new vistas and connecting to personal experience.

THE STUDENT'S DILEMMA

The student's dilemma, put succinctly, is this: How can I decide what I am to do when I do not know who I am? In an important sense, this has always been the student's dilemma, and the best education has often deepened it by acknowledging the centrality of the question "Who am I?" The most fascinating characters in fiction and real life are usually caught at some time in their lives by existential anxieties. But, I will argue, although the basic problem is perennial, the specific problems today are different.

The question "What am I to do?" can be asked at several levels. At its deepest level, it is the central question of moral life. It is at this level that Alasdair MacIntyre (1981) relates it to the "Who am I?" question and, thus, to traditions and life stories. For MacIntyre, the great mistake of modern ethics has been to suppose that people are wholly autonomous moral agents who exercise (if they will to do so) a universal capacity for reason. In contrast, MacIntyre describes people as embedded in traditions and dependent on those traditions for their moral vigor. The moral health of the traditions is, in turn, dependent on the exercise of virtues by their participants.

But the questions "What am I to do?" and "Who am I?" are also closely connected at the everyday, instrumental level. For example, when we find ourselves unexpectedly free for a few hours, we ask, at least implicitly, "What am I going to do?" The answer comes, perhaps unconsciously, out of earlier answers to the question "Who am I?" For instance, my own answer to the question what to do with those precious free hours would probably never be "go bowling" or "hang out at Rick's bar" or "go to church" or "read Shakespeare."

What we do and who we are are intimately related. In one sense, we become what we practice, what we do; and that is why parents and teachers make sure that children do certain things, practice certain virtues, and follow certain rules. However, in another sense, children are already identified with traditions and the life stories of adults before this shaping begins. It is the very power of these traditions that has in the past induced some aspects of existential anxiety in the young. Catholic teenagers have had part of the "Who am I?" question decided, at least temporarily, for them. Teenagers from conservative Republican families may rebel against traditional political values, and even become Democrats. Girls from families that believe "a woman's place is in the home" may strike out for themselves and prepare for professional life. In all these cases, there is some form of tradition, some reasonably stable set of life stories, that provides an initial identity—an initial answer to the "Who am I?" question.

The kids who have usually done well in school are those who have more or less accepted, for a while at least, that they are people of a certain kind. Those who resist—the "lads" described by Paul Willis (1977), for example—have accepted a different sort of identification. To suppose that we can effectively teach both sets of kids the same material simply by setting uniform standards, trying harder, and evaluating more creatively is illusion on a grand scale.

The traditions and reasonably coherent life stories with which we identify ourselves provide the continuity needed for learning and even for change. Mary Catherine Bateson writes:

> In all learning, one is changed, becoming someone slightly—or pro-foundly—different; but learning is welcome when it affirms a continu-ing sense of self. What is learned then becomes a part of that system of self-definition that filters all future perceptions and possibilities of learning. It is only from a sense of continuing truths that we can draw the courage for change, even for the constant, day-to-day changes of growth and aging. (Bateson 1994, 79)

I said earlier that today's problems and existential anxieties are somewhat different from those of the past. Earlier in this century, the task was to break free, to become an individual, and then, upon suffering a renewed longing for relation, to rebuild connections. Now we live in the age pre-dicted by Max Weber—an administered society cut loose from coherent life stories. Indeed, some would claim that we live in the nihilistic time forecast by Nietzsche. Increasing numbers of children enter adolescence with no recognizable traditions or coherent life stories to furnish the con-tinuity Bateson identifies as important. Others find nothing in school that connects to the traditions with which they do identify.

Before considering what might be done to help students with their existential dilemma, I want to say that, although I find the description of present social conditions offered by MacIntyre and other communitarians largely accurate, I do not entirely agree with their proposed solutions. I do not think it is either possible or desirable to revive Aristotelianism or return to the biblical and republican traditions (Bellah et al. 1985). So, what *can* be done in schools?

SHARING THE STUDENT'S DILEMMA

The first thing to do is to acknowledge the student's dilemma, bring it to the fore, and, perhaps, even deepen it. Kids who have answered the ques-tion "Who am I?" with "A college-bound, future professional" often do well in school, but they need to be shaken up. They need to explore the full range of human capacities and dimensions open to growth. They need to hear that we, their teachers, believe that the question of self-identity has intellectual, moral, social, and spiritual dimensions as well as ethnic and economic ones. Who am I? Am I a good friend? Do I see beauty in the world? To what traditions do I belong? Should I question them?

For those students who cannot find themselves at all in the usual academic settings, such discussion is even more important. They need to know that decency, reliability, friendliness, and a host of other qualities are highly valued. They need to hear reasonably coherent life stories that are recognizable as possibilities for themselves. We ought not to emphasize one model—alien to many kids—of a college-bound, well-paid future. Kids who will some day be salespeople, truck drivers, hairdressers, animal groomers, clerks, cooks, delivery people, custodians, and mechanics will perform such work not because we have relegated them to it by tracking or faulty teaching, but because we *need* people to do such work, and it will be available to them. But they need our respect and attention *now*, while they are students, and we need something in school *now* to include their life stories, to connect in a valued way with their current answers to the "Who am I?" question, and to suggest realistic possibilities for future answers.

I want to be very careful in this next set of recommendations because they are easily misunderstood. I believe that we should offer a variety of curricular strands conforming roughly to fairly distinct and identifiable human talents, or "intelligences," as Gardner (1983) refers to them. Each strand should be meticulously designed using the best knowledge we have about curriculum and instruction. (A spiral curriculum can be as effective in cooking or horticulture as it is in mathematics and physics.) Each strand should be enriched by lots of discussion of existential questions.

It is not a case of "relegating kids to plumbing" in the sixth grade. To begin with, we ought not to denigrate any honest form of work by talking this way. There are future plumbers, hairdressers, bus drivers, salespeople, waiters, cooks, custodians, and clerks in our classes. If the life stories of children include associations with people who do this kind of work, then we should acknowledge the dignity of this work and explore these life stories for admirable answers to the question "Who am I?" It should be all right to be a truck driver. It should *not* be all right to be a cheat, to be violent, or to be careless of one's companions on earth or of the earth itself. There is something deeply wrong with a society that does not recognize and respect the people who do its essential work and fails to pay them a living wage.

Many people are deeply offended by my recommendations for multiple curricular strands. If kids study, for example, carpentry starting in the ninth grade, might they not be trapped? Suppose they change their minds? Suppose they really are college-capable? (And today we suppose not only that almost everyone *is* college-capable but, more worrisome, that everyone who has such capability should *want* to go to college.) The answer to this well-intentioned objection comes out of our earlier discussion. If kids are occupied in legitimate studies connected to their own life stories, if they see themselves in what they are asked to do, then they are likely to acquire both the confidence and the skills to learn new material. Therefore they will not be "trapped." Cherished for who they are in every educational setting, they will learn how "to become" and how to learn.

We need to keep a world of possibilities open in all desirable directions, and this is where incidental learning can be powerful. As we share historical, biographical, and personal stories with students, as we openly discuss existential questions, we increase the possibility that each student will pick up something significant. Material of the sort I have described in a number of places on the meaning of life, the existence of gods, what it means to be in relation, immortality, eternity, and infinity is the connective tissue of the curriculum (Noddings 1992 and 1993). It connects the bits and pieces of the curriculum itself, the students to the curriculum, and the students and teachers to one another.

It should not be reduced to specific learning objectives. It should not be tested. It should not occupy the whole day, and it should not be allowed to degenerate into "shooting the breeze." But it has to become a legitimate part of the school day, of ongoing life in classrooms. As we help students to answer the question "Who am I?" their answers to the question "What am I to do?" should be more satisfying across the whole range of human experience.

Why do we not attend more fully to the existential issues that are central to human life? When I identify the obstacles, I cannot be optimistic. There are all the obstacles described by Larry Cuban (Chapter 1, this volume) and more: the pervasive obsession with control—uniform standards, specified outcomes, measuring and testing everything; the well-intentioned drive for equality that, tragically, gets translated into sameness; the widespread fear of open discussion in schools (what dreadful things will be smuggled in if we allow questions about gods or the meaning of life?); the narrow preparation of teachers; the structure of schooling that favors fragmentation and specialization; the proliferation of traditions clamoring to be heard; the growing number of life stories that are broken, incoherent, outrageous, and just plain horrible. And, finally, there is the enemy identified by Pogo—us. With the best of intentions, we get caught up in what some have called "middle-class welfare": grants, projects, and national committees. Much of what we do is self-serving. I could give lots of examples, but you know them as well as I do. It seems fitting here, in a volume sponsored by the Center for the Study of Ethics and Contemporary Moral Problems, that we resolve to reflect on our own part in the problem. What, perhaps unexamined, self lies beneath our actions and recommendations? In a rigorous self-examination, we, too, need to explore the connections between the questions "Who am I?" and "What am I to do?"

For me, as the mother of a large and heterogeneous family, as a former (perhaps forever) math teacher, as a philosopher, and as a teacher educator, I am outraged and disgusted that educators in New York and Newark have decided that all children must now study (and, presumably, pass?) algebra, geometry, and now—in Newark—calculus. We cannot even keep the kids safe, or help them to understand that the search for goodness and decency is worthwhile, that their own goodness and decency are appreciated, that the work of their parents and neighbors is valued, or that their suffering is at least recognized. When we fail at all these things, we decide to compensate by teaching them algebra, geometry, and calculus.

Who *are* we, that such solutions should seem reasonable to us? I know one answer to that question: We are well-intentioned, idealistic people who believe "all children can learn," that children should not be deprived of opportunities because of their race, ethnicity, gender, class, or any other academically irrelevant attribute. We are also people who want to be on the "right" side of social and political issues, and right now, I suspect, that desire is getting in the way of doing what is best for kids. We have our own existential crisis, and I urge some attention to it.

Beneath the math educator, administrator, politician, and professor, there is, we hope, a whole adult. That whole adult can see more clearly and widely than the specialist. We should not use children's initial motivations merely as hooks to drag them all along to the same fixed ends. Rather, as we enlarge the scope of possibilities for them by sharing our lives and interests, we also acknowledge their legitimate interests and talents. Kids should be able to choose vocational education, arts, or academic education proudly, confident that we respect their choice and that we will offer them a fine, rich course of study. Much of what they learn in any of these curricula will be learned incidentally from their teachers as whole persons. It takes a whole adult, acting as a whole adult, to teach a whole child.

REFERENCES

Bateson, M. C. 1994. *Peripheral visions: Learning along the way.* New York: Harper-Collins.

Bellah, R. N., W. M. Sullivan, A. Swidler, and S. Tipton. 1985. *Habits of the heart: Individualism and commitment in American life.* Berkeley: University of California Press.

Bruner, J. S. 1960. *The process of education.* Cambridge, MA: Harvard University Press.

Bruner, J. S. 1971. *The process of education* reconsidered. In *Dare to care/dare to act: Racism and education*, ed. R. Leeper. Washington, DC: Association for Supervision and Curriculum Development.

Buber, M. [1947] 1965. *Between man and man*. Trans. by R. G. Smith. New York: Macmillan.

Dewey, J. 1938. *Experience and education*. New York: Macmillan.

Gardner, H. 1983. *Frames of mind: The theory of multiple intelligences*. New York: Basic Books.

Jackson, P. W. 1992. *Untaught lessons*. New York: Teachers College Press.

MacIntyre, A. 1981. *After virtue: A study in moral theory*. Notre Dame, IN: University of Notre Dame Press.

Noddings, N. 1992. *The challenge to "care" in schools: An alternative approach to education*. New York: Teachers College Press.

Noddings, N. 1993. *Educating for intelligent belief or unbelief*. New York: Teachers College Press.

Willis, P. 1977. *Learning to labour: How working class kids get working class jobs*. Farnborough, England: Saxon House.

Habits of Mind: Democratic Values and the Creation of Effective Learning Communities

DEBORAH MEIER

WHEN WE TALK about the crisis of American schooling, we are discussing matters that lie at the heart of the nation's future. We are not just discussing literacy or numeracy, or the preparation of a twenty-first-century work force. What we are debating are our differing conceptions of what democracy is about and, for some, whether it is even all that important.

There is a close and inevitable connection between our confidence in democracy and our confidence in the power of people collectively to resolve problems. Democracy rests upon respect for the power and value of individuals and groups acting openly on the political stage, appealing to their fellow citizens in the name of their own immediate as well as the nation's larger self-interest.

In the past 10 years, our confidence in democracy, in any form of public politics, has been badly shaken. It somehow looked easier to defend when the challenges to it all seemed external, the threats "foreign." Then Churchill's warning that democracy was a thoroughly flawed system, except for the alternatives, seemed easier to swallow.

In 1949 when I entered adulthood, I saw history as a steady progression from lower to higher forms and democracy as the inevitable flowering of civilization. I was nervous about the appeal of communism because of its offer of a quick totalitarian solution to complex social problems, as well as about our new human capacity to wipe out the entire species through nuclear disaster. But with a little bit of luck, I thought at the time, the truth would set us free and the road to democracy would be confidently taken. In retrospect, I do not know if this was the naiveté of youth or the naiveté of the times.

I have not changed my mind entirely. But history seems a shaky reed on which to pin one's hopes, and the challenges to democracy are far more complicated than I had imagined then. Above all, I see more clearly today that democracy is not a "natural" form of human organization. It depends, in fact, on certain habits of mind and heart that have very insubstantial foundations in most societies. While such habits are compatible with human nature, they are not "natural" to it. They are possible, but not inevitable. They require conscious, intentional learning, and they require commitment.

What do I mean by habits of mind? It is a phrase we have come to use often at Central Park East Secondary School, one which is an underpinning for what we are trying to do at the school: to create informed citizens of a democracy. For us, this is an absolutely vital part of what our school is about. So, from the first day students enter our school, we begin to talk about our five habits of mind, or ways of looking at things, which we believe apply to all academic and nonacademic subject matter and to all thoughtful human activities. They are the kinds of questions, we believe, that well-educated citizens raise about their world:

- How do you know what you know? (Evidence)
- From whose viewpoint is this being presented? (Perspective)
- How is this event or work connected to others? (Connections)
- What if things were different? (Supposition)
- Why is this important? (Relevance)

To graduate from Central Park East, students are required to present evidence of their mastery of these five habits of mind not once but 14 times—in both traditional academic disciplines, including literature, history, math, science, and art, and in interdisciplinary fields, such as community service, media, and ethical and social issues. It is expected that in the work the students present, these questions underlie their way of handling the material. The evidence is presented and defended before a graduation committee consisting of faculty, another student, and an adult of the student's choice. The evidence includes a wide range of work in each subject area. These presentations, which are done over the course of the student's last two years, are judged according to criteria designed by the entire faculty.

BEHIND THE FIVE HABITS OF MIND

It is difficult to accept that with all the piles of pages of new standards and new goals that we are supposed to apply to our students, at Central Park East we have been able to compress them into those five basic understandings. Yet we have found that the five basic understandings are far more powerful and practical than the several thousand standards that tell us what every student is supposed to know or know how to do by the time they are 18 (and then forget). I sometimes think that these five habits can actually be boiled down to just two: skepticism and empathy. I do not mean, of course, that all other habits are unnecessary or irrelevant, only that these two encompass the most difficult and critical—and unnatural—of those necessary for the politics of democratic living. That is why they must be taught.

Skepticism is that difficult habit of keeping an open mind, accepting the idea that today's truisms may seem foolish tomorrow, and acknowledging that within the seemingly obvious "common sense" may lie some treacherous traps. It rests upon the assumption that even what we most deeply believe to be a fact may in time turn out to be otherwise. It behooves us, then, to listen carefully to others and to listen even to ourselves with a third ear. It enables us to develop a sense of humor and helps us to overcome our own self-righteousness. Skepticism does not ask us or expect us to abandon our cherished beliefs or to hold them or fight for them any less dearly. But skepticism may influence the way we fight, and certainly it will influence how rigidly we hold onto these beliefs. Skepticism pushes us to treat others who do not share our views with respect. Ultimately, it helps us to internalize that respect in order to insure that we do not, in a rash moment, eliminate ideas or peoples we may disagree with and even despise.

Skepticism, once developed, requires early and consistent reinforcement. Institutionalizing it works the same way. A school that values and tries to teach skepticism would always challenge itself to listen to its critics, to look at its failures, and to question its own assumptions. It would establish that its students be judged not on the basis of whether they agreed with its teachers, but whether they understood the nature of both the agreements and disagreements and could articulate them in a civil manner. It would insist that the students know what kinds of questions to ask, understand how to judge the credibility of evidence, and be able to imagine alternate scenarios. Students would not be afraid to read books that presented views they rejected or hoped were wrong. And while they might throw themselves wholeheartedly into the defense of their own ideas, after having acquired a healthy and well-developed habit of skepticism, they would also be able to keep a part of their mind open to the other person's ideas.

However, skepticism by itself can lead to cynicism. Skepticism, therefore, needs to be balanced by the equally important habit of empathy. Well-developed empathy makes it hard to feel untouched by the misery of others; it enables us to hear their voices inside our own head and to understand their explanations and their "side" of the story. Reading the newspaper, for example, thus becomes both more compelling and more difficult. Empathy makes us want to run toward and away from at the same time. In imagining ourselves in the shoes of others, the world gets reshaped before our eyes in a way that is both thrilling and uncomfortable. Home—wherever we started out—is changed forever by this encounter with the "other." Empathy subtly broadens our capacity for imagination; our natural childish playfulness is expanded, not obliterated. Good literature, great drama, and powerful art of every kind—all these help a person to develop empathy. Such is the purpose of a good education for democracy.

Skepticism and empathy are two continuously varying weights on opposite sides of a scale, and they form the very core of our five habits of mind. Whatever you choose to call them, those qualities of mind and heart have a crucial importance to our democracy that extends well beyond our present and former students at Central Park East. It is the absence of these habits in the larger population of our society that has created the current crisis for democracy; it is not just an "inner-city" crisis, but a societal one. In fact, it is also a worldwide crisis, and it challenges democracy's very underpinnings.

US AND THEM

It is often very easy for people cut off from the inner city to see this crisis as merely an urban, racial, or ethnic one. In more homogeneous communities, such as white middle- and upper-class suburbs, citizens think of themselves as typical. It is often difficult for them to imagine other ways of seeing the world. In such communities, the citizens' capacity to practice either empathy or skepticism is less severely tested. The boundaries around their world are invisible to them, and they tend to think that "everyone" is "like them" except those who are "deviants." They are able, at least for now, to imagine that they are the "norm," and everyone else is an "other." Even within our big cities, such as New York, powerful people speak casually about sending their kids to private schools, since "no one can use public schools any more." No one? Only a million of their fellow citizens do. In the next breath, they speak about the need for common sacrifices for "the public good" in the face of budget crises. Yet they do not imagine that these common sacrifices mean that their own children's schools will be less well funded.

Interestingly then, the task of "empathy" falls most heavily on those who are most vulnerable. They are the children I teach, surrounded as they are by images of a world that makes them strangers in it or that invites them to pretend not to be themselves.

To build a society in which we can speak across such boundaries, where everyone can imagine themselves in the shoes of others, can analyze the world, and develop different ways of seeing is hard enough. But to imagine a society so unlike our own, in which this is the ordinary way of living, is a tall order. That is why democracy seems less inevitable to me at the age of 63 than it did when I was 18. It is the attempt to create that democracy through our schools which is what we are after.

When I say "we," I am talking about more than those of us at Central Park East. We created a larger web of schools in New York City called the Center for Collaborative Education, which shares a similar philosophy. We are a piece of a much larger network, the Coalition of Essential Schools, which was started by Ted Sizer at Brown University. The Coalition itself is part of an even larger and older tradition of democratic schooling.

I believe that the way we are reinventing, not just reforming, education provides the foundation for creating young people who can be intelligent and responsible citizens in a democracy. Yet as strongly as I believe that, if I were suddenly put in the position to legislate change, I would feel just as strongly that it cannot, alas, be mandated.

WHY REFORM CANNOT BE MANDATED

It is not, as my colleague Ed Joyner of the Yale Child Studies Center notes (see Chapter 5, this volume), because all mandates are pointless. He reminds us that in his own lifetime, thanks to court rulings and civil rights legislation, mandates have liberated millions of people from subhuman conditions and enfranchised generations of previously disenfranchised black people. The Bill of Rights itself is a series of such mandates. Every piece of legislation is a mandate—a policy resting on coercion, not just moral suasion. Of course, mandates are often essential, but it is also important to remember that every mandate has its own forms of resistance and its own unexpected consequences. Despite the mandate for desegregation, for example, most black and white students still do not go to school together. Many schools that mandate the elimination of tracking—a reform that I also support—soon find themselves confronted with resistant teachers and parents who sabotage the reform and find covert ways to reestablish tracking. Mandates seem to offer easy answers, and we live at a time in which we long for such easy answers. Interestingly, conservatives who now so vocally rail against federal mandates on everything from affirmative action to free school lunches quickly seek top-down mandates when it comes to their own agenda—from school dress codes to teaching about abortion.

Historically, much of school reform has been of the mandate variety, and it breeds a form of covert, silent resistance that prevents the democratic discussion which is the aim of the reform itself. It undercuts its own purposes, for it is open, respectful debate that is needed and that will determine the outcome in the end.

An analogy helps me these days. I imagine that to average Eastern Europeans, their daily world appears more violent today than it was under communism. Nostalgia for yesterday, for an orderliness and predictability that once was, most probably lies beneath the surface for many citizens. It would be hard for it to be otherwise. Nostalgia, in this case and in others, is often accompanied by an understandable, if misplaced, yearning for a paternalistic, even totalitarian, dream. It is similar to the Joe Clark fantasy for governing our schools: use a bullhorn and declare "off with your head." It is easy to see how dangerous such nostalgia for communism might be in Eastern Europe. It is more difficult to see the danger closer to home.

At moments when we are faced with out-of-control and unruly youngsters, I, too, feel the blood rising, and draconian solutions have their appeal to me. It is then that I must remind myself that the solutions we seek, even under circumstances of stress and anger, must be compatible with where we want to go. A boot-camp mentality is not the way to develop in our students the kinds of habits of mind that lead to becoming active, informed citizens. We must say it over and over: When we give in to easy answers "just this once" or "temporarily," we are in more danger in the long run than we want to acknowledge. By doing so, we give in to the notion that democracy is a luxury that is only possible under the most favorable circumstances.

We also do not accumulate wisdom if we hide from each other, our perceived experiences, our understandings, or our assumptions—whether out of deference, fear, or scorn. To build a respectful school community requires open discussion, however inconvenient it might be. Open discussion, in turn, rests upon the presumption that we are members of a common species, belong to a common community with a shared destiny, and must hear each other out. It acknowledges that we are stuck with each other, even if not always happily, and we are bound to disagree at times. Hopefully, with the right kind of habits, we will be able to handle disagreements as they arise. Through give-and-take, our differences will not be unbridgeable, and the dialogue will work for us even in times of trouble.

Unfortunately, most of us have not had many experiences of such communities, especially ones that include the many "others" we busily and understandably avoid in our personal lives. Public schools are a critical place to create these communities and to learn the habits that help create and nurture those communities. If we abandon public education, we abandon a critical tool for the development of such habits, for outside of the public schools, where a diverse group of people have at least the potential to mix and rub elbows, we are very unlikely to create such uncomfortable mixtures and combinations. This is a crucial reason why vouchers, which are an attack on the very idea of public education, need to be resisted.

THE BEGINNINGS OF THE CENTRAL PARK EAST SCHOOLS

Creating a school to nurture democratic ideas is what we set out to do at Central Park East Elementary School 21 years ago. It was a task in the tradition of John Dewey's Lab School, founded almost a century earlier for the children of the faculty of the University of Chicago. Central Park East was the product, in part, of my own history and point of view, and also that of the small band of fellow teachers who joined me. Central Park East was also influenced by a hundred years of democratic school reform. But this time, it was for the children of East Harlem, who were mostly poor and mostly African American and Hispanic.

We hardly understood at first how such a school would challenge our own habits as well. We did not grasp how little we ourselves were accustomed to hearing others, to having to collaborate with colleagues, to taking responsibility for our community. We, too, had built our ideas in isolation, in institutions where we could blame "The Authorities," and behind closed doors where we could work secretly and unexposed. We spoke about creating a community and simultaneously yearned for a one-room schoolhouse in which we could just be left alone.

But we worked at it. We knew we needed to stay small—under 300 students. Size and scale were critical to our success for two reasons. First of all, we felt that only by staying small would we would be able to know our students and their families well, and then be able to create a shared community with them. Second, it would enable us, the teachers, to know each other well enough to take responsibility for each other's work and to be, in the current jargon, accountable. We also needed a school small enough so that shared governance of the school would not take on such a distracting life of its own that it would replace our concern for the education of our students. We prided ourselves on running a school without permanent committees.

As we became more popular, we created spin-offs, including Central Park East II and River East, the Brooklyn New School, Our Little School, and others. When we decided to tackle secondary education 10 years ago, we started a "new" school, rather than just adding on. We based the high school on much of what we read in Ted Sizer's *Horace's Compromise.* We soon joined forces with the growing number of other small high schools in New York City, and we helped nurture more into being. Today we are one of a band of more than 50 small, like-minded schools. And, thanks to a generous grant from the Annenberg Foundation, we are on the eve of seeing if together we can invent a new kind of system and a series of networks to support similar schools. Twenty years ago, however, we were not thinking of spreading our ideas; we only wanted to make sure our own school worked.

We began by taking Ted Sizer's dictum "keep it simple" seriously because both the kids and what we want to teach them are complex. The traditional school has reversed this. The structure and organization of the traditional school are so complex that only the full-time programmer, often with the help of a computer, knows how it fits together. On the other hand, the curriculum has been simplified into small sequenced bits and pieces that can be "easily" fed into the minds of children by interchangeable adults acting the role of teachers. In our school, by contrast, we tried to create as seamless a structure as possible so that very uninterchangeable adults would be required to exercise the most complex judgments. In our high school, most students deal with only two or three different adults at one time, and these adults remain with them for several years. Teachers work in small clusters and can change virtually any part of their schedule at a moment's notice, without checking with higher authorities. It allows us to focus our energies not on coping with the larger "system" but on coping with our own ornery natures and the complexity of what we are trying to achieve. Such a focus required us to rethink the issues of time and size.

TIME AND SIZE

Why are time and size so important? Thoughtful students must grow out of thoughtful schools, and thoughtfulness takes time; time must be spent on substance, not process. We did not merely want workshops on how to conduct meetings but workshops on curriculum, graduation require-ments, pedagogical styles, and shared readings. Teachers must know each other not only socially in the teachers' lounge, but as colleagues. They must be able to distinguish between the ones who talk well and the ones who teach well.

We knew from the history of past reform efforts that creating such a community required time for talking. Time was needed for "just talking" between teachers and students, time for "just talking" among staff mem-bers, and time for "just talking" between school and family. We designed our schedule for this. In our high school, we built in six hours a week between 8:30 A.M. and 3:00 P.M. for teacher-talk of various sorts. We in-cluded monthly retreats, day-long seminars, preschool sessions, and vol-untary meetings before and after official school hours. We also built in five hours a week in the high school for each adult over a period of at least two years to meet with a group of 10 to 15 students. These hours were for talking things over and for tackling all the loose ends of their intellectual and moral lives. We built in a minimum of two family confer-ences annually, each lasting at least half an hour and often much longer. These conferences are meetings in which every family member we can induce to join us comes together with the student's teacher or adviser to examine the student's work and discuss, argue, and plan together. The student, of course, is central to such a conference. We have built in time for others—colleagues from other schools that share our philosophy and from those which do not—to observe us, to look over our work and criti-cize it, and to reflect together.

Schools require an assumption of safety, but in small schools we look for safety not in expensive metal detectors (which are then foiled by clever students who discover back doors), or IDs, or patrolling police. The data overwhelmingly show that small schools, regardless of who their students are, are safer places because the kids know each other and the adults do, too. Their membership in a common community means that there are no strangers in the halls who are not quickly accosted with a friendly, "Can I help you?" When parents have fears, they know whom to call and do not hesitate to pass on rumors. The kids do likewise. They share "secrets" with adults whom they trust when the life of their class-mates or the safety of their school might be at stake. Word travels fast, and it travels to places and to people who can quickly and effectively respond.

In the end, small schools like ours are also in a better position to respond to the cry for accountability. Data are hard to hide in such schools. New York City may claim that 85% of its high school students attend school each day, but that is only because the methods for counting are so easily manipulated. But in a small school, we all know when we are fudging. Our data are not indirect and bureaucratic but easily checked out by direct observation. We have a host of cross-checking methods, all of which are easily and publicly accessible.

Above all, the kind of community the Central Park East Schools have built provides students with the experience of a shared culture, where adults and young people work out their dilemmas together. In most high schools, youngsters create a teen culture totally separate from the adults who most want to influence them. The two worlds live side-by-side, untouched by each other. Yet we know that young people learn most of what they know by being immersed in the culture created by grown-ups. They learn what it means to "grow up" from those they observe and imagine themselves being when they grow up. My brother and I spent hours and hours in our youth at baseball games. My brother learned a lot about how to play baseball by watching and imagining himself to be Joe DiMaggio. I knew how to drive, before I ever got behind the wheel, from being in the car with a mother who drove and whom I imagined myself growing up to be like. I took in "driving" before the first formal lesson began.

Since few young people in large, anonymous schools have ever been exposed to adults engaged in intense discussion of ideas, it is no wonder that they cannot imagine that such discussion is "for real." At Central Park East, we feel that we have no right to demand academic achievement from students who have not witnessed what academic achievement looks like in the hands of experts. It is like imagining kids who have never been exposed to a real ball game becoming great ballplayers. If it is just a charade, if we are not serious, then the price is too high. If we are serious, kids need to see what it is that we honor so much that we require them to spend 12 long years trying to acquire it.

WHAT WE ARE TRYING TO DO

Ultimately, what we are trying to do is to give all of our students what the top achievers get even in the worst of big-city schools, for even in the least successful of New York's high schools, there is a small group of students who do make it. These are the kids who are on the student council, editors of the yearbook, members of the debating club, and writers for the school's newspaper. They attend the honors and AP classes. They know each other, and they are well known by the faculty. They all admire each other. They belong to the same club. In the process, the teachers and the administrators who tout these students' achievements

tend to forget how many losers it took to create these few precious winners. It was a chilling but powerful moment when a youngster at Kennedy High School in the Bronx, with its 5,000-member student body,
noted on graduation day, "What happened to all the rest who came here
with us in ninth grade? How come only 150 of us are up here today to
receive diplomas?" Even at Central Park East Secondary School, we need
to force ourselves occasionally to take note of those whom we have lost,
for by understanding how it happened, we can help to build a more responsive and effective school.

    "It takes a whole village to raise a child" has become a frequently
quoted mantra, but it only works if there is truly a village. If it is a village
that studies together, it also celebrates and mourns together. But how
many schools can do that today? Our entire school came together to
mourn the passing of Josie Hernandez, whose children were in our first
graduating class and who had become a secretary at one of our elementary schools. Her sudden death could not go by unnoted. At all four
Central Park East Schools, we stopped to take stock of her life and its
meaning. We knew we had to respond to her death, personally and individually. We could do this not because we were more caring than other
teachers or other schools, but because we have a structure and style that
enables us to show our care effectively. Imagine if many of our big-city
schools tried to take serious and respectful note of the illnesses, tragedies,
and deaths among the families of their students. It would be a place of
perpetual mourning.

    Small and self-governed schools also change our notions of leader-
ship. They restore the word *principal* to its original meaning. Administration may still be needed, but the school head need not be "an administrator"; he or she could be instead a head teacher. It is no wonder that so
many of our most gifted educators do not aspire to be principals. They
rightly see that the skills required to be a principal have virtually nothing
to do with the skills acquired by those people whom they honor as outstanding teachers. But when schools resemble small, self-governing communities like Central Park East, the head teacher position calls for qualities much more akin to that which our best teachers already demonstrate.

    Small, autonomous schools are, in the end, a way for children, staff,
and parents to create for themselves the experience of community, good
conversation, and the riches of public as well as academic life. We are
faced with many crises today, and only such small, caring schools can
begin to involve the subjects of these crises in the solutions to them.

    It is exhausting work at best. It will become more fruitful work when
we also figure out and help to create the systemic supports such schools
require. We are on the brink of tackling that in many places throughout

this nation. In New York City, thanks to the Annenberg grant and a host of serendipitous forces coming together at the same time, we have gotten an agreement from the board of education, the teachers' union, the mayor, and the state to create a parallel structure—serving a population as large as that of Cincinnati, Newark, or Pittsburgh—to explore what it would be like to have a system of small, special schools. For quite some time, these small, successful schools have operated despite the system. But what would it be like if they operated in concert with a reinvented system? What kind of bureaucratic controls can we do without? How independent and autonomous dare we let such schools become? What trade-offs are involved? Can we build a system of exceptions so that we can truly say that, by the year 2000, every child in New York City can attend a "Central Park East" of their own choice?

Even such a transformed reality would not be a panacea for all our unsolved problems. Schools cannot create vibrant, growing local economies, provide decent shelter, or stop the drug dealers. But the right kind of school can make a difference. By engaging us as teachers, such schools stand a chance of engaging children, too. As we all become capable of being strong, powerful, and lifelong learners, as well as citizens of our schools, so all our students will stand a better chance of being lifelong learners and citizens of a free society.

We believe it is doable. We know such schools can be created; and we know they can work for all children. That has already been proven. What remains to be done is to insure that no child in America has to go to a school that neither you nor I would tolerate for our own children.

BIBLIOGRAPHY

Berliner, D.C. 1993. Mythology and the American system of education. *Phi Delta Kappan*, April, 74(8): 632, 634–640.

Bracey, G. W. 1991. Why can't they be like we were? *Phi Delta Kappan*, October, 73(2): 104–117.

Bracey, G. W. 1992. The second Bracey report on the condition of public education. *Phi Delta Kappan*, October, 74(2): 104–108, 110–117.

Bracey, G. W. 1993. The third Bracey report on the condition of public education. *Phi Delta Kappan*, October, 75(2): 104–112, 114–118.

Bracey, G. W. 1994. The fourth Bracey report on the condition of public education. *Phi Delta Kappan*, October, 76(2): 115–127.

Carini, P. F. 1993. Images and immeasurables. Occasional paper. Prospect Center, North Bennington, VT.

Cohen, D. 1972. *The learning child*. New York: Schocken.

Cuban, L. 1994. The great school scam. *Education Week*, 15 June, 13: 44.

Darling-Hammond, L. 1993. Reframing the school reform agenda: Developing capacity for school transformation. *Phi Delta Kappan*, June, 74(10): 753–761.

Delpit, L. 1994. *Other people's children: Cultural conflict in the classroom.* New York: New Press.

Dewey, J. [1916] 1965. *Democracy and education.* New York: Free Press.

Dewey, J. 1986. Experience and education. *Educational Forum,* Spring, 50(3): 241–252.

Duckworth, E. 1987. *The having of wonderful ideas and other essays.* New York: Teachers College Press.

Fine, M. 1984. *Chartering urban school reform: Reflecting on public high schools in the midst of change.* New York: Teachers College Press.

Freedman, S. 1992. *Small victories: The real world of a teacher.* New York: Harper-Collins.

Glickman, C. E. 1993. *Renewing America's schools.* San Francisco: Jossey-Bass.

Gould, S. J. 1981. *The mismeasure of man.* New York: Norton.

Hampel, R. 1986. *The last little citadel: American high schools since 1940.* Boston: Houghton Mifflin.

Holt, J. 1968. *How children fail.* New York: Dell.

Howe, H. 1993. *Thinking about kids: An agenda.* New York: Free Press.

Kohl, H. R. [1968] 1988. *Thirty-six children.* New York: NAL-Dutton.

Kohl, H. R. 1994. *I won't learn from you: And other thoughts on creative maladjustment.* New York: New Press.

Kozol, J. 1992. *Savage inequalities.* New York: HarperCollins.

Lieberman, A., ed. 1995. *The work of restructuring schools: Building from the ground up.* New York: Teachers College Press.

Little, J. W. In press. *Ties that bind.* New York: Teachers College Press.

Mitchell, L. S. [1934] 1991. *The young geographers: How they explore the world and how they map the world.* New York: Bank Street College of Education.

Paley, V. 1981. *Wally's stories: Conversations in the kindergarten.* Cambridge, MA: Harvard University Press.

Perrone, V. 1991. *A letter to teachers: Reflections on schooling and the art of teaching.* San Francisco: Jossey-Bass.

Powell, A. G., et al. 1985. *Shopping mall high: Winners and losers in the educational marketplace.* Boston: Houghton Mifflin.

Rose, M. 1990. *Lives on the boundary: A moving account of the struggles and achievements of America's educationally underprepared.* New York: Penguin.

Rose, M. 1995. *Possible lives: The promise of public education in America.* Boston: Houghton Mifflin.

Rossi, N., and T. Cole, trans. 1970. *Letter to a teacher by schoolboys of Barbiana.* New York: Random House.

Sarason, S. 1982. *The culture of school and the problem of change.* Boston: Allyn & Bacon.

Seletsky, A. 1985. Where the action is. *The Nation,* 25 May, 240(20): 634–638

Shulman, L. 1987. Knowledge and teaching: Foundations of the new reform. *Harvard Educational Review,* February, 57: 1–22.

Shulman, L. 1990. *Aristotle had it right: On knowledge and pedagogy.* Occasional paper #4 (May), The Holmes Group, Michigan State University.

Sizer, T. 1992. *Horace's compromise: The dilemma of the American high school.* Boston: Houghton Mifflin.

Smith, F. 1985. *Reading without nonsense.* New York: Teachers College Press.

ARTICLES, BOOKS, AND VIDEOS ABOUT THE CENTRAL PARK EAST SCHOOLS

Ancess, J., et al. 1993. The development of authentic assessment at Central Park East Secondary School. In *Creating learner-centered accountability.* Available from National Center for Restructuring Education, Schools, and Teaching. (NCREST), Box 110, Teachers College, Columbia University, New York, NY 10027, (212) 678-3432.

Bensman, D. 1987. *Quality education in the inner city: The story of the Central Park East Schools.* Available from Center for Collaborative Education, 1573 Madison Avenue, Room 201, New York, NY 10029, (212) 348-7821.

Bensman, D. 1994. *Lives of the graduates of Central Park East Elementary School. Where have they gone? What did they really learn?* Available from Center for Collaborative Education.

Darling-Hammond, L., et al. 1994. *Graduation by portfolio at Central Park East Secondary School.* Available from NCREST.

Fliegel, S., and J. MacGuire. 1993. *Miracle in East Harlem: The fight for choice in public education.* New York: Random House.

Graduation by portfolio—Performance-based assessment at Central Park East Secondary School. Video: 50 minutes. Available from Center for Collaborative Education.

Snyder, J., et al. 1992. *Makers of meaning in a learning-centered school: A case study of Central Park East 1 Elementary School.* Available from NCREST.

Wiseman, F. *High school II.* Video: 220 minutes. Available from Zipporah Films, 1 Richdale Avenue, Unit 4, Cambridge, MA 02140, (617) 576-3603.

Wood, G. H. 1992. *Schools that work: America's most innovative public education programs.* New York: Dutton.

Mobilizing Schools and Communities to Develop Ethics and Social Responsibility

EDWARD T. JOYNER

THE FOUNDERS of the United States recognized that universal, free public education was the cornerstone of democracy. Our early public schools were shaped by the collective wisdom that emerged from a powerful coalition of forces representing the family, the church, and the community that allowed schools to transform our nation's youth into fully contributing citizens.

Our notion of education for the common good was conceived and carried out by schools and communities that spoke with a common tongue with respect to what they wanted young people to learn and how they expected them to "behave." There was near-unanimous agreement among adults regarding the values that they wanted to pass on to children. My own life experiences reflect the consistent values and behaviors that adults in communities prior to the mid-to-late 1960s transmitted to children.

THE MORAL INFLUENCE OF ADULTS ON CHILDREN: A RECOLLECTION

I grew up in the 1950s and 1960s in a small town in North Carolina. During my third year in school, I was part of an event that profoundly influenced my development as an educator. Some girls and boys in my classroom were passing notes that ridiculed one of our fellow students because of his tattered clothing and poor hygiene. This behavior had also occurred in the past away from the watchful eye of our teacher, Miss

McPherson. On this eventful day, the teacher intercepted several of the notes, and after questioning the class, discovered that most, if not all, of the class had participated at various times in teasing this shy youngster. After having read all the notes, Miss McPherson announced that all but the bus students would remain after school and that the entire class would not be able to have recess the next day. Of course, the members of our class (myself included) who lived in town thought that this was unfair. We also could not understand why she kept the whole class instead of only singling out our "guilty" classmates.

When the bell rang to end the school day, our teacher dismissed the bus students, and the rest of us remained in our seats anticipating the possibility of a stern lecture, notes sent home to our parents, or—worse— the feared corporal punishment from the dreaded "board of education" that was a part of the standard equipment in nearly every teacher's classroom in the rural South during the 1950s. Instead, Miss McPherson employed a different strategy.

Our teacher asked each one of us if we believed that we should treat others as we wished to be treated? We all answered "yes." She then asked us to give her one good reason why any of us thought that belittling another student was a good thing. With all our collective wisdom, we could not think of one way in which ridiculing others contributed to human progress.

Miss McPherson continued by asking us to put ourselves in our classmate's place and to write a few sentences describing how it would feel if others made fun of our clothing or other personal characteristics. She ended the session by delivering a sermon on the importance of being kind to others. Our teacher made it clear that kindness, in her mind, was the most important human attribute and that it should be placed alongside respect, honesty, courtesy, responsibility, and love for self and others as the most important values in life. She said that doing well in school was important, but that it was equally important to become a good person. Miss McPherson was very straightforward and honest about our status as "little colored children" living in the segregated South of the 1950s. She said that if we were not loved and respected by others, we could at least love ourselves and should begin to prepare ourselves for a time when we could enjoy the full rights and responsibilities of American citizenship. We left that day with a sense of collective shame and guilt. That several of our peers had participated in the humiliation of another human being, and that others said nothing or did nothing to stop this cruelty, left everyone feeling responsible for what had happened.

In the days and weeks that followed, many of us felt obligated to compensate for the misdeeds of our class. We were especially nice to the boy who had been the object of our scorn. We recognized that most of us had laughed when he was the butt of the many jokes made about his appearance and personal hygiene. By laughing, we were as guilty as the jokesters. As I reflect back on this experience, I realize that we were unwittingly participating in the psychological destruction of another child either by direct involvement or by our indifference to his pain.

I found out later that Miss McPherson made a visit to the boy's home and very delicately talked to his mother about personal hygiene. She also took several items of clothing to him after discussing this with his mother. She made sure that our parents were made aware of why we had to remain after school, and we all got varying degrees of counseling and punishment at home as a result. I am also certain that it was not purely coincidental that my Sunday School teacher, who was a friend of Miss McPherson (and a fifth-grade teacher in our school), taught us the story of the Good Samaritan in our Sunday School class a Sunday or two after the incident.

This story from my childhood is an example of the power that adults have to influence the behavior of children. This power becomes greater when the adults share a common agreement about what is right and wrong and what is acceptable and unacceptable behavior. Dr. James Comer, the Maurice Falk Professor of Child Psychiatry at Yale University, suggests that "tight-knit social networks of approving and disapproving people are more effective determinants of a child's behavior than laws, policemen, security, and surveillance equipment. Eventually the attitudes, values, and behavior of adult authority figures become a part of the child's character" (Comer 1980, 10).

The norms and values in my community were set by parents, relatives, neighbors, community leaders, and the teachers and administrators in our school. Few of the adults in our town wavered in their support of the basic values that held our community together. When our parents and others were told that we had teased the young man, it was clearly communicated to us that to belittle another human being for any reason was cruel and unacceptable. The example of the Good Samaritan was placed before us to encourage us not only to be courteous and respectful to others but also to help people in need when we could. This family, school, and community support was the foundation for our growth and development.

CHILDREN AT RISK TODAY

We are faced today with a generation of young people of all racial and economic backgrounds who are growing up without the concerted support that many of the children in my generation received. Marian Wright Edelman, the president of the Children's Defense Fund, captures the plight of contemporary youth when she states:

> Too many young people—of all colors, of all walks of life—are growing up today unable to handle life in hard places, without hope, without adequate attention, and without steady internal compasses to navigate the morally polluted seas they must face on the journey to adulthood. Millions of children are drowning in the meaninglessness of a culture that rewards greed and tells them that life is about getting rather than giving. (Edelman 1992, 15)

There are many indicators that clearly support Edelman's point. The increasingly violent nature of our society graphically illustrates that we are a nation in rapid moral decline. The United States has the highest murder rate for 15- to 24-year-old males among leading industrial nations (Jacquet 1989). In 1985, according to the National Center for Health Statistics (1987), children 11 years of age or younger were responsible for 21 killings, 3,434 assaults, 1,735 robberies, and 435 rapes. A study by the Carnegie Corporation in 1994 found that our youngest children are not immune from this violence, as one in three victims of physical abuse are babies less than a year old. In 1990, more 1-year-olds were physically abused than in any previous year for which we have data. Almost 90% of children who died of abuse and neglect in 1990 were under the age of 5; 53% were less than a year old (Carnegie Task Force on Meeting the Needs of Young Children 1994). Children are both victims of and perpetrators of the senseless violence that is a relatively new phenomenon among our youth.

Growing up in a violent environment puts young people at risk in other areas. According to Mary Schwab-Stone, a prominent pediatrician at the Yale Child Study Center, exposure to violence is associated with more involvement in antisocial activities, with alcohol use, with lower social achievement, with less perceived harm from engaging in risky behaviors and more willingness to fight (Schwab-Stone 1995). She further reports that more than 55% of the eighth and tenth graders surveyed in a mid-sized New England city reported that they had engaged in sexual intercourse. These students were 4.4 times more likely to drop out than students who reported no sexual activity. National figures indicate that there have been more than 1 million teenage pregnancies a year since 1983. The infection of approximately 2.5 million adolescents annually with sexually transmitted diseases is a by-product of such frequent unprotected sexual activity (Schwab-Stone 1995).

The troubling statistics among our young are directly related to two factors: (1) the failure of adults to provide positive models worthy of emulation, and (2) a fragmented effort by the caregivers who share the responsibility for working together to create standards of behavior that encourage youth to behave in socially accepted ways. However, all is not lost. Schools working with families and communities can play a major role in changing the disturbing trends that presently characterize American society. We can teach our young people how to behave in constructive ways, but we must begin by providing better examples for our children and by supporting standards of behavior based on moral principles of justice, fairness, and a sense of responsibility for self and others. The African proverb, "It takes a whole village to raise a child," effectively captures the breadth and depth of the work that must be done.

When we say it takes a whole village to raise a child, implicitly we are recognizing that the way children learn to become adults is by having adult members of a community agree on the values they want children in the community to accept and practice. While this requires more effort today than in the past, teachers, parents, and community members must engage in a conversation of mission. What kind of schools do we want for our children? What kind of behaviors—academic, social, and moral— do we want from our children? What examples must we set to guide them? This kind of conversation is fundamental to the development of what Ted Sizer (1992) refers to as "habits of heart and habits of mind."

We know that the relationships between children and the adults whom they deem to be significant will either build or destroy a child's character. James (1890), Mead (1934), and Cooley (1902) agreed in principle that those with whom the individual identifies and who are important to him or her have the greatest potential for influencing that person's behavior. When related to the school, it becomes clear that, along with parents, teachers and other school personnel are significant in influencing the behavior of children. Since children are socially anchored in their families and immediate communities, it is important that schools initiate structures and processes so that they can collaborate with families and community groups to create a common set of values, principles, and expectations for students. Once critical stakeholders can agree on values, principles, and expectations, it becomes easier to create the programs and activities that provide the necessary experiences for students to develop their character and intellect.

When the home, school, and community can agree on the values and behaviors to be transmitted, the child can function better in all three contexts. If there is conflict and/or ambiguity, the child is likely to experience inner conflict in trying on the various roles required to move back and forth between conflicting social systems.

Both James Comer and Eric Schaps, of the Developmental Studies

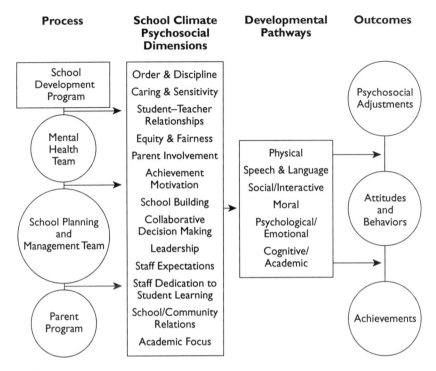

The model is the property of the Yale Child Study Center. Use of this model requires prior authorization of the SDP Director of Research

Figure 5.1. The Comer Process

Center in Oakland, California, have developed structures and processes at the school and classroom levels to help young people with their intellectual and moral growth. Comer has, over the past 25 years, developed a governance and planning process that uses systems theory and child development knowledge to create a "whole-village mentality" in stakeholders at the central office, school, family, and community levels (Figure 5.1). Eric Schaps has developed pedagogical approaches designed to create thoughtful, knowledgeable, competent, caring, principled, and self-disciplined students (Schaps et al. 1993).

DEVELOPMENTAL PATHWAYS AND THE WHOLE CHILD

Comer has identified six pathways that should serve both as a framework for analysis when assessing child and adolescent growth and develop-

ment and as focal points for activities and programs designed to facili-
tate such development. These pathways are the physical, the cognitive-
intellectual, the psycho-emotional, the social-interactive, the speech and
language, and the moral-ethical. Taken together, they constitute what we
popularly refer to as the "whole child." Optimum development is a function of balance and synergy between a child's physical, psycho-emotional,
social-interactive, cognitive-intellectual, speech and language, and moral-
ethical self. Development in any one of these pathways can have the effect
of enhancing functioning in the others. For example, a self-confident and
emotionally stable child will most likely be able to interact appropriately
in a variety of social settings. The ability to interact well socially may
allow a child to bond and attach to a powerful authority figure such as a
teacher, who, because of such a bond, may expend more effort to develop
the child's intellectual potential. Since intellectual growth is mediated by
language, the child may also experience growth in the ability to receive
and communicate written and spoken language. Hence we cannot single
out any one of the pathways for exclusive development. Moreover, the
stage for moral-ethical growth is set when we address the physical, intellectual, psycho-emotional, social, and language needs of students. Thus,
recognition of the developmental pathways as the framework for analysis
of student behavior and as focal points for schools and community pro-
gramming is a critical first step toward creating moral and ethical children and adolescents along with positive, nurturing relationships between children and significant adults who serve their needs.

The emphasis on the developmental pathways is at the heart of the
Comer Process, and that is what distinguishes it from other school reforms. Comer defines these six areas as follows:

1. *The Physical Pathway.* At the most basic level, the environment must
   meet the child's basic physical needs in order for the child to grow and
   to develop. These needs include food, rest, shelter, and freedom from
   pain and/or illness. If these needs are not met, the physical distress
   that results will affect the child's functioning in all the other areas of
   development. For example, being deprived of food and clothing can
   influence both children and adults to violate deeply held moral convictions. Victor Hugo illustrated this point through the character of Jean
   Valjean in his novel *Les Miserables,* the source of the current Broad-
   way musical.
2. *The Cognitive-Intellectual Pathway.* All children are born with potential
   that allows them to reason and solve problems. This pathway allows
   children to make sense of the world and to absorb the knowledge and
   skills (through experiences with other human beings) that allow them

to gain a measure of control over how development is expressed in the other five areas. For example, physical threat might create an impulse to lash out at the assailant. Depending on the reasoning level of the individual and the context in which the threat takes place, the person may override the instinct to strike back and use a strategy that protects the welfare of both parties. Gandhi and Dr. Martin Luther King, Jr., are examples of individuals who had tremendous control over such instincts. They used their cognitive and intellectual development as a means to control how they would express the other dimensions of their development.

3. *The Psycho-Emotional Pathway.* Children have the need to develop a sense of self-regard, an attitude which tells them that they "count," that they are important, and that they have talents and attributes which will allow them to contribute to the world in meaningful, socially approved ways. This developing self is largely determined by the quality of human interactions experienced first by children in the family and extended family and later in other social networks such as the school and church. When children are not esteemed by significant adults, their ability to function well in the other areas is impaired. For example, a young woman with low self-esteem may engage in risky sexual behavior that has the potential to threaten her physical well-being. This is also viewed as a moral and social issue.

4. *The Social-Interactive Pathway.* Children must develop the ability to interact in a wide range of social settings because their development in other areas is dependent on the transmission of the values, knowledge, and skills necessary to live successfully in a particular place and time. Powerful adults are more likely to engage in productive relationships with children and adolescents who respond to them in ways they deem to be "acceptable." On the other hand, children are dependent on these same adults to model and teach them that which is socially acceptable. Early in the child's development, the home and community provide the child with the knowledge of interpersonal interaction patterns or prescriptions for the appropriate attitudes, verbal responses, and gestures that are viewed as acceptable in particular social contexts. When behaviors learned in the home are congruent with those learned in school, a win/win environment is created. This allows for a bond among parent, child, and teacher that allows the child the favored status that most children need in order to learn in school and at home. When the child's social skills are viewed negatively, a lose/lose relationship ensues and neither of the parties benefits. Children are labeled as social outcasts, and their development in all other areas is threatened.

5. *The Speech and Language Pathway.* Language has two primary functions in human development: (1) communication and (2) the representation of knowledge. Early in life children learn that language can be used to convey messages to the self and others. They learn the oral and behavioral cues for imparting messages and simultaneously learn to interpret the messages of others. These acquired words and symbols also become the categories through which children express reasoning ability.

6. *The Moral-Ethical Pathway.* Crucial to all human interactions is the child's understanding and possession of sound moral and ethical standards, as well as the inclination to act upon these values. Such behavior is based on socially transmitted principles that not only delineate the acts for which the individual is held morally responsible but also prescribe just and fair consequences for moral transgression. Typically, moral standards are acquired from the family, religious institutions, and schools. Children are also motivated to behave in specific ways because of the modeling behaviors of significant adults.

In an age of great influence by mass media, children may also be motivated by individuals that they deem to be significant because of popularity and achievement in sports, entertainment, and other high-profile arenas. When role models behave in ways consistent with such values and when social institutions concur in these values, children are able to function across such institutions and exhibit the behaviors that reflect the collective wisdom of significant adults. However, when one or more of these institutions fail to instill common values or impart values that are in conflict with those of others serving the child, the child becomes confused and may make inappropriate choices with respect to what reasonable individuals would deem to be ethical behavior.

Working collaboratively with parents and school staff, Comer developed a nine-component process model that organizes schools, families, and communities in a way that allows them to focus their efforts on the development of students through the six pathways. The Comer Process consists of three structures, three operations, and three guiding principles. The three structures consist of (1) a *governance and management team* representative of parents, teachers, administrators, and support staff; (2) a *mental health team* consisting of social service professionals in the school and school district; and (3) a *parent program* that includes a broad representation of parents across social and economic groups in the school.

Since the governance and management team represents all of the various constituent groups within the broader school community, it carries out the three critical operations. This team is responsible for the development of: (4) a *comprehensive school plan* with specific goals related to the academic and psychosocial development of students; (5) *staff and parent development* activities based on building-level goals identified in the school plan; and (6) periodic *assessment*, which allows the team to *modify* the plan to meet identified needs and opportunities.

Successful implementation of the process requires that participants accept the guiding principles of: (7) *collaboration*, (8) *"no-fault" problem solving*, and (9) *consensus decision making*. Collaboration is necessary for all of the stakeholders to have a sense of ownership of the initiatives taken by the school to improve teaching and learning. People are more willing to support the goals in an organization when they own both the problems or challenges faced by it as well as the solutions necessary for continuous improvement. "No-fault" problem solving is employed because trying to affix blame rather than trying to fix the problem results in wasted time and energy. Finger-pointing also creates bad feelings that often linger and prevent the development of the levels of trust necessary for optimum group functioning. In addition, it sets a poor example for students. Finally, consensus decision making is employed to avoid winners and losers. Team members are asked to make decisions that they can all support with the understanding that any decision can be changed at any time if it does not achieve reasonably good results. Every participant is expected to honor the guiding principles of the program. Since respect, honesty, forgiveness, responsibility, and trust are embedded in the guiding principles, adults set a good example for the students in the school by modeling them.

Eric Schaps and his associates at the Developmental Studies Center have created a child-centered process designed to establish schools as caring communities (Schaps et al. 1995). Schaps has identified five goals for schools that will produce students who are thoughtful, knowledgeable, competent, caring, principled, and self-disciplined (Figure 5.2). These goals include:

- Stable, warm relationships
- A challenging, learner-centered curriculum
- Teaching for understanding
- Simultaneous focus on intellectual, ethical, and social development
- Focus on promoting intrinsic motivation

The Developmental Studies Center has identified the key experiences in school that contribute to children's growth as well as the developmental processes that help children and youth grow into adulthood as lifelong learners who practice high standards of ethical conduct (Figure 5.3).

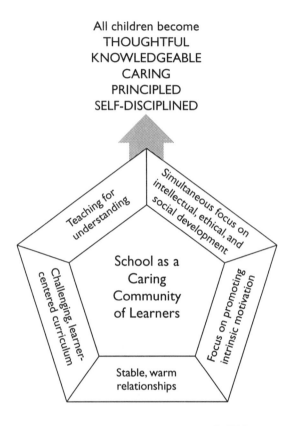

Figure 5.2. School as a Caring Community of Learners

THE COMER PROCESS AND THE CARING COMMUNITY

Both the Comer Process and the Developmental Studies Center use theory and applied knowledge about human growth to create an ecological support system that places as much emphasis on moral-ethical development as it does on cognitive-intellectual growth. They also recognize the role that adults play in this effort. Comer provides participation structures for key adult stakeholders and support mechanisms in the form of a comprehensive school plan that reflects the needs of the school in both the intellectual and social arenas. The process also provides ongoing staff development that helps parents and educators acquire needed knowledge and skills, as well as a modification process that allows for changes

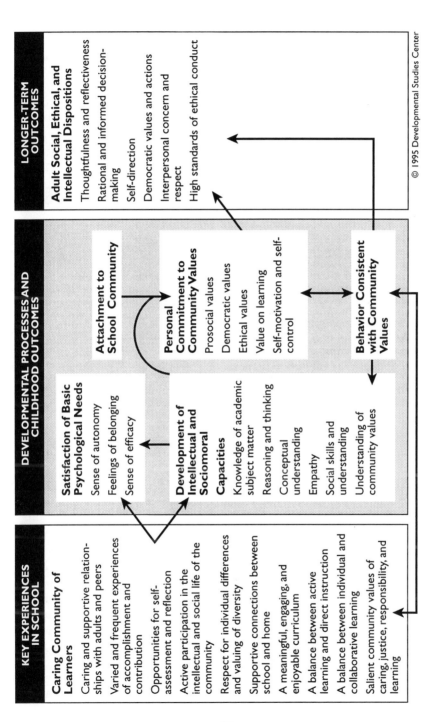

KEY EXPERIENCES IN SCHOOL

Caring Community of Learners

Caring and supportive relationships with adults and peers

Varied and frequent experiences of accomplishment and contribution

Opportunities for self-assessment and reflection

Active participation in the intellectual and social life of the community

Respect for individual differences and valuing of diversity

Supportive connections between school and home

A meaningful, engaging, and enjoyable curriculum

A balance between active learning and direct instruction

A balance between individual and collaborative learning

Salient community values of caring, justice, responsibility, and learning

DEVELOPMENTAL PROCESSES AND CHILDHOOD OUTCOMES

Satisfaction of Basic Psychological Needs

Sense of autonomy

Feelings of belonging

Sense of efficacy

Development of Intellectual and Sociomoral Capacities

Knowledge of academic subject matter

Reasoning and thinking

Conceptual understanding

Empathy

Social skills and understanding

Understanding of community values

Attachment to School Community

Personal Commitment to Community Values

Prosocial values

Democratic values

Ethical values

Value on learning

Self-motivation and self-control

Behavior Consistent with Community Values

LONGER-TERM OUTCOMES

Adult Social, Ethical, and Intellectual Dispositions

Thoughtfulness and reflectiveness

Rational and informed decision-making

Self-direction

Democratic values and actions

Interpersonal concern and respect

High standards of ethical conduct

© 1995 Developmental Studies Center

Figure 5.3. Development of Adult, Social, Ethical, and Intellectual Dispositions

85

in programs and actions based on new information that comes from formative and summative evaluation of results. Schaps provides direct training of teachers so that they can maintain a developmental perspective with respect to pedagogy and create a nurturing classroom environment. Both reformers reject the deficit perspective and focus on students' strengths rather than their weaknesses. Neither tries to isolate children from their community, but rather solicits the support of family and community to socialize children and provide a climate for overall growth. They ask adults to preach the work ethic, to teach respect for academic learning, and to exhibit the moral-ethical behavior they expect from children.

SUMMARY

While moral development is the responsibility of the whole village, the school can play a pivotal role in developing ethical behavior in children and youth. Schools attempting to take on this crucial task should be guided by the following principles gleaned from the work of two of our nation's most notable school reform programs:

1. Moral behavior cannot be addressed without considering the developmental needs of the whole child. Physical, intellectual, psychoemotional, social, and language development influence moral development. The developmental pathways are interactive, inasmuch as development in any one of them enhances development in the others. On the other hand, lack of development in any one of them *may* negatively influence development in the others. To promote moral development, programs developed by schools should reflect the "wholeness" of children and youth.
2. Optimum moral growth occurs when educators, parents, and members of the community can agree on the values and behaviors they expect from young people and practice such behaviors themselves.
3. Schools must adopt participation structures that engage stakeholders in problem solving, planning, implementation, and evaluation of the programs and activities that lead to high levels of performance in the intellectual, psychosocial, and moral realms. Such interaction should be governed by "no-fault" problem solving, collaborative planning, and consensus decision making.
4. Cross-training opportunities for parents, community members, and educators must be created to help adults keep pace with the attitudes,

knowledge, and skills that they need to help young people navigate a sea of life that is fraught with unseen dangers.

5. Schools must accept that all children bring with them the potential to learn and to succeed. There is no scientific evidence to support the validity of deficit models of school reform. The only exception would be children who have been identified as having specific physical or mental deficits resulting from congenital illnesses or abnormalities (Haynes 1993). Even in these cases, individuals have succeeded in various walks of life; Helen Keller, Stevie Wonder, Jim Abbott, and the late Wilma Rudolph are excellent examples of success. Such acceptance creates a moral climate of inclusion.

6. The development of ethical behaviors and social responsibility must be addressed in all areas of the school and must be supported by the school board and central office. This includes the curriculum, classroom practices, athletics and fine arts programs, organizations and clubs, and opportunities for peer, school, and community service.

We can create schools and communities that foster the development of ethical behavior in young people, but we must first examine our own behavior as adults. This is not a partisan effort. To accomplish this noble task, we must create coalitions that transcend such barriers as race, class, religion, and gender. We are running out of time, and the young people in our country deserve our best efforts.

NOTE

I wish to acknowledge the contributions of Dr. James P. Comer, Dr. Norris M. Haynes, Dr. Kimberly Kinsler, and Dr. Eric Schaps in assisting with the identification of relevant material in my preparation of this manuscript.

REFERENCES

Carnegie Task Force on Meeting the Needs of Young Children. 1994. *Starting points: Meeting the needs of our youngest children.* New York: Carnegie Corporation of New York.

Comer, J. P. 1980. *School power: Implications of an intervention project.* New York: Free Press.

Cooley, C. 1902. *Human nature and the social order.* New York: Scribner's.

Edelman, M. W. 1992. *The measure of our success: A letter to my children and yours.* Boston: Beacon Press.

Haynes, N. M. 1993. *Critical issues in educating African-American children.* Langley Park, MD: IAAS Publishers.

Jacquet, L. 1989. Juvenile sex offenders: Distressingly commonplace. *Our Sunday Visitor,* 25 June, 78(8): 3.

James, W. 1890. *The principles of psychology.* New York: Scribner's.

Mead, G. H. 1934. *Individual, self, and society.* Chicago: University of Chicago Press.

National Center for Health Statistics, U.S. Department of Health and Human Services. 1987. *Catalog of publications of the National Center for Health Statistics, 1980–1986.* Washington, DC: U.S. Government Printing Office.

Schaps, E., V. Batlistich, and D. Solomon. 1993. The child development project. *Educational Leadership,* November, 51(3): 46.

Schaps, E., C. Lewis, and M. Watson. 1995. Training materials on child development and school as a caring community. Developmental Studies Center, Oakland, CA. Duplicated.

Schwab-Stone, M. 1995. No safe haven: A study of violence exposure in an urban community. *Journal of the American Academy of Child and Adolescent Psychiatry,* October, 34(10): 1343–1352.

Sizer, T. 1992. *Horace's school: Redesigning the American high school.* Boston: Houghton Mifflin.

Professional Development: Learning from Experience

LEE S. SHULMAN

THE STORY IS TOLD about a schoolteacher, a *melamed* as we call him in the Jewish tradition, who sat late one evening next to the fire, ruminating with an unopened book in his lap. Suddenly he observed to his wife of many years, "You know, Yentl, I was just thinking. If I were the czar, I would be richer than the czar." Now his wife, after 25 years of marriage, had learned that many things come out of this fellow's mouth—not all of which are particularly profound—but she humored him and said, "I really don't understand; if you were the czar (that's a wonderful thought), you would be as rich as the czar." He replied, "No, no, no! I've been thinking. If I were the czar, I would indeed be richer than the czar." "How could that be?" she queried. "Because," he responded, "if I were the czar, I could still do a little teaching on the side!"

Why that story? In some ways, that wonderful story also reflects a deeper and more disturbing set of premises that many of us carry, including those of us whose lives are bound up as teachers and with teaching, with regard to the activity and profession of teaching. It is that teaching is something that one does "on the side." It is not particularly complicated. It is not particularly demanding. Anyone could do it, if they didn't already have something more important to do.

I have spent most of my scholarly career trying to understand teaching. I interrupted this effort for a period of about 10 years when I tried to ask similar questions about the practice of medicine. The question in both cases has been a very straightforward and simple one: How is this apparently simple, straightforward activity conducted? What are people really doing when they teach? Or when they meet a patient and make a diagnosis and prescribe a treatment? What I have found in years of studying the women and men engaged in these professions is that, of the two, teaching is by far the more complex and demanding. The more time I spend in classrooms with teachers—talking with them, observing, watching videotapes, talking some more, reflecting on my own teaching—the more I peel off layer upon layer of incredible complexity. After some 30 years of doing such work, I have concluded that classroom teaching—particularly at the elementary and secondary levels—is perhaps the most complex, most challenging, and most demanding, subtle, nuanced, and frightening activity that our species has ever invented. In fact, when I compared the complexity of teaching with that much more highly rewarded profession, "doing medicine," I concluded that the only time medicine even approaches the complexity of an average day of classroom teaching is in an emergency room during a natural disaster (Shulman 1987, 369–386). When 30 patients want your attention at the same time, only then do you approach the complexity of the average classroom on an average day.

For every strategy of reform, I believe that the engine of reform — its regulator and ultimately its bottleneck—is the classroom teacher. In Larry Cuban's terms (Chapter 1, this volume), this makes me a pedagogical rather than a systemic reformer, and I think he has me correctly pegged. I would argue that whatever your conception of reform—whether the classroom door is open or closed, whether the curriculum is mandated or invented—its success ultimately rests on the quality of the pedagogical interaction between teacher and students. And I say "students" rather than "student" because we do not teach in situations where we and an individual student are sitting on opposite ends of a tutorial log and thus can work clinically, one-on-one in the educational process. We are always working with groups of students, often several groups each day, and nearly always in larger numbers than we think is prudent.

I now offer this chapter's sole argument: Efforts at school reform must give as much attention to creating the conditions for teacher learning as for student learning. Any effort at school reform will ultimately fail if it does not ask itself: "As I design this grand plan for improving the quality of learning in students, have I designed with equal care and concern a plan for teacher learning in this setting?" The effective school must be educative for its teachers. The proposals for reform reported in this volume—the Coalition of Essential Schools, Central Park East Secondary School, Comer Project schools—share in common the commitment to creating the conditions for teacher learning.

You may ask, "What are the conditions for teacher learning?" I invite you to examine Jerome Bruner's propositions (Chapter 2, this volume) regarding the conditions that make student learning flourish: He suggests that these are agency or activity, reflection, collaboration or interaction, and culture or community. We teachers are just older members of the same species as our students. We do not suddenly change the necessary conditions for learning when we pass our 21st birthday and earn teaching credentials. Those principles, along with several more that I shall add, define the conditions for teacher learning as well.

To paraphrase the famous Rabbi Hillel in an analogous situation roughly 2,000 years ago, "That is the essence; the rest is commentary." That commentary now follows.

THREE QUESTIONS

I have three questions: What makes teaching so difficult? How can teachers learn to manage, cope with, and eventually master those difficulties? What forms of school reform can contribute to creating the conditions for teacher learning? These are difficult questions, so permit me to describe my approach to answering them. I stand correctly accused, as a university academician, of being a theoretician. I believe that theory is indispensable. However, my approach to theory is somewhat different from that of many of my colleagues.

Our usual sense of theory is that we invent theories and then we apply them to practice. I, on the other hand, am the kind of person who finds things that work in practice, and then I try to make them work in theory. I am thus utterly dependent on learning from what David Hawkins once dubbed "the wisdom of practice." Nearly 30 years ago, I edited a book entitled *Learning by Discovery*, to which Jerome Bruner and I were both contributors (Shulman and Keislar 1966). David Hawkins wrote a paper in that volume called "Learning the Unteachable," in which he argued that there are times in human history when there is much more wisdom in practice than in the academy, when gamblers know more about probability than statisticians, and when sailors know more about the heavens than astronomers (Hawkins 1966, 3–12). He claimed, and I think correctly, that we are probably at a time in the history of education when there is more, and indeed even a distinctive, wisdom about teaching among practicing teachers than there is among academic educators. But the wisdom of teachers is isolated and unvoiced. We as teachers indeed can become smarter about what we do, but we work in lonely circumstances that make it difficult for us to articulate what we know and to share what we have learned with others. The nature of our work habits and conditions is so unreflective that we even forget some of the understandings that we have achieved in the course of our practice.

How many times do we find ourselves teaching something that we have taught before, only to realize that we are making the same mistakes that we made the last time we taught the same topic? Because of the pedagogical isolation of teaching, even at universities, and because of our own lack of adequate discipline in documenting and reflecting on our own practice, we fail to incorporate what we have learned into our new practices. We continue to repeat the same mistakes. We suffer from chronic pedagogical amnesia.

We all know the old saw that there are two kinds of teachers: One has 20 years of experience; the other has 1 year of experience 20 times. There is a large difference between learning from experience and simply having experience. Many teachers have experience. It takes special teachers working under special circumstances to learn from that experience. Yet learning from experience is one of the requirements of any school reform. Most of our school reform efforts encourage teachers to create conditions in which students will be creative and inventive, both problem solvers and innovators. Teachers are asked to create conditions for learning that they themselves may never have encountered before. Under those conditions, teachers must learn to anticipate the unexpected, because they have created circumstances in which successful students have been given the freedom and encouragement to come up with surprises.

If such reforms are to flourish and grow, the teachers must be capable of apprehending those surprises, analyzing the extent to which they are educative for their students, and adapting their future teaching either to enhance or discourage such student performances. Teachers must therefore learn from the experiences they create with their students. In cases of school reform, the classroom becomes the educator's laboratory, a setting in which new forms of teaching and learning are painstakingly grown in a fertile culture of exploration. The teacher manages that laboratory and is responsible for detecting and reporting its lessons for improved educational practice.

When I study or conduct research on practice, I strive to mine the "wisdom of practice" that grows in the minds of those experimenting teachers. In mining that wisdom, I attempt to develop more powerful theories of practice, which I can then share with my fellow educator-academicians and classroom teachers—who in turn correct those theories and comment on them as we continue to refine them together.

In doing this kind of work, I often find that the theories developed independent of practice are either wrong or dangerously incomplete. I now invite you into that most intriguing of places, the valley where theory and practice intersect.

THEORY INTO PRACTICE . . . ALMOST

Let us take an example of an excellent theory, rooted in superb research, and how that theory must be adapted in the context of practice. I have a colleague at Stanford who I think is one of the most gifted practitioners and theorists in the field of science education during this past half-century. Her name is Mary Budd Rowe. She is a former president of the National Science Teachers Association and was an experienced classroom teacher for many years before she became a professor. She shares membership on the National Board for Professional Teaching Standards with Albert Shanker, Deborah Meier, and a host of classroom teachers around the country. She is widely known all over the world for her research on a phenomenon that is now part of the standard vocabulary of all teachers: wait-time (Rowe 1974a and 1974b). Rowe discovered in her classroom research that when teachers question students, the longer they wait for answers without either shifting to another student or saying something else themselves, the greater the likelihood that the answers the students eventually give will be of a higher order intellectually. The less time they offer students, the more probable it is that student responses will be at a "lower" level of rote or procedural understanding. Rowe and her students demonstrated repeatedly that longer wait-times promote higher-order and more creative responses in students. Since all school reform advocates prefer students to display deeper understanding, Rowe's findings have broad significance.

There is an important corollary to that finding. Not every question deserves long wait-time. If I ask you to tell me your phone number, wait-time is unlikely to enhance the depth of the answer. There has to be a proper fit between the depth or complexity of the question and whether it demands an answer worth waiting for.

Soon after the research became well known, entrepreneurs all over the country began developing wait-time workshops based on Rowe's excellent studies. Evaluators began doing studies to see whether, under training, teachers would subsequently lengthen their wait-times during interactions with students. They also asked whether teachers would learn to distinguish between higher-order and lower-order questions so that they would know when the longer wait-times would be appropriate. During the workshops, teacher wait-times and question discriminations de-

veloped nicely in the desired directions. However, when teachers returned to their classrooms, within a short time, their wait-times were back
to the usual fraction of a second. Evaluators often interpreted that finding
as evidence of teachers' resistance to change.

Those of us who are respectful of the wisdom of practice would not
readily accept that interpretation. When I see a teacher who rejects the
behavior of a recommended reform, my first question is: What is it about
what teachers have elected to do, instead of using the strategies the reform says they should, that makes their choice more sensible? Again, I'm
following the dictum that we treat teachers with as much respect as we
do students. In mathematics education, we learned years ago to ask,
when a pupil makes a mathematical error, what could be going on inside
the learner's head that would make that mathematical response sensible?
We need to ask the same thing about teachers.

As we began to research why teachers would not extend their wait-
time, we found ourselves converging on two different but mutually consistent responses. The first was: Can classroom life afford silence? If nature abhors a vacuum, classrooms abhor silence with a vengeance. As
classroom silences are created, students (and teachers) get very uncomfortable with them and fill them not only with responses to questions but
with other "creative" activity as well. Indeed, one reason why we teachers find ourselves so often engaging in machine-gun recitation is that if
we keep the pace of classroom interactions really fast, it serves as a powerful form of classroom management and control. Similarly, long wait-
times may become irresistible invitations to disruption and loss of control.

Nevertheless, there is another, deeper reason why longer wait-times
may be difficult to accomplish. Mary Budd Rowe was absolutely right:
The longer teachers wait, the higher the probability that the student will
come up with a higher-order response. What are higher-order responses?
They are, in principle, more unpredictable, more inventive, and more
likely to fall outside the range of responses that teachers expect students
to make. Therefore the longer we wait, the greater the likelihood that
the students will introduce into the classroom discourse ideas, concepts,
conjectures, hypotheses, and proposals that we teachers have not antici-
pated and for which we have no ready response. At one level, that is
exactly what we want! At another level, it creates enormous cognitive
strain, especially on the substantive understanding that teachers bring to
their teaching. Moreover, through no fault of teachers themselves, they
often enter classrooms without some of the deep disciplinary knowledge
that is increasingly expected of teachers by the new standards in such
areas as math, history, literature, and science. In large measure, these disciplinary gaps may be attributed to poor undergraduate liberal education

in universities. So when we are asking teachers to increase their wait-time, we may well be asking them to employ a strategy that is guaranteed to turn their safe classroom into an intellectual minefield. And they sensibly say that they cannot risk it. Classroom teaching is hard enough under current conditions.

This small example may be a metaphor for many of the dilemmas that accompany our preferred forms of school improvement and reform. Nearly all of these reforms call for more attention to deepened disciplinary and interdisciplinary understanding among students. They ask teachers to employ forms of instruction in which students are less passive, more collaborative in their interactions with one another, and given more opportunities for creative projects. These kind of experiences, in turn, require teachers to create far more complex participant structures in their classrooms. An unintended consequence of these proposed innovations is that there will be much more significant challenges to teachers' understandings, organizational skills, and capacities to learn and adapt from their experiences. Traditional forms of teaching help teachers maintain some modicum of control over the unpredictable quality of classroom life (Cuban 1993). The new reforms threaten that stability and create unusual challenges for teachers. A modest "reform," such as increasing wait-time, can produce significant elevations in the quality, and unpredictability, of student contributions. These changes are good for learning, but they add strain to the already heavy burden of teaching.

If the simple proposal that teachers extend their wait-times can render teaching far more difficult, what might the complexity of a full-blown classroom and curricular reform entail? One of the areas in which such reforms are most advanced is the teaching of mathematics. Deborah Ball of Michigan State University has been one of the nation's leaders in implementing and investigating the classroom teaching–learning processes associated with such changes. We can examine the work of Deborah Ball to see how classroom life might change if even more pervasive reforms were introduced. Many of the features of Ball's classroom are congruent with more general attributes of the new pedagogy.

Ball spent 10 years as an elementary school teacher with a special interest in mathematics. She then completed a Ph.D. but decided not to leave the classroom and mathematics teaching behind. Instead, she has spent much of the past few years of her career teaching mathematics in elementary school classrooms and conducting research on her own teaching (Ball 1993). She uses her own teaching experiences in a third-grade classroom as a way of trying to understand the complexities of mathematical teaching and learning. I have had the pleasure of sitting and watching Ball's classroom because she videotapes her teaching, analyzes it thoroughly, keeps her own journals, and gathers the mathematics portfolios in which her youngsters write daily. She can track how the pupils are thinking about the mathematics they are learning all during the process. Ball creates a mathematical community in her classroom where pupils work collaboratively to solve the problems they are presented with and the problems that they themselves create. They learn never to be satisfied with merely understanding procedures but to expect instead to understand the conceptual reasons behind mathematical processes. Ball steadfastly avoids saying "right" or "wrong" to the pupils when they offer a mathematical conjecture because she insists that the rules of mathematics be used to determine an idea's validity; students cannot depend on the teacher as an ultimate authority. Once they learn to turn mindlessly to authority, they forget that mathematics is essentially a way of thinking and reasoning, a language of analysis and representation, not an arbitrary system of rules in which only people with special talents or authority are permitted to have the answers.

The following episode reflects the type of teaching that Ball routinely pursues (Ball 1993). Ball had been teaching about the concepts of odd and even numbers for several weeks. The students had already passed a test on odd and even numbers. Just as Ball was preparing to make a transition to a new topic, she asked whether anyone had any other ideas they wanted to express about even and odd numbers before they continued with the next topic. Shea raised his hand. Shea was a pupil who had not been participating very much during the odd and even unit. He observed, "Some numbers can be both even and odd. Like six. Six could be odd and even." Most of us would now say, "No, that's not true; you remember the rule that distinguishes odd from even numbers. If a number can be divided by two and have nothing left over, it is even. Six is therefore even. Understand? Good. Let's move along to our next topic." Others of us might temporize and say, "That's a very interesting idea, Shea. Would you come and talk to me about it after class?" Ball was concerned about Shea; she wanted to make sure that he was included in the mathematics-making process. She also was curious about what he had in mind and always tried to show respect for student conjectures.

Ball's students had learned an idea that lies at the heart of mathematics, an idea we call factoring—which is that any number can be taken apart and put back together again in all kinds of ways. It is fundamental because it lies at the heart of everything that we do mathematically later; it is essential to dealing with equalities and inequalities, and in algebra, it seems that all we do is take things apart and put them back together in different ways. It is critical to learn this disposition and strategy early on. Shea proceeded to explain that six must be both odd and even because six is made up of three groups of two. He knows that an even number is defined as a number that can be divided into groups of two with nothing left over, but the definition says nothing about how many groups there should be. Shea thought that should be important. He observed that six has three groups of two, and while there is no remainder, there are three groups, so six is both an odd and even number. Ball recognized that Shea was engaged in authentic mathematical reasoning. Learning to reason and think mathematically was the most important goal of her mathematics instruction. He was certainly wrong about six being both an odd and even number, but he was working on the problem deeply and mathematically.

This incident occurred because Ball had created a classroom in which that kind of mathematical invention was both possible and encouraged. It was modeled and rewarded. The other pupils immediately engaged with Shea. Lyn ran up to the board and said, "Shea, if you say six is odd and even, if I use your logic, then so is ten!" Shea thought about her claim for a moment and responded, "Thank you very much; I hadn't thought of that. Yes, you're right. Ten is odd and even, too." Lyn became more exasperated, as befits a bright and tenacious third grader. "If ten is odd, then so's fourteen." After a moment's thought, Shea again agreed. Lyn finally declared, "But before you're done, every number is going to be both odd and even, and then if that's the case, why have we been having this discussion of even and odd numbers for the last three weeks?"

One of the things that happened in the classroom was that Shea's conjecture was posted on the wall with other student propositions that were under active consideration and debate in the classroom community. In the days that followed, some students began exploring the properties of "Shea numbers," as they called them. After a while, everyone was quite clear on which numbers were odd and which were even. But they arrived at those conclusions mathematically, rather than passively accepting them from an authority.

There are at least two interesting things to examine in connection with this account. First, notice the unpredictability inherent in classrooms where pupils actually have an opportunity to think and to display their reasoning. Educationally speaking, it is simultaneously a gold mine and a minefield! Ball and her counterparts have to be the kind of teachers who understand mathematics well enough to be able to handle that level of complexity, who are sufficiently skilled mathematical pedagogues to create the classroom conditions that produce and nurture such complexity, and who will not panic when their pupils produce surprising conjectures. Equally important, however, is the second feature of this account. It occurred in a classroom where Ball was able to take time to reflect on what had happened, not only to learn for her own benefit, but ultimately in ways that made her experiences and reflections accessible to countless educators who could thereby learn vicariously from her experience. Her private intellectual property thereby became community property when she analyzed this case, wrote it up, and published it. She has produced many other cases like this one, and they result not only in a growing case literature of mathematics teaching but also in an evolving theory of mathematical pedagogy.

All of us who teach encounter similar cases regularly. But, as I suggested earlier, we suffer from persistent pedagogical amnesia. And amnesiacs are incapable of learning from experiences because they just cannot hold their experiences in memory long enough to reflect on them. What can we learn from Ball's experience? One thing that we learn from this case is that we cannot trust "the test" as the basis for ensuring what pupils know. These pupils had all passed "the test" on odd and even numbers. Tests have limits as indicators of student knowledge for several reasons. It is not only because pupils forget tomorrow what they knew today. It is also because understanding something deeply means you can understand it when challenged by new situations to which it has to apply, in different representations, and under different circumstances. Learning is highly contextualized and situated. Any traditional test, however, selects a single "neutral" way to frame a question that it puts to students. The test results can not tell us how flexibly the knowledge is held. Because of the emphasis on multiple ways of learning and representing important ideas, it is important for all learners who wish to learn something deeply to continue to revisit it again and again.

There is a lovely Hebrew proverb that asserts, when studying holy texts, "Turn it over repeatedly, because there is so much within it." Almost anything worth teaching in classrooms should be worthy of being turned over repeatedly, because there is so much to it. The reason why we should be seeking to evaluate student learning through projects, performance assessments, and portfolios is because these approaches afford more opportunities to tap into learners' flexibility of understanding, representations, and applications. This insight also lies behind the repeated claim that, in curriculum reform, "less is more." Bruner's conception of the spiral curriculum also implies that some ideas are sufficiently pivotal that they deserve regular revisiting by students as they traverse the grades of the school.

I related the Deborah Ball example in such detail in order to support the claim that all teaching—even the ostensibly simple teaching of arithmetic—is incredibly complex and enormously demanding. It does not require the threat of violence in schools to make teaching complicated. It is not only the multiplicity of roles that we, as teachers, have to play—at times social workers, nurses, counselors, parents, and, yes, pedagogues—that makes teaching complicated. The pedagogy of subject matter for understanding is both a handful and a mind-full all by itself. We thus encounter two sources of complexity: the intellectual demands of deep disciplinary understanding paired with the social demands of coping with the unpredictability that accompanies such teaching. The examples from Mary Budd Rowe and Deborah Ball, taken together, help us to see that complexity more clearly. They also underscore the need for teachers to be continuous learners if they are to become capable of coping with the manifold challenges of these new, widespread classroom reforms.

TEACHERS AS LEARNERS

Under what conditions can teachers learn to teach in the manner of a Deborah Ball or consistent with other models of school reform? Are there a set of principles that can guide our efforts to support teachers to learn this kind of teaching? I believe that the conditions for teacher learning are directly parallel to those needed for pupil learning. Jerome Bruner, in Chapter 2 of this volume, has proposed a set of principles that account for why those reforms we call the "community of learners" work as well as they do. I will review my reading of Bruner's principles for student learning in a community of learners as my starting point for discussing the conditions of teacher learning. Although Bruner proposed four principles, I have elaborated them into five because as I work with teachers on these principles, they continue to teach me new ways of looking at what student and teacher learning are, and they have insisted that we add at least one more. What are the principles that account for why this kind of learning seems to be so effective? I will argue that there are at least these five: activity, reflection, collaboration, passion, and community or culture. I shall discuss them first in conjunction with pupils as learners and then extend them to teachers.

FIVE PRINCIPLES OF EFFECTIVE AND ENDURING LEARNING FOR STUDENTS AND THEIR TEACHERS

The first principle is the principle of activity. The students who are the learners in these settings are remarkably active most of the time. They are active in that they are writing, they are investigating, and they are at the computer getting information. They are talking to one another, shar-

ing information, and challenging one another's ideas. At every opportunity, the level of activity of the students is higher than in the average
classroom. This might not surprise anyone. We all know it from our practice as well as from theory—active learning results in more enduring
learning than passive learning. It is one of the key principles of all human
learning, equally relevant for adults as well as children.

Similarly, in the lives of teachers, authentic and enduring learning
occurs when the teacher is an active agent in the process—not passive,
not an audience, not a client or a collector. Teacher learning becomes
more active through experimentation and inquiry, as well as through
writing, dialogue, and questioning. Thus the school settings in which
teachers work must provide them with the opportunities and support for
becoming active investigators of their own teaching.

The second thing that we have seen in these classrooms is that they
are not merely active, because activity alone is insufficient for learning.
As Dewey observed many years ago, we do not learn just by doing; we
learn by thinking about what we are doing. Successful students in these
settings spend considerable time, as Bruner calls it, "going meta," that is,
engaging in metacognition. They are thinking about what they are doing
and why. Their teachers give them plenty of opportunities to talk about
how they are learning, why they are learning in these ways, and why
they are getting things wrong when they get them wrong and why they
are right when they get them right. A very high level of carefully guided
reflection is blended with activity in the work of the students.

As with students, reflection is needed in the lives of teachers. They
cannot become better teachers through activity and experimentation
alone. Schools must create occasions for teachers to become reflective
about their work, whether through journal writing, case conferences,
video clubs, or support for teaching portfolios. Such work requires both
scheduled time and substantial support.

Activity and reflection are hard work. If you are a typical learner,
you often find yourself working alone, intending to read an article or a
book. You sit down after dinner with a good reading light on, with good
music playing softly in the background, and with no distractions in the
room. Ten minutes later, you find yourself in the middle of a chapter,
with absolutely no recollection of what you have read up to that point. It
can be very hard to engage in active and reflective learning all by yourself. For students, it is even harder. This is one of the reasons why one of
the most important inventions of Ann Brown, with AnneMarie Palincsar,
is called "reciprocal teaching" (Palincsar and Brown 1984). Reciprocal
teaching is a process of enhancing students' reading comprehension
through working with one another, scaffolding each other's learning, and

helping each other focus, attend, and question actively, critically, and re-flectively as they jointly read complicated text. Thus active, reflective learning proceeds best in the presence of a third principle, which is collaboration.

With teachers, authentic and enduring learning also requires collaboration. When teachers collaborate, they can work together in ways that scaffold and support each other's learning, and in ways that supplement each other's knowledge. Collaboration is a marriage of insufficiencies, not exclusively "cooperation" in a particular form of social interaction. There are difficult intellectual and professional challenges that are nearly impossible to accomplish alone but are readily addressed in the company of others.

This kind of learning is not exclusively cognitive or intellectual in nature. Indeed, there is a significant emotional and affective component that inheres in such work. Authentic and enduring learning occurs when teachers and students share a passion for the material, are emotionally committed to the ideas, processes, and activities, and see the work as connected to present and future goals. Although the language of the reforms is heavily intellectual, the importance of emotion, enthusiasm, and passion is central to these efforts, both for students and for teachers. And there is a special quality to those affective responses that develop within individuals who have become interdependent members of well-functioning, cohesive groups. Simply observe the spirit that develops among the members of an athletic team, or the cast of a play, or members of a cabin at camp, and you can begin to discern the special emotional qualities associated with working collaboratives.

In that same vein, authentic and enduring learning works best when the processes of activity, reflection, emotion, and collaboration are supported, legitimated, and nurtured in a community or culture that values such experiences and creates many opportunities for them to occur and to be accomplished with success and pleasure. Such communities create "participant structures" that reduce the labor-intensity of the activities needed to engage in the most daunting practices that lead to teaching and learning. Classrooms and schools that are characterized by activity, reflection, and collaboration in learning communities are inherently uncertain, complex, and demanding. Both learning and teaching in such settings entail high levels of risk and unpredictability for the participants. Students and teachers both require a school and community culture that supports and rewards those levels of risk taking and invention characteristic of these new ways of learning for understanding and commitment.

What are the hallmarks of learning communities? It is one thing to declare the importance of community. It is quite another matter to accomplish one. Many teachers and teacher educators who wish to employ the power of learning communities in which the five principles of active learning can be learned, rewarded, and nurtured have found that creating such communities is a daunting task. Brown, Ash, Rutherford, Nakagawa, Gordon, and Campione (1993) have suggested that effective learning communities share certain salient features. First, the members must have something significant to offer one another; the basis for interdependence within a community is that its members represent an array of different talents, understandings, skills, and dispositions. This feature of "distributed expertise" is needed within such communities. It is present either because the community is formed through bringing together a diverse group of individuals, or because the community encourages a division of labor in which different members invest in developing their individual expertise for the sake of the larger group. Thus group members are characterized by "individuality"—in which members develop their individual talents for the sake of the community—rather than "individualism"—in which members develop their particular talents for the sake of maintaining their own competitive edge.

Individual talent once developed must be shared. A working community of learners, therefore, is not only constituted of diversely capable members, but its members engage in the kinds of dialogue, peer instruction, conversations, and collaborative work that permit knowledge to be transmitted and shared among the group members. Thus a second attribute of a learning community is a commitment to the sharing of expertise among its diverse members.

As learning communities begin to engage in such processes of discussion, dialogue, and sharing, another critical feature of their functioning becomes apparent. Members must hold one another in sufficient respect to trust the value of their respective contributions. They must be prepared to engage their peers with civility, patience, and regard if the trust that makes for authentic interdependence can be achieved. Thus trust and respect are additional attributes of the community.

Finally, I suspect that effective learning communities must be capable of moving from talk to action, and from deliberation to the joint pursuit of tasks that are publicly visible and whose outcomes hold real consequences for all of the group members. This is the feature that has been called developing a "community of practice." If members of a group are to work together effectively to perform a consequential task more complex and difficult than any of them could have accomplished alone, they will have to form a learning community in which distributed expertise is nurtured, the sharing of that expertise is actively pursued, and the respect needed to fuel that sharing is developed.

I am prepared to assert that the same principles that explain learning among students can also be used to explain learning among teachers. That is, if we are to design teacher education and professional development activities that will assist teachers to learn to teach in these reform-oriented ways, then we must employ teacher education approaches in which teachers will be active, reflective, collaborative, impassioned, and communal. The communities in which such processes can flourish will be characterized by diversity, dialogue, respect, and mutually valued practices. We can use these principles to design our interventions and to construct the instruments that we use to evaluate our efforts. We can use the results of those evaluations to critique and revise our approaches.

ORGANIZATIONAL CONTEXTS AND COMMUNITIES FOR TEACHER LEARNING

What are the necessary organizational contexts and conditions for all teachers to learn to teach in these new ways? One never learns to teach once and for all. It is a continuous, ongoing, constantly deepening process. We would not want to depend on teachers who would, for the rest of their careers, only continue to implement what they had learned even in the best preservice program we can imagine. Similarly, we would not want to teach in a university whose library was constituted of all the books ever published up to the day the university was opened but that had never acquired another book or journal for the rest of the history of the institution. Thus any school that wishes its teachers to teach well had better provide the conditions for them to be learning continually.

My colleagues, Milbrey McLaughlin and Joan Talbert (1993), whose work is frequently cited, have studied the conditions that are associated with teachers who regularly teach for deep understanding in secondary schools. Their findings confirm our claim that teaching of the sort we are discussing is not only complicated but also risky. It leaves teachers open to uncertainty and, quite frankly, to failure. A classroom in which the kind of complexity we have just described is commonplace is one where teachers are taking worthwhile risks. What kind of organizational and institutional conditions permit that kind of risk taking?

Teachers who were found to teach for understanding had been members of high school departments in which faculty members were collaborative and supportive of one another in trying out new ideas. They were truly participants in teacher learning communities. This is a finding of the greatest importance, because it points to the critical nature of school-based opportunities for teachers to work together on matters of curriculum, teaching, evaluation, and mutual support. In addition, most of the teachers who were systematically and consistently displaying teaching for understanding were also part of out-of-school networks. Whether it was the National Writing Project or a local affiliate of that project, a math collaborative, or a union-centered teacher research effort, they were not solely dependent on the persistence of a powerful learning community within their own school. Our educational institutions can change dramatically and rapidly when the principal or a department chair moves, a critical partner/teacher retires or takes a leave, or a school district shifts its policies for political reasons. Under such circumstances, the functioning of an outside teacher network can sustain the commitment to reform. Teachers can have other people to talk to, to inspire them, to share a vision, to share a dream, to boost their spirits, and to offer constructive suggestions. As I contemplate the reforms discussed in this book, reforms that were created to sustain student learning of a high order, many of them reflect the organizational conditions of groups of collaborating teachers who talk to one another about their work, support one another's efforts, and are affiliated with a broader network of institutions and of teachers that interconnect to provide a scaffolding for their common efforts. The functioning of faculty and administrators in Deborah Meier's Central Park East Secondary School, and their networked connections to the Coalition of Essential Schools and other collaborative efforts, provides a vivid illustration of these principles.

SUMMING UP

I will sum up with a series of assertions. We cannot be satisfied with school reform efforts that focus exclusively on student learning, even though all the rhetoric claims that student learning is the bottom line of every reform effort. I think of school reform as an ellipse, not as a circle. An ellipse has two foci that define its orbit, not just one. For me, the two foci that define the orbit of school reform are student learning and teacher learning. If you do not have both of them as real foci, the orbit will be askew and off-course. I do not argue for the priority of teacher learning over student learning because that is equally untenable. The two purposes mutually define the orbit.

We also must recognize how much risk is entailed in doing the kind of teaching we are advocating, and why we must create structures within our schools that permit teachers to take those risks and then celebrate them, not bury them. One of the lessons we can learn from the medical community is the character of a ritual called the clinical pathological conference. A clinical pathological conference (CPC) is a weekly conference in which a member of the medical staff or the medical faculty presents a case that did not go well. The CPC is not built around a story such as: "I did an ideal appendectomy last week." Instead, the CPC will attest: "I did an appendectomy last week and some things happened that I didn't think were going to happen. We ought to discuss these unanticipated findings and see what we can learn from them." Within the culture of that community, there is a value placed on examining what happens when mistakes are made, when problems arise, and when surprises occur. These become occasions for learning, not opportunities for shame.

We all know that the more we teach well, the more surprises we will encounter. Those are special moments for learning. I have never learned much from planning a lesson that runs smoothly. I learn when I have to confront the discomfort of a lesson that did not go quite the way I had intended, whether because it was poorly designed or because someone like Shea came up with a surprise conjecture. Under these conditions, if I have achieved the conditions of deliberation, reflection, and collaboration, my colleagues and I can learn from one another. Where are the CPC-like case conferences in our public schools? One of the most important books written on medical education was Charles Bosk's *Forgive and Remember* (Bosk 1979). Writing about the surgical residency, his point was that if the principle was "forgive and forget," it would be a recipe for safety and stasis, not for learning from experience. If you want to learn from experience, you must both forgive and remember. The entire organization and the organization of the profession have to be organized so that learning from your reflective memories becomes the essence of the community's commitment to teacher development and teacher learning.

I return to my central theme. If we wish to create schools where reform will be enduring and not evanescent, we need to ask: Is this a school where teachers can learn? Unless we create the conditions for teacher learning, every single reform that we initiate, even if it looks like it is working at the beginning, will eventually erode and disappear. An effectively reformed school is a setting that is educative for its teachers. That is the essence; the rest has been commentary.

REFERENCES

Ball, D. 1993. With an eye on the mathematical horizon: Dilemmas of teaching elementary school mathematics. *Elementary School Journal*, March, 93(4): 373–397.

Bosk, C. L. 1979. *Forgive and remember: Managing medical failure.* Chicago: University of Chicago Press.

Brown, A. L., D. Ash, M. Rutherford, K. Nakagawa, A. Gordon, and J. C. Campione. 1993. Distributed expertise in the classroom. In *Cognitions: Psychological and educational considerations*, ed. G. Solomon. New York: Cambridge University Press.

Cuban, L. 1993. *How teachers taught: Constancy and change in American classrooms, 1880–1990*. New York: Teachers College Press.

Hawkins, D. 1966. Learning the unteachable. In *Learning by discovery: A critical appraisal*, ed. L. S. Shulman and E. R. Keislar. Chicago: Rand McNally.

McLaughlin, M. W., and J. E. Talbert. 1993. *Contexts that matter for teaching and learning: Strategic opportunities for meeting the nation's education goals*. Stanford, CA: Center for Research on the Context of Secondary School Teaching, Stanford University.

Palincsar, A. S., and A. L. Brown. 1984. Reciprocal teaching of comprehension-fostering and monitoring activities. *Cognition and Instruction* 1(2): 117–175.

Rowe, M. B. 1974a. Relation of wait-time and rewards to the development of language, logic, and fate control: Part II—Rewards. *Journal of Research in Science Teaching* 11(4): 291–308.

Rowe, M. B. 1974b. Wait-time and rewards as instructional variables, their influence on language, logic, and fate control: Part I—Wait-time. *Journal of Research in Science Teaching* 11(2): 81–94.

Shulman, L. S. 1987. The wisdom of practice: Managing complexity in medicine and teaching. In *Talks to teachers: A Festschrift for N. L. Cage*, ed. D.C. Berliner and B. V. Rosenshine. New York: Random House.

Shulman, L. S., and E. R. Keislar. 1966. *Learning by discovery: A critical appraisal*. Chicago: Rand McNally.

Preparing Teachers for Twenty-First-Century Schools:
Teacher Learning in Global Perspective

ALBERT SHANKER

PREPARING TEACHERS for the twenty-first century: Your view of what that means obviously depends on the direction you think schools should take. Over the past several years, we have been shown visions of schools that are radically different from most of our current schools and encouraged to see them as the schools of the future for some, if not all, of our children. At one time, I was in that camp myself, but I have gradually changed my mind. It is not that I think these visions are unimportant or that I oppose their having a bigger place in our thinking about schools. However, I have come to think that the assumptions underlying the call for radical change are just plain wrong.

The call for change is based on the idea that the traditional model of schooling does not work. When people speak of the traditional model, they are thinking about classrooms where the teacher stands up front talking and asking questions, and all of the children are supposed to learn in the same way and at the same time. As we know, this is not the way children learn. And so, the thinking goes, we need to throw out the whole system and put something totally different in its place. But what will replace the traditional model?

There is currently a good deal of experimentation, but no one has yet found an alternative to the traditional model that has been tested by time. Moreover, this traditional model seems to work quite well in other industrialized countries. So I think we need to ask ourselves whether we can afford to junk our current system when we have no substitute for it and, indeed, whether it is the model itself that is wrong or the way we are using it.

WHAT SYSTEM?

One of the assumptions about our current system is that it is extremely well organized and even rigid, and that it needs to be made much more flexible because it does not fit our times or our youngsters. Another assumption is that there is a heavy emphasis on academics. However, a look at our schools will show that academics are very low in the order of priorities and that socialization comes first. Take, for example, the current crusade for total inclusion—that is, including all youngsters with disabilities in regular classrooms regardless of the nature and severity of their disability. Total inclusion is an argument for socializing disabled youngsters and others with the assertion that full inclusion, if "done properly," need not result in the sacrifice of academic achievement (Shanker 1993 and 1994).

Another assumption is that because our students are subjected to lots of tests, we run a high-stakes school system that is very hard on students and teachers, and we need to get rid of these extrinsic systems of motivation. But if you look at our system, you see that there are no visible stakes. Schools can fail on every indicator with no consequences for the principal or the teachers and no visible consequences for the kids: They move on, they get promoted, they graduate, and 95% of the colleges and universities in the United States will accept them no matter what their level of achievement.

My parents used to tell me, almost every day, "If you want to go to college, you've got to do better than that," and they really pushed hard. Later, when I tried to tell my children that they were not working enough or achieving enough, they just laughed at me. They said, "Dad, no one works at school, and they are all going to college." Of course, if you want to go to certain selective schools, you have to work; my children knew that, but they had made up their minds that they did not care about getting into Stanford or Harvard.

In other words, all our assumptions call for relaxing a rigid system and moving away from academics and high stakes when, as a matter of fact, our current system is hardly a system at all. Far from being rigid, it is almost anarchic.

When I was teaching, I was given some thick curriculum manuals put out by the state of New York. There was so much material in them that it would have been impossible to cover it all, but you were not expected to. Indeed, the instructions at the beginning indicated that the material was just illustrative. It showed the kinds of things that students studied in the various grades, and you, as the teacher, were to feel free to select on the basis of your youngsters' interests or what you thought they were able to do or what interested you. If you did not find anything in the manual, you were free to pick something else. And many teachers did just that. Some teachers did not work very hard—they got a copy of the *Instructor* or *Grade Teacher* and used the ready-made plans. Others did a tremendous amount of work on their own. But there was very little direction from the outside, and that is still the case. There are some exceptions. In Texas, for example, teachers are given checklists for almost every class period, and they check off which areas and skills they have covered. But for the most part, there is no system. If there is rigidity, it comes from the inside. That is, teachers tend to do things the way they remember things being done when they were students.

THE QUESTION OF STUDENT ACHIEVEMENT

There is some dispute as to whether the kids in our educational system are generally doing well or poorly. Many educators view negative reports about student achievement as somewhat hysterical—perhaps even part of a right-wing conspiracy. However, most of them do not bother to look very closely at the evidence, such as that provided by the National Assessment of Educational Progress (NAEP). NAEP, one of the most important indicators of student achievement, has been testing representative samples of American students in grades 4, 9, and 11 for more than 20 years, and most people have confidence in its findings.

NAEP tests are not norm-referenced, so you do not get test results showing that 53% of the kids are above average. A NAEP exam has four or five different levels of proficiency and no quotas for how many kids can be at a given level. Also, NAEP makes available examples of questions and answers so you can see, for example, what is meant by "elaborated" writing—the term for the highest level of achievement—what is "adequate" and what would be considered "poor." The same is true for NAEP exams in reading and mathematics and the other fields in which NAEP tests students.

When you look at the results for 17-year-olds, you have to remember that NAEP is not testing the 20% of students who have dropped out of school by then, most of whom would probably not do very well. At this level, it is testing only the relatively successful kids, the ones who are likely to get a high school diploma and the majority of whom will go on to postsecondary education. What you find when you look at these students' scores in the NAEP writing examination is that only about 3% of them can write what is considered an "elaborated" answer. "Elaborated" just means a good essay or letter; it is what used to be considered a good answer on a New York State Regents' exam and what is expected all over the world from kids who expect to be admitted to university. Three percent—and this figure has remained stable since 1969 or 1970.

If you go down to the next level, where the writing is less thoughtful and has some grammatical and spelling errors but the youngster can still do a fair job developing an argument, you find that only about 20% have achieved it. This figure, too, has remained stable over the years. In other words, 75% of students who are still in school when they are 17 years old will graduate with a writing achievement level that is very low. They are not able to persuade or describe or tell a story; their writing is hard to understand, and it is loaded with spelling and grammatical errors (Applebee, Langer, Mullis, & Jenkins, 1990, 13, 17, 28, 42).

Moving on to reading or mathematics, you find that about 6% are able to perform at the highest levels. The cut points at the next level are similar to the ones for writing. This means that a large majority of our students who graduate from high school are achieving at an elementary school level (Mullis, Dossey, Foertsch, Jones, & Gentile, 1991, 75–79, 121–126).

One of the important results of education is the ability to engage in lifelong learning. But if you do not reach a certain reading level, you will read only if you have to. People who read for pleasure are proficient enough to lose themselves in what they read. If you have to stop every sentence or so to figure out what a word is or if you read very slowly, it is like reading a foreign language. Most of us who have had three years of Spanish or French or German could make our way through an article, but we would never do it for pleasure because it is just too hard. So we are graduating youngsters who will probably not continue to read for pleasure, and, as a result, they will lose whatever proficiency they acquired in school.

What about youngsters who attend private schools? We hear that they perform at high levels, but as a matter of fact, they do not do much better than public school students. Private schools do have certain advantages. A higher percentage of parents of private school students are college graduates, and a much smaller number of parents were themselves dropouts (Benson 1991, 47). Also, private school parents are likely to be concerned with their children's education because they are directly paying for it.

Private schools also have the advantage of deciding which students they want to admit and keep. Catholic schools make up the largest private school system in the country—about 81% of students who attend private schools go to Catholic schools—and most Catholic high schools have entrance examinations (Center for Education Statistics 1987, 22). Catholic schools, like all private schools, have the option of getting rid of students who are not working out. When I was teaching, the toughest kids I had were the Catholic school kids who had been kicked out because they did not behave.

Nevertheless, public and private schools are very close in terms of student achievement.[1] If you say that other industrialized democracies with good school systems are three miles ahead of us, private schools are three feet ahead of the public schools—a difference that does not mean much educationally (U.S. Department of Education 1991).

Why are we not seeing more dissatisfaction with our educational system—even a revolution? It is because we are taking care of the problem at the top end. More and more colleges and universities are devoting time, space, and energy to remediation. And college texts have been dumbed-down in order to meet the students at their level. Institutions of higher learning are playing this game because they are competing for students, which means there is pressure on the faculty to be accommodating so they do not lose any customers. The result is a system in which huge numbers of students are getting their junior high and high school education in college. But parents and teachers like to be proud of their graduates, so we say that 55% go on to college and 35% are getting a degree, and we avoid looking at what is behind those figures (U.S. Department of Education 1992, 304).

FOREIGN COMPARISONS

How does this compare with achievement levels in other countries? These data sound very bad, but perhaps that is the way things are around the world.

It is not possible to compare exactly the performance of children in the United States and other countries. Exams differ from country to country, and the international comparisons that have been set up to answer this question have many problems that make their results inconclusive. However, you can get a pretty good idea by looking at the textbooks used in other countries. For instance, the textbooks for Japan's national system have been translated, so you can see what Japanese children at the equivalent of our sixth-grade level are doing and compare it with what our sixth graders study. You can also get textbooks from Russia, France, Germany, and the United Kingdom.[2]

Most of these countries have some form of school-leaving examination for the youngsters who are in the college-bound track; and by looking at the German Abitur, the French baccalaureate, or the General Certificate of Secondary Education in the United Kingdom, you can find out what is required of youngsters going to college. The American Federation of Teachers, in cooperation with the National Center for Improving Science Education (NCISE), has put out a study comparing school-leaving biology exams in England, France, Germany, Wales, and Japan with the Advanced Placement (AP) biology exam in the United States. The exams in these other countries are more sophisticated and more difficult than the AP, although most adults would feel pleased to pass the AP. But if you consider how many kids take and pass the AP and how many pass these other exams, the differences are staggering. In England and Wales, 31% of the kids graduating from high school take the biology exam, and 25% of the entire cohort pass. In France, 43% try the biology baccalaureat and 32% pass. In Germany, 37% take the Abitur in biology and 36% pass. In Japan, if you count first and second tries, 58% take the biology exam and 36% pass. In the United States? Only 7% of our youngsters take the AP and 4% pass (American Federation of Teachers and National Center for Improving Science Education 1994, 96).

All of this has important implications for the area of teacher training. Every teacher in Germany, for example, has passed four subjects in the Abitur before entering college or university. These exams are very demanding, and it is no exaggeration to say that anyone passing them would meet the standards for entering most of the elite colleges in the United States. In other words, everyone who becomes a teacher in Germany might have gone to Harvard or Stanford in the United States. When I visit American schools, a lot of elementary teachers tell me that they themselves have never really understood arithmetic or science. When I go to Germany and meet with German teachers and ask them how many never understood arithmetic, they look at me waiting for the punch line to this American joke.

ELITISM AND DIVERSITY

There are a number of arguments to explain why a system that works well in other industrialized democracies could not possibly work for us.

People often say that the excellent education some of these countries offer their children comes at a price we would not like to pay. These countries, the argument goes, educate only a tiny percentage of their students. They have elitist systems, whereas ours is egalitarian. But which is the elitist system? Is the German system, in which 36% of the graduating class can do something as difficult as the Abitur in biology, elitist? Or is elitist a better word for our system, which produces only 4%, who pass an easier exam? And biology is not the only thing these youngsters abroad are taking. In England and Wales, students who want to enter college or university have to take three different exams like this in three different subjects; in France, seven to eight baccalaureat exams; in Germany, four subjects in the Abitur; and in Japan, three to four exams depending on what field students plan to enter. In the United States, not all students are required to take AP exams; for that matter, some colleges and universities do not even require students to take either the Scholastic Assessment Test (sat) or the American College Test (act) in order to qualify for admission into a college or university. That is a tremendous difference.

What about the youngsters who are not bound for college? Maybe these other countries do a good job educating the elite, but do they not throw away all the others? If you look at the German system and include the apprenticeship program and the programs preparing students to enter technical schools, you see that this is just not true. They not only do an excellent job with their top youngsters, but they also do very well with those in the middle and those at the bottom—and that goes for all their tracks. We do a much poorer job with all of our students—top, middle, and bottom—except for the very top 3% or so. In the United Kingdom, they also throw away those who are not college bound. Like us, they have not quite figured out what to do with them (Green and Steedman 1993).

People also use "diversity" to explain why an educational system similar to the German, Japanese, or French system would not be feasible for us. Is *diversity* some kind of code word, and do we mean that a diverse population is not as capable of learning biology or mathematics as a homogeneous one? In fact, this argument will not wash either because the populations in these other countries are no longer homogeneous. There has been an immense flow of refugees into Europe from Africa, Asia, and Eastern Europe.

Some demographers are predicting that, because of the difference between the birthrates of the native French and the Muslim immigrants from North Africa, France will become a majority Muslim country within the lifetimes of most of the current population. The French response to this prediction is to use their school system to make sure that Muslim children will become French men and women. Instead of bowing to multiculturalism, the French have decided that, while they may move from being a Catholic country to being a Muslim country, they will still be French.

But there has also been a lot of unrest because of the increase in immigration. That is why you have the so-called skinheads in Germany attacking Turkish workers and their families, many of whom have lived in Germany for years. Indeed, diversity poses greater problems in some of these other countries than it does here in the United States. In Germany, for example, it is not expected that Turks will become German citizens, and in Japan, it is extremely difficult for immigrants to become Japanese citizens. When people come to the United States, the expectation is not just that they will become citizens; they are supposed to become Americans because being American does not come through the bloodlines the way being German or Japanese does. So the argument that the diversity of the United States makes it hard for us to educate all of our students does not hold up.

A useful way to think about the problems we are having with our educational system is to ask ourselves how we would go about solving a problem in which we had a great personal stake. Suppose that for many years we had been in business and done pretty well. Then our business started slipping very rapidly. What would we do? We might decide to alter radically everything about the way we did business. And we might try a lot of things that no one had ever tried before or some other things that had been tried without much evidence of long-term success. Still, I do not think anybody whose livelihood depended on solving the problem would handle it in any of these ways. A much better idea would be to look at the competitors' operations and see what they were doing that we were not. We might even engage in some form of industrial espionage—like hiring somebody who works for the most successful of our competitors. But has anybody ever heard of educational espionage? Here we are, in the middle of what most people believe is a crisis in education, and almost nobody is doing what they would do in their own lives, which is to look at what others are doing who are involved in the same enterprise and who seem to be more successful.

This does not mean there is a single model of the successful educational system that we should try to import into the United States. The French system is different from the German, which is different from the British, and so forth. All are models that developed in accordance with their histories, their cultures, and the tensions within their societies. Whatever we do here will also reflect our politics and history. Nevertheless, we should be able to discover some common elements that help explain the success of these other systems and that we can consider adapting for our use.

STANDARDS AND STAKES

What do all these systems have in common? They all have explicit standards for what students should know and be able to do at certain ages. They have fairly standardized curricula, sometimes national and sometimes state or provincial. They do not test and retest kids using standardized tests the way we do—nobody else uses these kinds of tests the way we do. But they do use tests at certain critical junctures to make decisions about what students will do next—because all of these systems do track students quite explicitly. In Germany, tracking starts very early, in the fifth grade; the Japanese start tracking in the ninth grade; and other countries start somewhere in between. So, though students in these countries do not take many examinations, the ones they do take have high stakes attached to them. There are stakes in the elementary and secondary system in terms of the track into which students are put, and there are stakes involved when students leave secondary school and move on to higher education or to apprenticeship or further training in some kind of technical school or to a job.

I am not saying that only external stakes are important. There are many other things that are critical in educating children, such as the motivating power of ties with one's peers, parents, and teachers. But external stakes constitute a powerful incentive for working and achieving. We have just seen the collapse of a huge experiment that took place in the Soviet Union and Eastern Europe, based on the notion that intrinsic incentives are sufficient and the extrinsic ones are not needed. I agree that it would be a good thing if people acted responsibly because they knew it was the right way to behave; but abandoning external standards did not work under communism, and it is not working in our schools.

What happens in American schools? Suppose that I am a teacher and I give my youngsters an assignment that is pretty demanding. The kids start yelling and screaming, "Mr. Shanker, that's not fair. My sister didn't have to do that last year when she was in this grade. Other teachers aren't this hard. They don't give this much work." So I am forced into negotiating with my students. If they believe I am some kind of ogre because of the amount or difficulty of the work I give and they start ganging up on me, there is nothing I can do—especially since the parents are likely to side with their kids. In other countries, if the kids start in with this kind of thing, the teacher can say, "Look, here's what you are required to learn.

You'll be tested on it and expected to pass, but it's the same for kids your age all over the country. Anyway, I'm here to help you." The relationship between teacher and pupil is like that of a coach preparing athletes for the Olympics rather than some ogre who takes pleasure in overworking students.

Similarly, external standards would have strengthened my position with my own children when they told me they did not have to work to get into college. Because external standards did not exist, the onus of convincing them that learning is important and that learning more is better than learning less was on me, the individual parent—just as it is on the individual teacher. Parents are isolated, and, in most cases, they are not going to win. But there are other reasons for having a certain amount of standardization.

We have more mobility in this country than in any other society, so it would make sense to have a curriculum that allows students who move from one school to another to go right on with the work they were doing. Also, teachers constantly report that they have to waste time at the beginning of a new school year going back over last year's material because they have no way of telling what the new kids in the class know. This is boring for the kids who already know the material, and it means that our students learn much less than students in educational systems with external standards, where teachers do not have to waste time reteaching last year's curriculum.

Furthermore, if you have decided what the curriculum is, you can prepare textbooks. Textbooks in Germany or Japan, for example, are about one-quarter the size of ours, and many of them are models of clarity and brevity. Why? Because people in these other countries have figured out what they want their students to learn, and we have not. Texas has decided one thing and California another, and publishers want their textbooks to be sold in several states. So we end up with huge, unfocused, and confusing books.

And how do you prepare teachers if you do not know what the kids are supposed to be learning? Harold Stevenson, a scholar and researcher who has studied elementary schools in the United States, Japan, and China, describes the way Asian teachers who are teaching the same grade meet together to plan how they are going to teach a particular lesson— for instance, what examples they are going to use and which questions they will ask. Then, when the lesson is over, they meet again to talk about which explanations worked and which ones were confusing. They think in terms of perfecting a lesson over time, in much the same way that you might polish a stone (Stevenson and Stigler 1992, 156–173; Stigler and Stevenson 1991, 12–20, 43–47).

Many American teachers might object to this notion of teaching because they consider themselves artists. For them preparing a class is like standing in front of a blank canvas and deciding what they want to paint on it. Stevenson's response would be that Asian teachers also think of themselves as artists, but as performing artists. They are like pianists performing a concerto. They do not think they have to write the music while they are playing it. It may well be that our idea of creativity in teaching has to change. Writing the music at the same time as you perform it is too much to ask of most practitioners. I think that holds true whether you are talking about music or medicine or accounting. The general procedures to be followed are decided through practice or the buildup of knowledge. There is a range of possibilities; there is leeway for individual practitioners; but other professionals do not have the freedom to improvise that we have in American education.

HOW DOES TEACHER TRAINING FIT INTO THIS SCHEME?

One of the main issues in American education is how well our teachers are prepared in the subject matter they teach. David Cohen, who has been studying and writing about American education for a number of years, recently visited a number of California schools to see what happened to the state's new curriculum frameworks when they reached the classroom. He describes, for example, how one teacher enthusiastically embraced the new math curriculum; but when push came to shove, she could not handle it because she did not have a solid foundation in math herself. For instance, when kids questioned her about why they were supposed to multiply in a given problem instead of dividing, she would say something like, "I don't know why, but I know that if you do this, you will get the right answer" (Cohen 1990, 327–345). That lack of knowledge is a direct result of the failure of our elementary and secondary education system as well as a failure in how well we select teachers.

As I have already mentioned, only 3% of high school graduates are able to write a decent letter or essay. Since 55% go on to higher education, the number probably increases to 15% or even 20% of college graduates. But the rewards and the prestige connected with being a teacher are such that most people in this elite group are not interested in entering the teaching profession. Thus, many classroom teachers are going to be like the one David Cohen observed. In Germany, you have well-qualified people lining up to get teaching jobs. The problem there is that most of the students are going to be taught by 60-year-old teachers, and many qualified young people will never get a chance to teach. But another way of looking at the situation in Germany is to say that when you have a large number of people who are well educated and well prepared, then you are able to select.

One of the things that we need in the United States is a system of assessments to test prospective teachers. We have exams for lawyers and doctors and accountants and others, but in teaching we basically accept a college degree as an indication that the person is qualified to enter the profession. It is true that a test will not tell you if a person is going to be a good teacher. But it will tell you if somebody who is going to teach mathematics does not know any math. In other words, it will reveal people who are bound to be bad teachers because they do not know their subject matter. Furthermore, I am sure that if prospective teachers were tested on their knowledge of subject matter, the people who train teachers would pay more attention to whether or not their students have a solid grounding in the subjects they are going to teach. There is no pressure on education school professors to insist on mastery of subject matter now. They are meeting all the requirements that are being imposed on them.

I would not give up on those who are already teaching. They may have been hired without the appropriate background, but there are steps we could take to help them overcome that deficiency. For example, instead of giving teachers money to go back and take 30 or 60 or 90 credit hours in pedagogy or whatever they choose, we could give them a salary differential if they passed an examination that showed they really knew their field. Though we tend to focus on what happens to people before they begin teaching, most important teacher education and training takes place after people have started to teach.

We could also help teachers improve if we got them out of self-contained, isolated classrooms so they were able to interact with their colleagues. I am not talking about the kind of bull sessions that go on in teachers' rooms. I mean giving teachers the time to share ideas about teaching and problems they are having—time to ask such questions as "What are we doing with our students? What are our expectations? What is this textbook like? Is it better than that one?" Without this kind of chance to reflect on their practice and discuss it with colleagues, teachers are likely to go on doing the same thing they have always done—and, incidentally, the same thing their own teachers did.

We talk a lot about new educational models, but teachers and future teachers have very little experience with any model except the one they grew up with. Every teacher was once a student, and unlike most new practitioners in other professions, teachers come in with a very definite picture in their minds about the nature of school and teaching. We need to give them other pictures and models. If we had enough schools like Deborah Meier's Central Park East, we could give every new teacher an internship in a school that is very different from our traditional schools. But there are other ways as well. Prospective teachers could spend a year with a Boy Scout or Girl Scout troop and observe the merit badge system for motivating and assessing learning. Time in a summer camp that offers educational programs would also be useful. Or they could intern in certain industries where there is a good deal of internal mobility and the opportunity to develop new skills.

Teachers need a chance to discuss theoretical issues when they become practitioners. Most teachers are critical of the pedagogical courses they took when they were in college. It is not necessarily that these were bad courses—though some undoubtedly were. But when you are in the middle of the coursework for your bachelor's degree and you have never taught, there is a certain unreality about discussing issues with which you have had no experience. They are just words—and they will not be anything more until you find yourself in the classroom. We need to develop a system of professional practice schools or internships of the kind doctors undergo to give prospective teachers extensive practical experience.

Finally, I think that we need to develop incentives for teachers that encourage these changes. It is difficult to get teachers out of their self-contained classrooms. At first, a teacher may find the situation very isolating and lonely, but later it becomes a protection.

How do you get people to work together? If you have small schools with a small group of teachers, you let your new teachers know in advance that they will be working together. But we are a long way from a system where this kind of collegiality will be the rule. So you may need incentives. You may need to say that schools making a substantial amount of progress over a certain period of time will receive some sort of financial reward. This will not be like the old individual merit pay, which was based on the principal's judgment. It will be a reward for everybody, and it will be based on student outcomes. If you do that, you will force people to get out of their rooms because the teachers who are interested in getting the reward will start challenging those who make no effort to improve their teaching. I do not think external incentives are the only way of making these improvements; over time, we could develop professional norms. But much needs to be done.

THE VALUE OF THE TRADITIONAL MODEL

When I talk about looking again at the traditional model instead of simply discarding it, I do not mean we should abandon looking for new and different ways to solve our educational problems. But while we are looking wildly around for alternative models, most of the world does a lot better than we do with what is considered a traditional educational model. Therefore, in the absence of another model that is clearly better or even as good as theirs, we should look seriously at the model they follow and the results they get.

These traditional systems connect a certain number of things: They connect standards with stakes with curricula with teachers who know their stuff. The result is a large number of students who achieve at high levels using a teacher-centered system. It is foolish, and even immoral, to argue against such a system unless you have an alternative that is clearly better. And we do not have an alternative that has been tried on any sort of mass basis. Of course we should continue looking for and experimenting with alternative models—especially since there are kids for whom the traditional system does not work very well. If 70% of students do well with a traditional model and 30% do not, it is wrong simply to abandon the 30%. But this works the other way around, too. In medicine, if you have a treatment that works on 70% of patients but fails on 30%, you do not throw that medicine away until you have found something that works for a greater percentage of patients. That should be true in education, too. Maybe one of the alternatives we look at will do even better with the 70% as well, and if we find such a system, we should embrace it. But we should not refuse to take advantage of a system that we know works or to stay with it until we have something better.

We have never really tried the system that other countries have. We may have used bits and pieces, but we have never put it all together: standards; curricula and textbooks and assessments based on the standards; and teachers trained to be able to teach the curricula. I do not know if we can. The Russians have an expression: "It is very easy to take an aquarium and turn it into fish soup, but very difficult to do the opposite." We already have the fish soup. I hope that we can also do the impossible and turn it into an aquarium.

NOTES

1. On the 1990 NAEP mathematics examination, for example, the average proficiency for public school seniors was 295 in contrast to 302 for Catholic school students and 301 for students from other private schools—a relatively small difference on a 500-point scale. The real significance of these scores does not lie in the six- or seven-point difference between average scores for public and private schools but in the fact that a score of 300 represents mastery of material that NAEP says students are supposed to learn in seventh grade. This means that half of

these graduating seniors, in both public and private schools, were still functioning at a seventh-grade level (U. S. Department of Education 1991).

2. Translations of Japanese (grades 7–9) and Russian (grades 1–3) math textbooks are available from the University of Chicago School Mathematics and Science Project, Department of Education, University of Chicago, 5835 S. Kimbark Ave., Chicago, IL 60637.

REFERENCES

American Federation of Teachers and National Center for Improving Science Education. 1994. *What college-bound students abroad are expected to know about biology: Exams from England and Wales, France, Germany and Japan, plus a comparative look at the United States.* Washington, DC: American Federation of Teachers.

Applebee, A. N., J. Langer, I. V. S. Mullis, and L. Jenkins. 1990. *The writing report card, 1984–88: Findings from the nation's report card.* Washington, DC: U. S. Department of Education, Office of Educational Research and Improvement.

Benson, P. 1991. *Private schools in the United States: A statistical profile with comparisons to public schools.* Washington, DC: U.S. Department of Education, Office of Educational Research and Improvement, National Center for Education Statistics.

Center for Education Statistics. 1987. *Private schools and private school teachers: Final report of the 1985–86 private school study.* Washington, DC: U.S. Department of Education, Office of Educational Research and Improvement, National Center for Education Statistics.

Cohen, D. 1990. Policy and practice: An overview. *Educational Evaluation and Policy Analysis* 12(3): 327–345.

Green, A., and H. Steedman. 1993. *Educational provision, educational attainment and the needs of industry.* London: Institute of Education, University of London.

Mullis, I. V. S., J. A. Dossey, M. A. Foertsch, L. R. Jones, and C. A. Gentile. 1991. *Trends in academic progress: Achievement of U.S. students in science, 1969–70 to 1990; mathematics, 1973–1990; reading, 1971–1990; and writing, 1984–1990.* Washington, DC: U.S. Department of Education, Office of Educational Research and Improvement, National Center for Education Statistics.

Shanker, A. 1993. "A rush to inclusion," Where we stand. *New York Times,* 19 September, sec. 4:9.

Shanker, A. 1994. "Inclusion and ideology," Where we stand. *New York Times,* 6 February, sec. 4:7.

Stevenson, H. W., and J. W. Stigler. 1992. *The learning gap: Why our schools are failing and what we can learn from Japanese and Chinese education.* New York: Summit.

Stigler, J. W., and H. W. Stevenson. 1991. How Asian teachers polish a lesson to perfection. *American Educator,* Spring, 15(1): 12–20, 43–47.

U. S. Department of Education. 1991. *The state of mathematics achievement:* NAEP's *1990 assessment of the nation and trial assessment of the states.* Washington, DC:

U.S. Department of Education, Office of Educational Research and Improvement, Educational Resources Information Center.

U. S. Department of Education. 1992. *Digest of education statistics*. Washington, DC: U.S. Department of Education, Office of Educational Research and Improvement, National Center for Education Statistics.

Bringing Success to Scale in Public Education: Strategy, Designs, and New American Schools

JOHN L. ANDERSON

NEW AMERICAN SCHOOLS (NAS) was established in July 1991 by American corporate and foundation leaders with the mission of creating designs for new, high-performance schools that address the learning needs of all children and can be used in communities across the country. NAS is led by Chairperson of the Board David T. Kearns, former Deputy Secretary of Education and retired CEO of Xerox Corporation, and NAS's board of directors, consisting of 22 leaders in the American business community.

THE EMERGENCE OF NAS

NAS began with an unprecedented approach to education reform: a call to all citizens to become architects of a new generation of American schools, to cast aside assumptions about how schools should operate, and to submit their vision of new schools that should set the pace for the nation and the world. Only two constraints were imposed: that the design help all students achieve world-class standards and that, after initial investment costs, the new schools operate at costs comparable to conventional schools. In response, NAS received 686 design proposals from thousands of citizens in schools, community groups, and businesses, with organizations in many cases working together in unprecedented partnerships.

Every proposal was reviewed by experienced education, business, and community leaders in a thorough evaluation process. Eleven design teams were selected for the first phase of a five-year, four-phase approach:

- *Phase 1*: a one-year development phase to refine the design concepts and develop effective implementation strategies (1992)
- *Phase 2*: a two-year implementation phase at school sites to test the effectiveness of the designs and the potential for wide-scale adoption (1993–1995)
- *Phase 3*: a two-year national dissemination and scale-up phase to foster systemic reform through an intensified school implementation effort in selected jurisdictions around the nation (1995–1997)
- *Phase 4*: a three-year effort to complete the work we started, expand nationally, and show that entire districts can become places where good schools are the norm (1997–2000)

Based on their performance in year 1, nine of the eleven teams were selected to proceed into phase 2, after which seven teams continued on the project (see Appendix).

DESIGN TEAMS AS CATALYSTS FOR CHANGE

NAS's seven design teams, combining the talent, energy, and vision of today's most creative thinkers in education, business, science, and the humanities, have created academically rigorous and supportive learning environments that provide students with the intellectual and technical skills necessary to succeed in the twenty-first century.

The designs re-create and integrate all elements of a school's life, rather than improve only selected aspects of schools. The designs include:

1. New curricula and instructional approaches, such as multi-age grouping and learning through thematic or project-based units
2. High achievement standards and innovative means of assessing student performance, including portfolios, exhibits, and individual student plans
3. Extensive professional development with planning time during the school week and in-depth summer development activities
4. New governance and organizational structures, such as an extended school day, longer blocks of learning time, and managerial concepts borrowed from the corporate community
5. Stronger ties to the community through parental and business involve-

ment, community advocates for students, and collaboration with local social and health service providers

The design teams today are working with nearly 500 schools across the nation, testing their designs in diverse settings, ranging from rural Mississippi, to inner-city Los Angeles, to a Native American reservation in Arizona. NAS is helping the design teams, as they implement their breakthrough innovations, by providing opportunities to collaborate on common challenges through workshops and conferences, exchange of materials, and the use of electronic mail and bulletin boards.

While the purpose of phase 2 is to prove that the designs work, phase 3 is the opportunity to accomplish something that this nation has been unable or unwilling to do: Leverage individual school improvement by extending reform outward into districts and states.

In conjunction with the Education Commission of the States (ECS), the Annenberg Institute for School Reform, and other national organizations, NAS has begun to plan for scaling up its effort. The goal is to enable the creation of hundreds and then thousands of transformed schools across the United States, thus changing the fundamental character and practice of American education.

Three important assumptions underlie NAS's planning to meet this goal. First, NAS's design teams will be part of a unified effort. Second, long-term success will require important, systemic changes in the policy and operating environment within which individual schools exist. Finally, because systemic changes will be required, NAS will work with jurisdictions within which schools are found—namely, state and local school systems.

STRATEGY FOR SCHOOL REFORM

NAS's strategy is consistent with its commitment to impact school reform in a substantive and significant way. NAS seeks to demonstrate persuasively that the designs developed by the seven design teams can help other sites develop transformed, high-performance schools; and, in so doing, NAS seeks to foster the transformation of many schools in ways that make such transformed and transforming schools the norm rather than the exception. The above three assumptions reflect this extended goal and distinguish our approach from other model-school projects.

In formulating our strategy, we were very moved by the fact that there is not a single school district of any size in the United States with a diverse student population in which a large proportion of students achieve academically at very high levels. For school reform to have any meaning, we must confront both sides of the equation: school practices and systems practices. In thinking about the school-level side of the equation, NAS consciously chose to support many—rather than just one—school improvement designs, thus demonstrating an important belief on our part: that there should be a diversity of schools that respond to the individual interests and capabilities of students, parents, and professional staffs. The opportunity to make a choice between a number of designs provides an impetus to schools, and the communities they serve, to think deeply about what they want their students to be and to be able to do, and what pedagogy, curriculum, and school organization are most likely to provide students with these attributes. The designs, along with the technical assistance given by the teams, provide the outside nurturing and assistance most schools need to begin and sustain the transformation process.

But a school-level focus is not enough. We know that high-performance schools exist today but that they tend to be the exception rather than the norm. There are many reasons for this. One reason is that the existing policy and operating environments in which they find themselves contain many barriers to the development of such schools. The education policy environment has tended to promote uniformity rather than diversity. The result has been the practice of dividing students into groups according to perceived abilities in order to educate children most efficiently. The unintended effect is that a significant proportion of children do not acquire the skills needed for success in our modern society. School environments have been created that cater more nearly to the interests and needs of adults than to those of students. Too few technical support, professional development, and other sustained capacity-building efforts are in place. And the nation's human services systems, an important element of the operating environment, too often fail to help children come to school prepared to learn. As we set about defining the "scope" of our strategy, two important definitions emerged. We wanted to create a critical mass of transformed schools. We defined this as occurring when so much change has taken place that it would take more effort to revert to the old than to maintain the momentum toward the new. (We have adopted a goal of 30% of a jurisdiction's schools.) We defined a transformed school as one in which a significant proportion of its students—including those who are low income, belong to racial or language minorities, or have disabilities—know and can do whatever is necessary to function effectively as citizens and workers. To accomplish this, we assessed our resources and design teams' capacity and decided to seek partners in states or cities willing to work with us in creating a critical mass of transformed schools within their own jurisdictions.

IDENTIFYING A SUPPORTIVE OPERATING ENVIRONMENT

Currently, we are working with ten jurisdictions, including two states, to create supportive operating environments, thereby enabling a widespread transformation of their schools to occur. From our discussions to date with school and district personnel, we remain convinced that, on the basis of their work to date, a supportive operating environment must provide considerable autonomy to individual schools. In particular, schools require:

1. Control over budgeting and spending within the school; substantial power to hire, train, organize, and release staff
2. Control over the curricula and instructional strategies used in a school, consistent with public standards for school performance
3. Freedom to organize the school's schedule and the teacher and student assignments
4. Freedom to extend performance standards beyond those required by the locality or state
5. Substantial freedom to devise the specific means by which they demonstrate their accountability to their community beyond those means required by the state or the district
6. Opportunities for students (and their parents) to choose to attend or leave the school

Clearly, these elements add up to profound modifications in the way in which we govern and manage our schools.

However, the changes in governance and management are only part of the changes in the operating environment that are required for NAS designs—in fact, for all good schools—to succeed. A supportive operating environment also is likely to possess the following attributes:

1. Common, publicly supported standards of achievement for all students
2. Rich and reliable systems of assessment that help schools demonstrate that they are meeting the standards and help teachers make improvements in their programs
3. A transformed set of curricula and instructional strategies that are consistent with the standards and responsive to individual needs of students
4. A solid system for professional development and certification which is responsive to the needs of schools and school professionals and which assures that the instructional staff possesses the skills required to help students to meet high standards

5. Sources of assistance in choosing and developing curricula and instructional strategies
6. Technology that supports teachers and students in the instructional process and assists in the management of schools
7. A community services and support system that strengthens community and family engagement in the school and reduces health barriers and other nonschool obstacles to learning
8. An array of means by which a community and its schools engage the public to develop broad and deep understanding and support
9. A capacity and willingness to allocate the resources necessary to transform individual schools

Most of the suggested changes in schools require changes outside individual schools and often outside school districts. This is the reason NAS believes that successful initial scale-up efforts require jurisdictional partners who can provide or plan to develop operating environments in which the NAS designs are likely to thrive. In negotiation with potential jurisdictions, NAS is looking for evidence of the following:

1. A demonstrated commitment to put an effective operating environment in place
2. A commitment to achieving a critical mass of transforming schools within five years
3. A willingness and ability to acquire and allocate significant resources to the investments needed to restructure schools using NAS and other designs
4. The presence of institutions and processes that provide continuity in the face of changes in political and educational leadership
5. Widespread support for and participation in reform efforts by local educators, teachers' unions, businesses, higher education and community leaders, human service workers, and political leaders

These criteria are fundamental if change is to endure over time. Change cannot be implemented solely from one source or from the top down.

LESSONS LEARNED

During its lifetime, NAS has learned some important lessons: School change works best when there is a vision and design for improving the whole school; when specific deadlines and accountability measures are implemented to push change forward; when a whole school is transformed, not just a class or a department; and when strong emphasis is placed on professional development for teachers. These elements are fundamental to NAS designs and to the strategy for broadly replicating them. However, we also have learned that changes in individual schools alone will not create systems of excellent schools. There must be changes in policy environments, changes in the system, and support from the general public to foster the widespread school change this country requires to effectively provide all children with the education they need and deserve.

NAS's program is just one part of the larger national effort to change these policy and operating environments. The historic agreement to a set of national education goals by the governors and the president (the America 2000 program of the Bush administration and the Clinton administration's Goals 2000 program), Ambassador Annenberg's challenge to the nation, the reauthorization of the Elementary and Secondary Education Act (ESEA), the recent National Education Summit with governors and CEOs, the increasing number of state and local efforts seeking to bring about systemic change, and a variety of school reform networks are all part of this national effort. The nation's teaching organizations, along with professional associations of administrators, teacher training institutions, and a variety of business groups, are also proposing or implementing activities that they feel will create more effective operating environments. NAS's program must be seen as a component of such efforts and must seek ways to work with them.

NAS has accomplished an extraordinary amount in three short years and is well positioned to achieve even more. By the end of 2000, NAS plans to leave a legacy of design teams with the continuing capacity to assist large numbers of schools in their transformation and with many bold new schools throughout the country—indeed, a new generation of American schools for the twenty-first century.

APPENDIX: NEW AMERICAN SCHOOLS DESIGN TEAMS

The following are brief descriptions of seven NAS design teams working with 500 schools in 24 states.

The Audrey Cohen College System of Education completely redesigns the curriculum using an interdisciplinary approach that focuses on specific purposes for learning that lead to constructive social actions within the community. Instruction is project-based and highly motivated by the purposes. Students learn civic and personal responsibility while improving their community. For grades K–12.

Authentic Teaching, Learning, and Assessment for All Students (ATLAS) melds the visions of four important reform organizations. ATLAS requires a participatory governance structure focused on a pathway (a K–12 feeder pattern). While it has strong principles of interdisciplinary curriculum and instruction, the unique focus is on the consensus-building governance needed to lead away from fragmented, bureaucratic learning environments to unified support for a community of learners. For grades K–12.

Co-NECT Schools employ computational and communications technology enabling students to pursue an interdisciplinary, individualized curriculum with hands-on instruction in a school without walls that runs 24 hours per day. For grades K–12.

Expeditionary Learning/Outward Bound is dedicated to the complete development of students and teachers by extending the values of Outward Bound into schools. Curriculum and instruction move toward expeditions of learning that develop students' intellectual, physical, and civic skills. Teachers become learning guides and are provided with continuous, innovative professional development. For grades K–12.

The Modern Red Schoolhouse blends elements of traditional education with new instructional methods to provide all students with a strong foundation in American culture, as well as the skills necessary for future employment. The design is intended for potential schools of choice within multicultural communities. For grades K–12.

The National Alliance for Restructuring Education is an alliance of states, districts, schools, and expert organizations created to effect systemic change at all levels by promoting ambitious standards and accountability mechanisms. The focus is on outcomes-based governance with decentralized decision making and the provision of strong professional support to teachers and schools. For grades K–12.

Roots and Wings is a relentless and organized approach to ensuring that all children will leave elementary school with the skills required for success. The design reallocates existing federal, state, and local resources into a research-based system of curriculum, instruction, and family support designed to completely eliminate special education and low achievement. For grades K–6.

Design Team Contacts

Atlas Communities Education Development Center, Inc.
55 Chapel Street
Newton, MA 02160
(617) 969–7100, ext. 2436
Ms. Linda Gerstle, Project Director

Audrey Cohen College
75 Varick Street
New York, NY 10013
(212) 343–1234
Ms. Alida Mesrop, President

Co-NECT Schools
BBN Corporation
70 Fawcett Street
Cambridge, MA 02138
(671) 873–2000
Bruce Goldberg, Director

Expeditionary Learning/Outward Bound
122 Mount Auburn Street
Cambridge, MA 02138
(617) 576–1260
Mrs. Margaret Campbell, Executive Director

The Modern Red Schoolhouse
5395 Emerson Way
Indianapolis, IN 46226
(317) 545–1000
Dr. Sally B. Kilgore, Director

The National Alliance for Restructuring Education
700 11th Street, NW, Suite 750
Washington, DC 20001
(202) 783–3668
Dr. Judy B. Codding, Director

Roots and Wings
3505 North Charles Street
Baltimore, MD 21218
(410) 516–0274
Dr. Robert Slavin, Project Director

CHAPTER NINE

Building Bridges: How to Make Business–Education Partnerships Work

ROBERT L. WEHLING

"IF YOU ARE ON THE WRONG train," it is said, "every stop along the way is the wrong stop." Some may think this metaphor regarding the wrong train describes public education in America today, but I am convinced that most of the ongoing efforts to improve student achievement are on track. I believe we *are* on the right train and that the stops along the way are, in fact, the right stops. It is just that we have a long way to go to the end of the line.

Getting there successfully will require patience, persistence, vision, and passion—not just from those within the education community but also from those who have an equally high stake in the success of education reform. The business community is one such stakeholder; business–education partnerships can be an especially effective way to implement the necessary changes in education.

All too often, however, business–education partnerships fail to live up to their potential. Task forces are created. Studies are conducted. Recommendations are published. But then, with the glaring lights of publicity behind them, these high-profile partnerships do not get the job done. Why do these partnerships fail? What can be done to make them work? What can happen when they succeed? I believe these are important questions and will attempt to answer them here, drawing on my 35-plus years of experience in business and public education.

WHY DO BUSINESS–EDUCATION PARTNERSHIPS FAIL?

Business–education partnerships are important because schools and companies have so many success factors in common. Good schools and successful companies, for example, recognize that their most valuable assets are their people and that they must invest in those people with meaningful professional development programs. Similarly, the most innovative schools and the most innovative companies attract—and nurture—individuals who take personal and passionate responsibility for outstanding results. And the most effective schools and businesses understand that to promote change, they must involve all of their stakeholders.

Clearly, business leaders and educators have much in common and much to learn from one another. Yet too often, business–education partnerships fail. Why? I believe it is because businesspeople and educators come from dramatically different cultures. In fact, most of the failed business–education partnerships I have seen have failed because one or both sides would not give them enough time to build the kind of trust necessary to make progress.

This cultural gap can create many barriers. One of the most common is created when businesspeople arrive with their "idea of the month." They create a lot of momentum, like a whirlwind, and then they are gone, leaving educators shaking their heads and growing ever more skeptical about whether these partnerships can work.

Another frequent obstacle is the dramatic difference in the way businesspeople and educators approach a project—especially when it comes to how long it should take to get an initiative started and what the finished product should look like. Businesspeople, by and large, want things to happen very quickly. Consequently, they are generally willing to have something about 80% to 90% right and get going with it. "We will figure out what needs to be fixed as we go along" is a common attitude among businesspeople.

Educators, on the other hand, tend to want to get everything right in advance, even if it takes five years to do it. Then, they figure, they can put a program or model in place, confident that it will work and will not need to be tinkered with any longer. The best approach, in most cases, lies somewhere in between these two extremes. You have to give a project enough time to find that middle ground.

Another barrier that I have seen undermine far too many partnerships is the involvement of businesspeople who propose radical solutions when, in fact, they really do not know what they are talking about. We have made much progress in this area over the years, but there are a lot of business leaders involved in school reform who pontificate from their ivory towers and do more damage than good.

What I generally tell my business colleagues is that we desperately need their help, but unless they are willing to take the time to come into our classrooms, to sit down with our staff, to meet with administrators and students—to really get a firsthand feeling for the problems we are up against—we do not need their solutions. However, if they are willing to do all these things, we invite them in, and it can be a very positive, productive experience.

However, some fault lies on the school side of this issue as well. Historically, the message from schools to businesspeople has been: "We would like you to get involved in our levy campaign. We would like you to study our buildings and make recommendations about our maintenance needs—and, by the way, help us get the money to meet those needs—but we draw the line at the classroom. You are not allowed inside the classroom door. *We* will take care of the classroom; *you* take care of the outside shell." It is as counterproductive for educators to keep businesspeople out of the classroom as it is for businesspeople to offer solutions without ever having been there.

Fortunately, I think we are reaching a point where both sides are beginning to see that we need everyone whom we can recruit, rolling up their sleeves and working constructively for the benefit of our teachers and our children. I have seen this attitude adopted by people with whom I have worked in Ohio, particularly on two initiatives that are models for what effective business–education partnerships can achieve.

THE CINCINNATI YOUTH COLLABORATIVE: BUILDING BRIDGES ONE GENERATION AT A TIME

The Cincinnati Youth Collaborative (CYC) is a consortium of education, civic, business, and labor leaders. It is co-chaired by Cincinnati's mayor, the superintendent of the Cincinnati public schools, and the chairman and chief executive of Procter & Gamble.

When the CYC was formed in 1987, its members agreed on a shared vision: for all Cincinnati youth to graduate from high school with the training, knowledge, work habits, and motivation to realize their full potential, whether they would be entering the workplace in a productive and satisfying job or continuing with their higher education.

Agreeing on the vision was easy; achieving it was not. We needed a "big idea"—breakthrough thinking—if we were to achieve our vision for Cincinnati's children. That big idea came only after Collaborative members had spent literally five years building bridges between their respective cultures. As a result of that bridge building, we stopped trying to persuade each other to see classroom problems from either the business or educational point of view and started, instead, to look at these problems from the students' point of view. That was a fundamental shift, and it provided us with the insights we needed to develop programs that work.

For example, students at Taft High School, Cincinnati's core inner-city school, told us they see little connection between what happens in school and their own futures. We also learned that many of Taft's "at-risk" students had no positive adult influence in their lives.

With this understanding, we had a clearer picture of how the CYC could achieve its vision for these kids. We developed a program called T-CAP, the Taft Career Academic Program, to make education more relevant to what the students will experience later in life. T-CAP is a career-focused program within a solid academic framework, and it involves not only what is taught but how and where that instruction occurs. More than 100 adult mentors serve as role models, providing students with guidance, encouragement, and assistance. In addition, a system of Youth Advocates offer additional adult influence and support.

It is too early to declare victory, but we are already seeing tangible results. For example, the first-year students in T-CAP were promoted at a rate 14% higher than the previous year's class. And, on average, T-CAP students missed a week less of school during the year than other disadvantaged students who have not participated in the program.

The CYC is a true business–education success story made possible because Collaborative members were committed to closing the gaps between their respective cultures. They saw themselves as bridge builders, and they are building a better future for a generation of students as a result.

OHIO'S BEST:
BUILDING BRIDGES TO EVERYONE WITH A STAKE IN EDUCATION

Another good example is a relatively new initiative called the Ohio Education Improvement Consortium. This statewide school improvement initiative is making fundamental structural changes in school funding, community involvement, and classroom standards. It is a terrific example of closing cultural gaps, not only between business and education but also between literally dozens of groups and organizations that have an interest in Ohio's public education system.

The Consortium was formed in 1994 after school improvement leaders performed a "gap analysis" to determine whether Ohio's schools were achieving the six national educational goals established by President Bush and all 50 governors in 1989. At the end of this effort, the group, of which I was a member, asked, "If we don't do anything differently, do we have a legitimate chance to meet the national goals?" The answer was "no." It was clear that closing the gap would require leadership not only from education and business but also from literally everyone who had a stake in Ohio's public school system.

This was an important realization, and it led to more than 80 organizations becoming involved in the statewide effort to improve schools. Virtually every educational group was represented: the Ohio Federation of Teachers, the Ohio education system, the Ohio School Boards Association, the Buckeye Association of School Administrators, and the Ohio PTA. Many other groups participated as well, including the Business Roundtable; the Chamber of Commerce; the Farm Bureau; the NAACP; the Council of Churches; individual companies such as Sprint, United Telephone, and Procter & Gamble; parents; nonprofit organizations; professional trade associations; and others. To my knowledge, no other state has brought together such a diverse group of organizations to help improve schools.

Building this diverse group has been and continues to be a tremendous undertaking, but the Consortium is working because everyone involved has come to the table recognizing that bridges needed to be built and genuinely wanting to learn from one another.

Much has happened as a result. The Consortium quickly established a clear and far-reaching agenda known as Ohio's BEST (Building Excellent Schools for Today and the 21st Century).

The agenda has five core strategies:

1. Create high-performance education by raising standards for all Ohio students, teachers, and schools
2. Improve accountability for results
3. Increase the involvement of parents, businesses, and communities— including neighborhood and civic groups, labor organizations, and institutions of higher learning—in the education of Ohio's children
4. Create orderly, safe schools—free of drugs, alcohol, and violence
5. Ensure that every child has equal access to a quality education

It would not be possible to achieve such a far-reaching agenda without the Consortium's broad base of leadership because this initiative requires coordinated efforts at the state, community, and individual school levels.

At the state level, for example, we are using the governor's and legislature's budget authority to drive change. One strategy is to expand the state's use of seed money to encourage schools to adopt exemplary programs and practices from other schools. The state of Ohio has dedicated about $20 million in its biennial budget as venture capital grant money. Schools throughout the state are using these education venture grants to employ the Effective Schools model, Success for All, or a total quality model. And many of the schools are using the money for professional development as well. This initiative is working, and we hope to expand it in the years ahead.

BEST is also working at the community level to encourage neighborhood involvement in school improvement activities. A community that implements 10 specific initiatives is designated as an "Ohio's BEST Community," which recognizes the neighborhood's commitment to better schools and showcases the most innovative and effective improvement ideas. Finally, progress is underway at the individual school level. Two of the most promising initiatives are individual education plans and individual achievement portfolios.

The individual education plans are being developed for every Ohio student in the eighth grade or earlier and are updated throughout the student's schooling. There is ample evidence that students who have meaningful goals, who have some direction for their lives, achieve at a higher level than students without such goals. It does not cost anything to help students develop such goals, and yet very few schools have made the development of student goals a priority. Ohio's BEST is helping to change that.

Another important change is the creation of individual achievement portfolios. Through this initiative, all Ohio high school graduates will receive achievement portfolios along with their diplomas. This portfolio will highlight the student's academic and vocational accomplishments and abilities for prospective employers or postsecondary institutions.

Many other BEST initiatives are underway, but even these few illustrate the pace and breadth of activity going on in Ohio's schools. Progress is being made at every level—from the governor's office to individual classrooms—and it is being led by virtually everyone who has a stake in public education.

STAYING ON THE RIGHT TRACK

The Cincinnati Youth Collaborative and the Ohio Education Improvement Consortium are making a difference in Ohio. Business and other leaders outside education have spent plenty of time in Ohio classrooms, talking with students, parents, teachers, and administrators. Their perspective has broadened as a result. On the other side, educators have not only invited but welcomed the perspective these "outside parties" bring to their schools. As a result, their classrooms are better learning environments.

Most important, however, is that everyone involved in these efforts is committed for the long term. They recognize that meaningful change will not happen overnight, and they recommend long-term solutions, not "ideas of the month."

I think all of us working for better schools in Ohio feel confident that we are on the right track, and we understand that it does not matter if the track is not yet completed to the end of the line. Bridges need to be built wherever there are gaps so that our kids will make it to the end of the line.

SELECTED BIBLIOGRAPHY

Fosler, R. S. 1990. *The business role in state education reform*. New York: The Roundtable.

Kidder, T. 1989. *Among schoolchildren*. Boston: Houghton Mifflin.

Lund, L., and C. Wild. 1993. *Ten years after* A Nation at Risk. New York: The Conference Board.

Marshall, R., and M. Tucker. 1992. *Thinking for a living: Education and the wealth of nations*. New York: Basic Books.

Newman, F. 1990. *What business can do to achieve educational change in a community*. Denver: Education Commission of the States.

Rigden, D. W. 1994. *Sustaining change in schools: A role for business*. New York: Council for Aid to Education.

Schorr, L. B., and D. Schorr. 1988. *Within our reach: Breaking the cycle of disadvantage*. New York: Anchor Press/Doubleday.

Sizer, T. R. 1985. *Horace's compromise: The dilemma of the American high school*. Boston: Houghton Mifflin.

Wentworth, E. 1992. *Agents of change: Exemplary corporate policies and practices to improve education*. Washington, DC: Business Roundtable.

Wigginton, E. 1985. *Sometimes a shining moment: The Foxfire experience*. Garden City, NY: Anchor Press.

CHAPTER TEN

Equity and Liberty in Education Funding

KERN ALEXANDER

ACCORDING TO THE Vicar of Wakefield, the poor and downtrodden have a vast advantage over the rich because, upon entry to heaven, the contrast with their earthly condition is so great. The raptures and pleasures of heaven are relatively unknown to the poor on earth, but to the rich they are commonplace. Thus, according to the vicar's feckless analysis, poverty on earth is the preferable condition. The vicar himself, benighted and poverty stricken, confidently justified his condition: "Thus Providence has given the wretched two advantages over the happy in this life, greater felicity in dying and in heaven all that superiority of pleasure which arises from contrasted enjoyment" (Goldsmith [1766] 1961, 156). For such a man of poverty to discover happiness in his wretchedness is a bit unusual, for it is more frequently the affluent who glorify the joys and virtues of others who are in perpetual penury. To believe that money does not buy happiness normally requires some experience with both money and happiness.

Reinhold Niebuhr has explained to us that those persons with the advantage of great financial resources will normally go to substantial lengths to justify their advantages and invent proofs to defend inequalities of privilege (Niebuhr [1932] 1960, 117). All such justifications, acceptance, resignation by the poor, and moralizing by the affluent are found both implicitly and explicitly in considerations of funding of the public schools. In no forum are these conflicts more readily apparent than in the school finance equity litigation that has now touched virtually every state in the nation. Here the proponents of equality of funding come face-to-face with those who seek to maintain the status quo and retain educational advantage preserved by local school tax prerogatives.

In 1994, a notable legal struggle was begun in Ohio between children and parents of property-poor school districts and the state of Ohio (*De-Rolph v. State of Ohio*, 1 July 1994). Evidence indicated that revenues among the school districts ranged from the extremes of $22,625 in Perry Local, the richest school district, down to $3,114 in Huntington Local, the poorest school district. The children in the top 5% of the wealthiest school districts had an average of $6,204 in state and local revenues spent per pupil, per year, while the poorest 5% had an average of $3,423 spent. The courtroom contest lasted for several weeks, producing thousands of pages of testimony. Even though this type of litigation has become commonplace among the states in recent years (Alexander and Salmon 1995, 26–38; Hickrod and Anthony 1994), the Ohio case bears special attention because the Ohio Supreme Court, in an earlier 1979 case (*City of Cincinnati Board of Education v. Walter 1980*), had cast doubt on whether education is a fundamental right. In that decision, the Ohio court had ritualistically deferred to the legislature, vesting in that body plenary control over public school funding. The present case, challenging this unlimited judicial deference to the legislative branch, presents a two-part legal question: (1) Is education a fundamental right under the Ohio constitution? (2) If so, does the constitution tolerate wide disparities in per-pupil funding among public school districts?

The plaintiffs alleged that the Ohio public school funding scheme effectively denied equality of educational opportunity to those children who live and attend school in property-poor school districts. Except for the legal glare cast by the 1979 precedent, resolution of the issue appeared to be relatively simple. Yet external simplicity can often become exceedingly complex and convoluted when differing interpretations of law and fact are opened to litigation. Moreover, political consideration inevitably plays a role in the most objective judicial proceedings. The Ohio Supreme Court has not yet ruled on the question. That final court decision will ultimately affect the flow of billions of tax dollars and greatly impact the extent and nature of educational opportunity provided throughout Ohio for generations.

At the heart of the issue in the Ohio case is the intent and application of the education clause—Article VI, Section 2—of the Ohio constitution, which requires the General Assembly to secure a "thorough and efficient system of common schools throughout the state." The importance of the case as a precedent is enhanced by the relative antiquity of the Ohio constitution, enacted in 1851. This constitution's date becomes of greater significance when one considers that the constitutional language of that era was strongly influenced by the enlightened philosophical conceptualizations of the role of government in educating the masses that had swept

Europe and America from the late eighteenth century through the mid-nineteenth century. The wording of the Ohio constitution reflects the consequences of these philosophical reflections on the relevance of education to the republican form of government.

In rendering its decision, the lower court found that the funding method for the common schools in Ohio results in wide disparities in school revenues per pupil, which, in turn, produce widely variant educational opportunities. According to the court, these disparities are caused by the statutory method of funding that involves both local taxation and the state school finance formula. The court concluded that the level of funding provided is insufficient to "afford an adequate education program to pupils in plaintiff school districts" (*DeRolph v. State of Ohio* 1994, 455).

The issue in Ohio, as in other states, is far from settled. In all states, such litigation continues to be a major public policy issue. In each circumstance, when a judicial declaration is rendered, the complex issues pertaining to a remedy usually produce protracted proceedings in both the courts and the legislatures. If meaningful educational reform is ultimately to evolve from these cases, it is important to know and understand the underlying principles that form the foundation of such decisions.

This chapter attempts to provide some insight into both the legal and educational finance issues undergirding these cases. The constitutional intent in Ohio, as in other states, is most meaningful if the terminology of the constitution is understood in the context of the conditions of the era in which it was promulgated and the assumptions regarding the nature and role of public common schools in America. This chapter specifically addresses the bases for assuming that education is a fundamental right, the importance of universal education to the republican form of government, and the rationale of both dissenters and advocates in the debate over the need for equality of school funding. Further, the chapter attempts to explain how the two pivotal issues of human rights, liberty and equality, relate in the context of the school-equity litigation.

EDUCATION AS THE BASIS FOR REPUBLICAN GOVERNMENT

State constitutions in the United States assume a republican form of government and prescribe foundational principles to effectuate that end. Notable among these and pertinent to school finance are the provisions for education. There is implicit in these constitutions the reasonable assumption that educated people are better able to govern themselves than uneducated ones. Self-government and an educated citizenry are interrelated.

Republican government is hypothesized to be the best governmental form, effecting the greatest happiness of the greatest number of people. The idea that education plays a vital role in the support of a republican government is a concept that is traceable to founders of this country, with philosophical foundations in the writings of French Enlightenment scholars.

The role of education in relation to government is not merely of historical concern; it is integral to several current themes on the nature and form of government. Today, many subscribe to the notion that education should be privatized and the government's role should be minimized. Others believe that education should be privatized but that government should provide the financing, giving public tax dollars to families and/or to private and religious schools. Still others propose that education should be financed by government but that various types of enclaves should be permitted where local tax dollars can be retained for exclusive use of the particular locality. In each of these circumstances, there exist elaborate reasons justifying the obtaining of better-quality education for one's own preferred ends and for the systematic conveyance of one's own philosophical or cultural interests. In this regard, the nature of education to be provided is of great concern to government; the more limited the government and the more narrow its goals, the greater the necessity to control the context of education. Additionally, control of education is of major importance to the vested interests of various groups, and all administrations place education high on their lists of priorities.

Education as the means to elevate man and woman above the state of nature and the beasts of the forest is most desirable, but for education to contrarily advance particularized self-interest and to create social separation is highly undesirable. To recognize that education can be used for good or evil and that it can even foster meanness in government is not a revelation for anyone old enough to remember World War II; Germany was a country of well-educated people. Montesquieu early observed that the laws of education will be different for different forms of government: "In monarchies they will have honor for their object, in republics virtue, in despotic governments fear" (Montesquieu [1746] 1977, 127).

Problems arise when government perceives education not as what we owe to others but rather as what we owe to ourselves (Montesquieu [1746] 1977, 128). It is well known that monarchies and despotic regimes can be sustained without universal education; in fact, it may even be asserted as a tenet of political science that limited and selective access to education is most valued by the most undesirable types of government. Montesquieu noted that the republican form of government requires the whole power of education (Montesquieu [1746] 1977, 130). The broader the base of education, the more limitless its context and the greater its value to a republican government. The broad base of mass education reflects the primacy of the public good over private interests. Montesquieu further asserted that because virtue in government requires "a constant preference of public to private interest, the public interest is the principal business of education" (Montesquieu [1746] 1977, 130).

EDUCATION AND VIRTUE IN GOVERNMENT

The role of education is to advance virtue in government, and it is the consensus of history that the republican form of government best ensures virtue. A virtuous government prefers the public interest over self-interest and is characterized by a commitment to the social bond. By definition, virtuous government is grounded in morality and premised on the interaction of human beings. Morality exists only in interaction with others. Durkheim best summarized this idea when he said, "There are not genuinely moral ends except collective ones" (Durkheim [1925] 1973, 82). A person detached from the collectivity of others will be underdeveloped as a human being: "He cannot fully realize his own nature, except on the condition that he is involved in society" (Durkheim [1925] 1973, 68). Language is social; religion is social; government is social—"Man possesses all the less of himself when he possesses only himself" (Durkheim [1925] 1973, 69). In this regard, Dewey pointed out that if individuals were alone in the world, they would form habits relative to physical nature, but they would be in a moral vacuum due to the absence of relationships to other human beings (Dewey [1922] 1994, 85). Virtue and morality can exist only relative to other fellow beings. A republic requires universal education in order to instill a consciousness of moral necessity and demands of duty. Montesquieu said that virtue is *the* principle of the republic (see Rousseau [1762, 1758] 1978, 85).

Primitive impulses of self-interest may lead parents and neighbors in one community to attempt to capture and retain financial resources for their own school districts and to use financial means to sustain academic superiority for their own children. In the particular instance of state school financing schemes, parents in affluent school districts attempt to skew the wealth of the state toward support of the education of their own children and to the detriment of others. This is a direct and obvious contradiction to the requirements of moral government. In situations of government-aided parental preference, enhanced parental vanity, or the *amour-propre* (Dent 1992, 239), we can clearly see the Hobbesian desire to make oneself superior to others and to take precedence over others. Virtue requires a will and a commitment to principle beyond natural and primitive inclinations, a conquering of such affections, a resort to reason and conscience, and an obligation to duty (Dent 1992, 241). One can see that school finance litigation involves these natural human propensities. Where legislatures fail, the courts are faced with the difficulty of convincing self-interested parents to consider the education of all children of the state, not just their own.

Barlow, in an insightful but little-known treatise on government, wrote in 1792 that persons formed governments not to require virtue but rather to restrain vice. He argued that "if all men were disposed to mutual justice and benevolence" (Barlow [1792] 1983, 818), then government would not be needed; a government without virtue simply reinforces the human being's less civilized instincts. Assuming this is true and that government by expression of a nobler general disposition elevates the moral level of humanity, then government itself, by its own laws, should not create conditions that encourage the meaner and more primitive instincts of individuals. Thus, if government should seek to prevent vice, it is difficult to argue that it should establish systems of school finance that give more to the rich than to the poor. As a matter of moral principle, government should use its financing mechanisms to effectuate greater equality in education, not to increase inequality through its own financing schemes.

It is the primary function of education to link the child to a moral society and to imbue in every child desirable principles of government. Education shapes state and national morality (Barlow [1792] 1983, 818). An educational system that is individualized, particular, and sectarian cannot advance moral and virtuous ends. By definition, such an education separates its participants from the larger society. Thus special enclaves of property-rich parents who separate their children from others in quasi-private systems of publicly supported education foster separatism to the detriment of the moral ends of government. Such immorality is magnified by voucher schemes that give public funds to parents, thereby encouraging them to send their children to private and parochial schools.

Education is thus essential to a republican form of government, and in order to sustain republicanism the educational ideal must be premised on the common interest, not particularized self-interest. Education should bring the individual and particular wills into conformity with the transcending general will. The litigation involving public school finance in Ohio and in other states seeks to shift public resources from the control of special and particularized interest toward enhancement of the common interest. The issues as joined in the school finance cases serve as legal and philosophical battlegrounds for these opposing positions. These legal contests also reflect broader questions regarding the appropriate balance among state, localized, and individual interests.

THE LAW OF RECIPROCITY AND A BILL OF DUTIES

Political and moral philosophy operate on a vast balance wheel that is constantly readjusting itself between self-interest and moral and ethical responsibilities to others. There is always a natural weight of self-preference to pull against the moral considerations of benevolence to others. Virtue is a nobler and necessary corrective device enabling people to moderate their tendencies towards self-interest (Niebuhr [1932] 1960, 45). Helvetius observed in his *Essays on the Mind II* that a person's "virtues and vices are wholly owing to different modifications of personal interests" (quoted in Niebuhr [1932] 1960, 45). He argued that a human being's basic instincts of self-interest that cause one to enter mutually beneficial relationships are at the bottom of all virtue. Similarly, Bentham, in his later writings, perceiving reality to sway more toward self-interest than toward general utility of social interests, concluded that the "principle of self-preference" probably dominates human nature in that one "prefers his own happiness to that of all other sentient beings put together" (quoted in Niebuhr [1932] 1960, 46). A government of virtue moderates selfishness (Barry 1989, 157) and raises all persons above the state of nature. Hume suggested that if people pursued the public interest naturally, "and with hearty affection," then there would be no need for the rules of justice that a virtuous government prescribes (Hume [1740] 1978). Experience tells us, however, that without such government people would pursue their own self-interest, without precaution, and "would run headlong into every kind of injustice and violence" (Hume [1740] 1978).

Because individuals contrive for their own protection, self-interest intertwines with external collective interests, making mutual and common accord not only desirable but necessary. This is Hobbes's justification for Leviathan, and it is the basis for Kant's "categorical imperative" that "I ought never to act in such a way that I could not also will that my maxim should be universal law" (quoted in Sullivan 1994, 29). This is Kant's first principle. Herein lies the overarching rationale of justice: That which is good for the general will is ultimately best for the individual. A duty is owed to others for the preservation of one's own liberties. We therefore cannot exempt ourselves from the requirements that we place on others, and we cannot claim for ourselves "permissions we are unwilling to extend to all others" (quoted in Sullivan 1994, 46). Kant's categorical imperative, the requirement of universality, thus reasons that it is obligatory for all to serve the needs of all others. This is the law of reciprocity—"What is forbidden to one is forbidden to all, what is permissible for one is permissible for all, and what is obligatory for one is equally obligatory for all" (quoted in Sullivan 1994, 46).

The law of reciprocity suggests the importance of obligations and duties as concomitants to individual rights. It argues that there may be an even stronger moral rationale for a "bill of duties" than for a "bill of rights." A bill of rights is a constraint on government's encroachment on individual liberties, while a bill of duties more comprehensively prescribes expectations of both government and individuals. Where obligations to one another are fulfilled, personal liberties are not constricted but rather are protected as the moral norm.

Thus morality assumes a duty owed to others if for no other reason than that it constitutes a reciprocity of interest to protect one's self. As Hume states, the test is whether one "shares all [my neighbor's] joys and sorrows with the same force and vivacity as if originally my own" (Hume [1777] 1975, 185). Fuller called this the "golden rule" or the "pervasive bond of reciprocity," premised on the Kantian categorical imperative (Fuller 1979, 20). It does not fail to comport with the logic of Bentham's utility principle of the "greatest happiness for the greatest number of people," for the simple reason that if a duty is so unpleasant that the majority see it as constituting a substantial loss to the collective self-interest, then the duty would be less obviously necessary.

A bill of duties cannot simply represent the will of the majority because the will of the majority may result in a direct denial of the obligations owed to a minority. It is precisely here that the categorical imperative is essential, that a law acceptable to one's self must be translatable into a universal principle that affects all equally. In this regard, the clearest and most concise explanation of the essence of morality and virtue is enunciated in Matthew 7:1 and 12: "Therefore all things whatsoever ye would that men should do to you, do ye even so to them" (quoted in Fuller 1979, 20).

Whether this principle is termed the categorical imperative, the law of reciprocity, or the golden rule, one can easily see its application to the issues pertaining in school financing litigation. Can the people of one school district in a state conclude within the bounds of moral obligations that they do not have a duty to educate the children in other districts in a way equal to the education of their own children?

FUNDAMENTALITY OF EDUCATION

Universal free education is claimed as a uniquely American idea. The fundamentality of education may be viewed from many perspectives. It is, of course, argued that tyranny is cultivated and nourished by an intellectually inept people, made so by a lack of knowledge and limited access to information. The First Amendment to the United States Constitution guarantees "freedom of press," but such a right assumes, a priori, that the people are educated well enough to read and understand what they are reading. Moreover, the written nature of the Constitution itself implicitly assumes that the protections assured therein are interpretable by the people, generally. The Dark Ages were unnecessarily extended by the refusal of the few who were literate and the church to expand education and to translate Latin texts into the vernacular (Heer 1962, 103–104).

Later Horace Mann attributed to the Pilgrim founders "the magnificent idea of a Free and Universal Education for the People" (Mann 1847, 108). According to Mann, they held foremost in their minds an appreciation for life everlasting and knowledge on earth. He observed that "two divine ideas filled their great hearts—their duty to God and to posterity. For the one, they built the church; for the other, they opened the school" (Mann 1847, 108).

It was said that both religion and knowledge were founded on great and glorious truths, securing both "immortal and mortal happiness" (Fuller 1979, 20). The Puritan founders, stimulated by intellectual observations complemented by the widely disseminated reform ideas of Comenius and others, increased the initiative in pursuit of universal education. The great Massachusetts Statute of 1647, commonly referred to as the first public school law in America, reflected the educational fervor that accompanied the ideology of universal education. Accordingly, it was held that education should be extended to everybody to the end that all would be able to comprehend nature (*pansophia*) through reason (Lawson and Silver 1973, 154). During that era from 1640 to 1660, Cambridge economists William Dell and William Petty argued that none should be excluded from education because of poverty or parentage (Lawson and Silver 1973, 155). Petty asserted that "it hath come to pass that many are now holding the plough, which might have been fit to steer the state" (quoted in Lawson and Silver 1973, 155).

Such exertions, however, came to no avail in England, and Commager's observation that "Europe imagined and America realized the enlightenment" (Commager 1978) was nowhere more evident than in the field of universal education. It is true that the Puritans advanced the cause of learning in order to enable all to read and understand the Bible; however, it must be added that intellectuals of this era saw the importance of Baconian and Newtonian enlightenment in ushering in a new time when a person's own store of knowledge not only aided its possessor in facing the immortal and mortal truths, but more pragmatically enabled all persons to exercise basic rights.

Indeed, it was argued that knowledge is the condition precedent, i.e., prerequisite, to the obtaining of civil rights. The juxtaposition of ignorance and freedom to which Thomas Jefferson referred illustrated the a priori need for education as a precondition to the attainment of all freedoms.

Beyond the ability to exercise basic rights and freedoms or to assure economic sufficiency and utility, education must be assumed to be a fundamental right purely on moral grounds. This particular position was most adroitly expanded by Horace Mann in 1847. Mann argued persuasively that education is a natural right, a basic tenet of natural law on which the performance of all "domestic, social, civil and moral duties" are predicated (Mann 1847, 112). A life lived without the opportunity to obtain knowledge reduces the human being to a level that is indistinguishable from that of animals in the primitive state. The higher plane of humankind assumes some systematic acquisition of knowledge. Such an assumption, though not clearly enunciated, was not entirely foreign to the Hobbesian explanation of humankind's movement from the state of nature to the social structure of government.

In the final analysis, the issue of whether education is fundamental can be reduced to the simplest of considerations: of the importance of knowledge and whether the systematic expansion of knowledge is of foundational importance to the individual and the state. For the individual, knowledge is essential to the exercise of liberty. Education is the prerequisite to freedom. Even in its most primitive state, knowledge of the alternatives that freedom provides is necessary before one can conceive of the options that are incumbent in liberty. If one were born in the forest and able to run free, then confinement would be untenable; but if one had been born in and always lived in confinement, and had no knowledge of freedom in the forest, then one's relative perspective on liberty would be entirely different. There was no great outcry for freedom of the press before Gutenberg; the ignorant who could not read Latin did not complain of the lack of religious liberty in medieval Europe. Persons today who do not know how to use the Internet are not generally concerned about the extent to which censorship might limit the use of electronic mail. In short, the possession of knowledge has much to do with the sophistication and extent of the demands for liberty. The most obvious recent example is the great outcry for liberty that was launched in China, only to be quelled at Tiananmen Square. When young Chinese learned of the freedoms and options available to youth in America, they became dissatisfied with their own restricted state of affairs and demonstrated. Thus it may quite plausibly be argued, from evidence both historical and contemporary, that education and the acquisition of knowledge are fundamental to basic freedoms.

Mann cut to the essence of the issue when, in 1847, he designated education as a basic fundamental principle of natural law and an *absolute right*:

> I believe in the existence of a great immutable principle of natural law,
> or natural ethics—a principle antecedent to all human institutions and
> incapable of being abrogated by any ordinances of man—a principle of
> divine origin, clearly legible in the ways of Providence as those ways
> are manifested in the order of nature and in the history of the race,
> which proves the *absolute right* of every human being that comes into
> the world to an education; and which, of course, proves the correlative
> duty of every government to see that the means of that education pro-
> vide for all. (Mann 1847, 112; emphasis added)

EQUALITY OF EDUCATIONAL OPPORTUNITY

The school finance cases provide an opportunity to delve into the meaning of the concept of equality of educational opportunity and to discern
from it the measures to which the state must adhere in the provision of
education. States defend their allocations of school funds by citing various justifications for the disparities in funding among school districts. In
few other places does the tendency toward self-preference become more
obvious than in these cases. When the advantages of one's own children
are at stake, human beings are least able to transcend their own interests
(Niebuhr [1932] 1960). True to Niebuhr's admonishment, the more affluent will seek excuses to justify their privileges and will invent "specious"
proofs that the inequalities visited on others are justified and moral (Niebuhr [1932] 1960, 117).

In the school finance cases, the state usually defends the inequalities
by arguing that the differences in funding are justified because the state
should not intercede to deny the privileges that one's own local fiscal
ability bestows. The state thus maintains that the differences in local
wealth and income that produce funding disparities are justified; some
children benefit from attending well-funded schools, while others are
destined to have only minimal resources available in their schools. The
state, in defense of funding inequalities, effectively argues that because
local wealth differences are due reward for individual initiative and
greater motivation in wealth acquisition, the more affluent are entitled to
greater educational advantage for their children.

In further justification for inequality in funding, the state employs
the input-versus-outcome argument, maintaining that equality of educational funding cannot, in fact, create equality in individual productivity.

It is argued that even if resources are equalized, the state cannot guarantee the same educational outcomes. Moreover, if the state could guarantee the same educational results, it could not equalize the prospects in life, as all persons will end up with different lifetime outcomes anyway.

The plaintiffs respond to these defenses of inequality with a consistent and predictable logic. The logic flow goes something like this: (1) All persons are by natural right entitled to equal treatment. (2) Education is a state function, not a local one; the governmental entity in question is the sovereign state. (3) Every child is a child of the state, not the locality. (4) All taxes are state taxes, levied directly or under the delegation of state authority. The underlying rationale leads to the conclusion that it is the state itself that is responsible for any disparities in funding that may exist. The plaintiffs assert that public education is state-created, and it must be assumed that such a state function should impart its benefits impartially. Dworkin states the matter very simply when he says, "I assume that we . . . accept as fundamental, the principle that people should be treated as equals in the matter of distribution. That is to say that they should be treated as equals unless they are, in fact, not equal in some relevant way" (Dworkin 1986, 269). Of course, if one does not accept that people should be treated equally in the first place, then there is little room in which to pursue any aspect of the plaintiffs' assertions in the school finance litigation—or any other litigation.

TYPES OF INEQUALITY

The evidence in these school finance cases very clearly shows that the state's scheme for funding results in widely disparate educational opportunities. This inequality, on its face, seems to be unjust, and there is ample philosophical rationale to support such a conclusion. The primary and most grievous case against the state is that the state does not merely tolerate natural inequality, but rather actually causes the inequality. Rousseau in his famous dissertation on inequality observed that there are two kinds of inequality. One kind is caused by nature or physical circumstance, such as "differences in age, health, bodily strength and qualities of the mind or of the soul." The second kind of inequality is caused by "moral or political inequality" (Rousseau [1762, 1754] 1973, 49). The latter is caused by human convention and results from the consent of human beings in their social and economic relations and interactions.

Rawls defines three types of inequalities: (1) the natural lottery, which distributes genetic or individual abilities; (2) the social lottery, which distributes more or less favorable home and school environments;

and (3) the lottery of God, called by Hobbes "the secret workings of God, which men call Good Luck" (Hobbes [1651] 1968, 150). This lottery of life's chances distributes good and bad, wellness and illness, fortune and misfortune arbitrarily, including being in the right place at the right time (Rawls 1971, 75). In all these instances, inequality is the result of happenstance or conditions that may be considered morally arbitrary and thereby beyond the power of the state to correct on the basis of equity or justice. The school environment to which Rawls refers apparently constitutes conditions that are not state-controlled but rather result from social or economic conditions that affect the school. Barry adds to Rawls's list a fourth dimension of inequality, resulting from the distribution of primary goods (Barry 1989, 226). Education must, of course, be considered a primary good, and, as such, its distribution as something controlled by the state must be made with consideration of equality.

It is in the context of these authorities providing a basis for the categorization of inequalities that the allegations of the plaintiff school children in school finance cases can be best understood. The plaintiff children who suffer from unequal public school resources maintain that they are suffering from a more invidious inequality: "state-created" inequality. In view of this assertion, inequality in education can be best explained in four dimensions: (1) inequalities due to luck; (2) inequalities attributable to genetics; (3) inequalities caused by the social and economic environment; and (4) inequalities created by state laws that prescribe the way tax resources are allocated for public schools. The first three are the results of conditions that are not directly controlled by the state. The first and second are entirely external to state action. It can be maintained that the state should take steps to correct for genetic deficiencies that are harmful to education, and this is now done in statutory laws for disabled children. Yet these educational enhancements for the benefit of the disabled are benevolent and desirable, but not required. The disabilities are not caused by state action, and the state is thereby not required to institute corrective intervention, except in a charitable or altruistic sense. With both of the first two inequalities, remedial action by the state, even though highly desirable, is not required. Only where the state itself, by its own acts, creates the vice of inequality is remedy absolutely required.

The third kind of inequality is manifested in the educational disadvantage of children who live in blighted and poverty-ridden neighborhoods and, as a result, may be denied even minimal prospects of social and economic success in life. These children, lately labeled "at risk" and earlier called "educationally deprived," have a great need for government intervention to correct the effects of poverty visited upon them by the economic marketplace. Undeniably, government should provide compensatory education to correct the ravages of economic discrimination caused by laissez-faire competition, especially where it can be shown that such conditions are strongly influenced by tax laws and other means that favor the more affluent. Yet such educational deprivation is not caused by direct action of government. Government probably contributes indirectly to the problem but does not cause it exclusively and directly. Thus government cannot be required to correct the condition because government itself is not the direct cause. Such disadvantage, while highly detrimental to some children and to society, is nevertheless not invidious. To be invidious, the discrimination must be traced to intentional governmental action.

The fourth kind of inequality, which is created by law, is the result of direct state action. This type of inequality, state-created inequality, is invidious because it emanates from action of the legislature. Here, under statute, state and local tax resources are combined in such a way as to give some children substantial educational privilege while others are disadvantaged merely because of their geographic location and economic circumstance. This inequality is not merely an omission by the state but rather a commission—a direct result of state action.

STATE-CREATED INEQUALITY

This last type of inequality, state-created inequality, results when state and local tax dollars are malapportioned to favor one child over another. The state typically defends this inequality by maintaining that funds distributed from the state level act to reduce local revenue disparities and to some degree mitigate property tax disparities. This defense ignores the fact that the public school system is a state system and all taxes, whether collected at the state or local level, are, by law, state taxes. Taxes, whether levied at the state or local level, are under the authority of the legislature, unless in rare circumstances a tax provision in the state constitution supersedes legislative prerogative. Thus the combined effect of all taxes, state and local, creates wide disparities in per-pupil funding among children depending on whether they attend school in poor or affluent school districts. If, on its face, equality is virtue and inequality is vice, then such state-created inequality is morally objectionable.

What is the state's obligation to effect equality? The most obvious answer with regard to the school finance cases is that the state should not create inequality in the first place. The state has responsibility to promote the common interest and to mitigate perpetual and innate adverse tendencies of self-interest. Because human altruism is limited in range and intermittent, government must manifest a general will to moderate the human desire toward personal preference and advantage. The state should be the guarantor of equality and, in that role, should at the minimum divide all valuable things equally. If equal splitting cannot be done, then as surety the state should give all parties an equal chance of obtaining equal shares.

The most cogent explanation of equality as a goal of virtuous government and of its corresponding necessity is given by Berlin in his simple axiom that "a society in which every member holds an equal quantity of property needs no justification; only a society in which property is unequal needs it" (Berlin 1978, 84).

THE ETHICAL PRIMACY OF EQUALITY

According to Berlin, and a host of other political and moral philosophers, persons should be treated as strictly equal in the division of all valuable goods unless there is some special reason for departure from this rule. Yet, when one views any discourse on equality, it is usually colored or obscured by one's own experience and particular circumstances. Thus parents who live in more affluent neighborhoods can justify departures from equality by various perceptions of what special reasons may exist. Attempts to find special reasons to justify inequality in funding are variously propounded; the affluent are said to be more interested in education, to have higher aspirations to attend more prestigious institutions of higher education, and to be more talented or more gifted. In short, the more affluent are entitled to their just deserts, a perspective manifested in a multitude of ways when parental desire for educational opportunity for their children is at stake. Regardless of the reasons, however, one can be sure that the better educated will always desire more education for their offspring than the less educated. Such is the nature of education; its value is seldom understood by those who have not acquired a sample of it. The problem, therefore, is to make education available in equal amount to all who are equally able and can benefit from it, not to deploy benefits in greater quantities to some simply because they already have more.

Rakowski states the issue in another way but with equal clarity: "Although we come into the world at different times, and somebody was always there before us, we enter in the same way, without more right to the bounty of nature than anyone else who sees daylight for the first time. It therefore seems sensible to ask how the world should be carved up among people who are equally able but equally undeserving" (Rakowski

1991, 65). Thus, if we are all equally undeserving, then there is little doubt that adherence to strictly equal shares of education should be the rule.

Of course, the most tenacious of arguments to justify the retention of greater funding for children in property-rich school districts is that the wealth belongs by some inherent right to affluent families and that they should therefore be able to retain all its advantages solely for the education of their own children. Horace Mann in the early 1840s, when considering the statutes and financing of public schools, pointed out that it is an "arrogant doctrine" which propounds that people can claim that they have earned their present possessions and that those who happen to live in rich school districts have, by their own hands, earned the advantage that the property wealth of that district bestows upon them and their children. Mann said that it was absurd to conclude that the more affluent have an exclusive claim to the advantages of the wealth of that particular place on earth. Such exclusiveness ignores the fact that we all enjoy the benefits and suffer the detriments of our predecessors, and of infinite time, and that all generations are recipients of the common bounty of natural conditions that have contributed immeasurably to some being rich and others being poor. The benefits have accrued from the accumulated knowledge made possible by reading and writing, and by physics, chemistry, agriculture, philosophy, arts, and economics—the investments in learning of all those who have gone before us. "Surely all these boons and blessings" belong to others' children as well as to our own and to posterity as well as to ourselves (Mann 1847, 118). He also states: "The society of which we necessarily constitute a part, must be preserved; and, in order to preserve it, we must not look merely to what one individual or family needs, but to what the whole community needs; not merely to what one generation needs, but to the wants of a succession of generations" (Mann 1847, 120).

According to Mann, as observed above, the claim of each child to education is as natural as the claim for sustenance, shelter, care, and breathing; and "society at large—the government—having assumed to itself the ultimate control of all property, is bound" to distribute its bounty fairly and equitably (Mann 1847, 124). In elaboration, he set forth what he called the "eternal principles of natural ethics" that govern education and the state's responsibility to treat all children equally. He says:

1. The successive generations of men, taken collectively, constitute one great Commonwealth.
2. The property of this Commonwealth is pledged for education of all its youth. . . .
3. The successive holders of this property are trustees, bound to the

faithful execution of their trust by the most sacred obligations.... (Mann 1847, 127)

These principles enunciate an ethical standard for education that requires equality of opportunity and challenges the assertion of a special interest in preserving educational advantage merely because of location or current economic or social condition.

DEVIATING FROM STRICT EQUALITY

Plaintiffs in the school finance cases do not claim that all state and local tax resources should be distributed precisely equally, as it were, "one dollar for one scholar." Rather, they maintain that deviation may well be desirable for educational reasons, but a special reason for deviation cannot be wealth. Distribution must not be skewed to provide more for the advantaged to the detriment of the disadvantaged. Deviation from strict equality is not only permissible but desirable in appropriate circumstances. Initially, though, we must proceed from the assumption that all children are of equal talent and worth and are equally deserving and should therefore receive equal resources. The principle is that all equally deserving persons are entitled to equally valuable shares. Berlin has illustrated this maxim, the primacy of equality as a principle of human behavior, with his famous example of cakes and shares: "If I have a cake and there are ten persons among whom I wish to divide it, then I give exactly one tenth to each; this will not, at any rate automatically, call for justification; whereas if I depart from this principle of equal division, I am expected to produce a special reason" (Berlin 1978, 84). If, however, some persons are more deserving than others, then departure from equal distribution of equally valuable shares is justified. The problem, of course, is to determine a just rationale for departure from equality. An equally able and equally thirsty group of hikers have the same claim to equal portions of water; none has a greater claim. Yet if one is stricken by fever, then a different rationing of the store of water may be in order.

Special reasons must be relevant reasons. In matters of educational funding, relevance must have to do with legitimate educational issues. Unequal funding is justified if educational needs are different. A child with learning difficulties may be entitled to a disproportionately greater amount of funding than the average child. Rawls has maintained that an unequal distribution of goods "to the advantage of the least favored" comports with requirements of justice (Rawls 1971, 62). Departures from equal treatment must be justified on the same principles and with the same rationale that applies to all beneficiaries. All children are entitled to have their educational needs measured by application of the same criteria as are applied to all other children.

Relevant criteria in departing from equality to achieve justice must be based on educationally compelling grounds. It is not sufficient to assert reasons for deviation that are merely educationally related; they must be relevant to the end that a legitimate educational need is addressed. Moreover, as Rawls observes, the more favorable funding must go to the least advantaged, not to the most advantaged. It is difficult to conceive of a circumstance where departure from equality is justified by giving the more advantaged still greater resources to increase their advantages. It is thus doubtful whether a state is justified in funding gifted-and-talented programs if the same funds could be provided for children who are disadvantaged.

ADEQUACY AND THE VALUE OF MONEY

Affluent school districts at times defend their preferred funding status by asserting that the districts with less are nevertheless adequately funded, not underfunded. At what point does an adequate education decline to a minimum education? Plaintiffs may be forced to show that the funding they receive is not just unequal but also inadequate—and proving inadequacy is usually more difficult than merely showing financial inequality. Resolution of the issue must hinge on whether deviation from equal division advantages one child over another. If one child has adequate resources and another has more than adequate resources, does educational inequality really exist? Do financial differences really matter, or, as Rakowski puts it, is it "morally important whether one person has less than another regardless of how much either of them has"? (Rakowski 1991, 66). One school of thought maintains that what really matters "from the point of view of morality is not that everyone should have the same but that each should have enough"; past a certain point, everyone might be "so comfortable that nobody cares about remaining inequalities, and questions of justice would be aridly academic" (Rakowski 1991, 66). If this were the case, the relative difference between those merely adequately funded and those more than adequately funded would not become a contentious issue because the difference would be valueless. However, as long as resources have value and are unequally allocated, then providing adequate funding for some and more than adequate funding to others would appear to pose a moral dilemma. The value of the inequality then becomes the vital question. Are the resources distributed beyond designated levels of adequacy valueless? If they are valueless or of insignificant value, then departure from equality is inconsequential.

Yet common sense suggests that financial resources for education do have value. Defense teams in school finance litigation have attempted to show that educational inequality results not from insufficient money but from other, more ethereal educational factors. Yet because few can rationally believe that money makes little difference and thus has little value, it would appear to be difficult for the state to show that money is valueless or of such insignificant value as not to affect education. Equal division of something that has little or no value would presumably foster little acrimony or debate; this has not been the situation in school finance litigation. Wise has observed that if merely adequate funding for some children is all that is required, then one must ask how the state can justify providing some school districts with more than adequate funding: "Strictly speaking, total funds cannot be adequate (while inequity exists) unless one assumes that [the high-spending] districts are wasting resources" (Wise 1983, 311).

To sum up, the adequacy issue must ultimately rest on the moral question of whether some suffer unmerited disadvantage while others are entitled to unmerited advantage. "Moral equality entails an equal distribution of (unearned) resources" (Rakowski 1991, 39). To provide additional funding for some and not for others, based on wealth or economic condition or some designated level of adequacy, violates any reasonable definition of justice unless it can be shown that the additional funding is valueless, or nearly valueless, and educationally meaningless.

THE PRIMACY OF LIBERTY AND EQUALITY

Local control is often said to be a foundational and essential feature of the public school. Indeed, most thoughtful persons must conclude that subsidiary control, at the lowest level possible, is most efficient in a bureaucracy. States, in defense of disparate funding, frequently argue that inequality is the price one pays for local control. Local control is often placed in the broad and hallowed context of personal liberty: the freedom to have better and more abundant education for one's own children. The question therefore must arise as to whether liberty and equality are compatible or whether they are naturally and inevitably in conflict in the provision of education.

Fukuyama, in his popular work *The End of History and the Last Man*, observes that the "twin principles of liberty and equality" are the bases on which modern democracy is founded (Fukuyama 1992, xi). That liberty and equality are cornerstones of a republican form of government is well known to those who have read Madison, Jefferson, and Adams. If, however, one considers which comes first in a pantheon of rights and which takes precedence over the other—liberty or equality—then the issue becomes more complex. Is liberty more basic than equality? Which is more necessary to a republic? To consider the congruence—or incongruence—of liberty and equality is a formidable philosophical issue. Unfortunately, the question has not been fully resolved in any known treatment of political philosophy, and the school finance litigation is certainly indecisive on the issue.

To contend that movement toward fiscal equality for public school children must correspondingly reduce liberty is a popular and powerful philosophical position that is advanced by libertarians and many conservatives. Liberty, as in "Liberty, Equality, Fraternity," the great triad of the natural Rights of Man, was recognized in the Enlightenment and the French Revolution. Liberty captures the moral high ground in any consideration of political and moral rights. Moreover, a government of virtue seeks a priori to ensure liberty for the greatest number of citizens to the greatest extent possible.

The state, in defending unequal funding in the school finance cases, usually maintains that an expansion of equality necessarily requires a diminution of liberty. The state asserts that equalization of funding necessarily causes a loss of local control and that such loss is tantamount to a reduction in liberty. Ultimately, the state claims that the expenditures of wealthy local school districts would be reduced in order to spread the resources more evenly across the state. The disparities in local tax capacity among local school districts would have to be mitigated by either reducing local taxing authority or by greatly increasing state funds to overcome the local wealth differences. The state maintains that restrictions on local taxing authority in order to effect greater equality of funding would restrict local control and, thereby, restrain liberty.

The state argues that the alternative to greatly increasing state funding to reduce variations in local fiscal capacity would be both prohibitively expensive and highly questionable as tax policy. In short, the state asserts that inequality of funding must remain because the alternatives are untenable. The first alternative, loss of local taxing authority, strikes to the heart of liberty, and the second alternative, to greatly increase state funding, is unwise fiscal policy.

Moreover, it is maintained that restricting local tax prerogatives might lead to uniform mediocrity and a dismal sameness, with individual initiative stifled and the education and quality now experienced by the affluent sacrificed for the uncertain benefit of raising education levels for the poor to an inadequate average. Quality would thus be sacrificed

for equality. Defendants ask, "Is it better to have equality for all but quality for none?"

It is also implicitly maintained that equalization of resources would
prevent the exercise of choice and liberty, thereby limiting access to more
excellent levels of education. This idea is sometimes interpreted in educational parlance as the "lighthouse" concept, wherein certain school districts are given greater resources in order that they may illuminate the
horizons of knowledge. Without the guidance of such lighthouses, it is
argued, the mass of schoolchildren in average school districts might wan-
der about aimlessly, misguided and inefficient in their own pursuit of
knowledge. Those who have more should thus have the liberty to move
forward and explore and spend as their intuitions dictate.

THE PARADOX

A dichotomy is therefore presented: Does movement toward greater
equality result in a corresponding decline in liberty and local choice? Can
equality and liberty be reconciled? The answer to this conundrum is
found in the realization that the dichotomy is a false one. Paradoxically,
neither equality nor liberty can take precedence over the other. Rather,
they are complementary, intertwined, and mutually dependent. The relationship between liberty and equality is probably best stated by a little-
known but incisive commentator on both the American and French revolutions, Joel Barlow, who in 1792 observed that equality is required to
ensure the enjoyment of all rights and freedoms. Barlow explained that
liberty cannot be exercised without equality: "Every individual ought to
be rendered as independent of every other individual as possible; and at
the same time dependent as possible on the whole community" (Barlow
[1792] 1983, 823). This dependence on community as the surety for the
exercise of liberty is a concept implicit in the civil contract as expressed
in the writings of Locke in the *Second Treatise of Civil Government*, Rousseau in *The Social Contract*, and Kant in *The Metaphysics of Morals*. The
nature of the civil contract is that (1) there is an obligation to others generated by voluntary acts of each citizen, and (2) the contractee has relin-
quished certain rights and privileges in order to secure more extensive
and additional advantages and liberties (Dent 1992, 67–68). In other
words, the social contract is based on a commonality of interests and
fulfillment of obligations to others. The mutual exercise of those obligations expands the liberties of all.

That liberty and equality are mutually dependent is best explained
by Kant in his concept of "natural perfection." He observed that people's
duties to others and benefits to themselves become one. The necessity of

equality derives from each person's desire to extend his or her own free-doms and liberties. According to Kant, "self-love cannot be separated from need to be loved by others as well, we therefore make ourselves an end for others" (Kant [1797] 1993, 196–197). The goal of happiness for others is a duty because our happiness is dependent on their duty to us. Virtue is the strength of one's commitment in fulfilling this duty to others. The principle may be stated succinctly: "Every human being, as a being with needs and hence with inclinations, makes his own happiness his end and that, in so doing, he makes himself an end for others." Everyone desires "a maximum benevolence" toward themselves; each individual "wants others to be bound to benevolence toward him independently of their natural feelings." Individuals can, therefore, only obtain their own happiness by adopting the goal and fulfilling the duty of happiness to all other human beings (Kant [1797] 1993, 23–25).

It is true, of course, that individual liberty and state authority can come in conflict, although state authority is not synonymous with equal-ity. Locke and Mill maintained that state authority should be strictly lim-ited "to leave as much room as possible for individual liberty" (Raphael 1989, 136). It is argued that it is not possible for undeterred liberty to coexist with complete authority. Yet this conclusion cannot constitute the answer to the dilemma of liberty versus equality. If state authority is exer-cised in expansion of equality, then the authority is a means to a moral end (Raphael 1989, 136). If equality makes individuals more free, then the authority to effect that end expands liberty. On the other hand, if the machinery of the state is misused, then it may not expand liberty but instead create inequality by the state's own acts.

The common good should be the aim of the state, and if it is, its achievement requires extensive liberty and equality. Raphael points out that the conclusion to be drawn is the paradoxical one that compulsion by the state can make individuals more free, not less so, and that, in fact, those who are constrained by the law for the sake of moral ends can be, in Rousseau's phrase, "forced to be free" (Raphael 1989, 136). Thus, a citizen constrained by just laws is more free than one in a society with no laws. "Real liberty is the result of moral action by the government" (Ra-phael 1989, 137). Thus, if the state uses its authority to pursue the specific common good of educational opportunity, then it not only enhances equality but also materially extends the scope of individual liberty.

LIBERTY AND RIGHT

The mention of liberty always conjures in one's mind the freedom to do what is right. Freedom implicitly presumes right, yet freedom may also permit doing what is wrong. The exercise of liberty achieves a moral end only as it relates to the treatment of others. As observed earlier, moral ends are determined by the common good. If freedom of choice and liberty are exercised in a way that bring about results contrary to the common good, then by definition these exercises are wrong. In our own society today, we know that the exercise of liberty may be wrong if it results in racial segregation, economic and social stratification, religious discrimination, or ethnic discrimination. Individual liberty that seeks to harness the power and authority of government to reinforce such wrongheaded ends is subversive to equality and detrimental to liberty.

Thus, if we assume that all persons desire that their own children have full educational opportunity in order to have access to all the lifetime prospects and options in the exercise of liberty, then equality would be absolutely necessary. This mutual duty, with its corresponding distribution of benefits among all in society, becomes exceedingly important when one considers the desirability of equalizing school funding among school districts.

To achieve equality is to do right because social morality decrees that everyone has a duty to be the conveyer and recipient of benevolence. Each child is therefore entitled to the same advantages as other children regardless of where they live and attend school. This equality of treatment is not required because equality is an end in itself, but rather because it ultimately increases everyone's liberty. Equality, therefore, fosters choice, expands options, and thereby generally extends liberty. Inequality is thus inimical to liberty. The conventional wisdom, then, that a measure of inequality is necessary for the existence of liberty, is unsupported by political philosophy. The existence of the former is a menace to the latter.

LOCAL CONTROL AS A FRANCHISE

The issue of local control is invoked in yet another context by the state in defending unequal school funding. It is said that wherever there is intervention to create greater equality, there is always a reduction in local prerogatives. The plaintiff, however, points out that if local taxing powers of the affluent are not restricted, then the rich can always levy local rates that produce revenues far in excess of those of poor school districts. Thus the question emerges as to whether local taxing prerogatives of the rich should be limited.

In this regard, one must distinguish between individual liberties naturally derived and collective prerogatives that are bestowed by law. The organizational structure of public schools and the power to tax are determined by legislative authority. If that authority is exercised in a manner that advantages some and disadvantages others, then it is not a question of liberty but one of malapportionment of power. Because our structure of government is made up of sovereign states in which local school districts operate in a collective subunit, constituting the school government in the sovereign state, the legal government unit is the state.

Every individual is presumed to be a member of some sovereign governmental unit. Modern states have boundaries, "official languages, school systems with specific curricula, etc.," and various other laws governing individual relationships (Wallerstein 1992, 191). In the United States, these governmental entities—their boundaries, attributes, and relationships—have been decided; there are 50 state school systems operating under the laws of 50 state governments. The group, for educational purposes, is the state, not the local school district. This is relevant because the nature of duties and obligations may vary with the extent and size of the group. For example, the duties and obligations all the people in the Western Hemisphere owe to one another are less extensive than those owed by all people within the United States to one another; similarly, those duties owed to others among the states, within the United States are less intensified and less complex than those owed to fellow citizens within a single state. This cannot be changed without a reformation of our federal system of government.

Therefore persons living in the various school districts cannot presume to be separate and independent from the state as a whole. The resources of all the school districts, including the property wealth and the income, make up the capacity of the whole state. Each school district does not have a collective liberty to be excepted from the whole. All persons within and among those districts have the same rights and freedoms, none of them more or less extensive than those of others.

Thus the concept of local control is not founded on any accepted notion of individual liberty. Rather, it is in the nature of a franchise established by the state. A franchise is a special privilege conferred by government "which does not belong to the citizens . . . generally as a common right" (Black 1968, 768). In defending disparities in revenues among school districts, parents in property-rich school districts cannot assert any particular personal liberty or freedom in the retention of their district's affluence. However, people in rich school districts implicitly argue that they have a special privilege to be treated differently from the common whole simply because the state has given preferential treatment to them as a franchise. Thus the issue of individual liberty, to keep local control, is mistakenly regarded as a collective liberty. Groups do not have liberties—individuals do. Local control of taxation is therefore a special privilege, or a franchise, given by the state, allowing the affluent an educational advantage and denying equality of opportunity to those children in poorer school districts.

CONCLUSION

The Vicar of Wakefield would be familiar with the social and economic conditions in the United States today. He would still find the affluent conjuring up reasons to justify their advantages over the less fortunate. Perhaps he would discover conditions improved in some sectors, but he might well find the situation as bad or worse in others. He might possibly find it an anomaly that the egalitarian frontier of the American colonies of his day now has greater wealth differentials between rich and poor than his native England (World Bank 1991, 263). Indeed, he would not be surprised to discover that in America the economic elite have "achieved a virtual dominance of the legislative process" by their ability to shift the balance of power in the political system (Edsall 1984, 108). The vicar might even recognize the tendency of those in penury to abandon hope of earthly rewards and to look forward to a measure of equity and happiness in some heavenly haven. With these persons, as with the vicar, it is only in the hereafter that the poor and rich will have "equal dealings," but the poor thereafter will have "the endless satisfaction of knowing what it was once to be miserable"—a condition of bliss the rich will never experience (Goldsmith [1766] 1961, 156).

The poor vicar readily illustrates what Galbraith has called the "equilibrium of poverty": the creation of a condition in which the poor are not cognizant of their options because of intergenerational deprivations, especially in education (Galbraith 1979, 43). In such situations, "people do not strive, generation after generation, century after century, against circumstances that are so constituted as to defeat them. They accept"; they "reconcile themselves to what has for so long been the inevitable" (Galbraith 1979, 56). Aspiration becomes progressively more fruitless as incentive for self-improvement is excessively remote or nonexistent. "Such resignation by the poor provides the rich with what they believe to be a moral justification for their lack of sympathy; the poor do not even try" (Galbraith 1979, 57).

Education destroys this accommodation and acquiescence to poverty. Unlike the vicar, those who are educated do not accept that they must be poor. In this regard, Galbraith has observed, "It is by universal education that individuals gain access to the world outside the culture of poverty and its controlling equilibrium" (Galbraith 1979, 84).

For those who have been exposed to education and know its value, hope is not abandoned in earthly pursuits. Those who are challenging disparate allocation of school funding in court actions have not abandoned hope; but they have lost faith in the legislative process and turned, instead, to the courts for redress of their grievances. It is in these courts, where the issues are exposed, that there is a genuine opportunity to reveal the actions by the states that have tended to exacerbate the inequality of educational opportunity rather than mitigate or resolve it.

If the defense of these inequitable state laws is successful, then plaintiffs' children in disadvantaged economic circumstances will have no avenue for obtaining the rights inherent in the ideal of equality of educational opportunity. As a result of presidential appointments during the Reagan and Bush administrations, the federal judiciary has increasingly become less sympathetic to the educational plight of the poor. The state judiciary appears to be, quite literally, the court of last resort. Should the plaintiffs' appeals before the Ohio and other appellate state courts fail, then progress toward social cohesion and betterment will be most seriously retarded.

REFERENCES

Alexander, K., and R. G. Salmon. 1995. *Public school finance.* Boston: Allyn & Bacon.

Barlow, J. [1792] 1983. A letter to the national convention of France on the defects in the Constitution of 1791. In *American political writing during the founders' era, 1760–1805,* ed. C. S. Hyneman and D. S. Lutz. Indianapolis: Liberty Press.

Barry, B. M. 1989. *Theories of justice.* Berkeley: University of California Press.

Bentham, J. 1843. *Works.* Vol. 10, 80. Edinburgh: W. Tait.

Berlin, I. 1978. Equality. In *Concepts and categories: Philosophical essays,* ed. H. Hardy. New York: Viking.

Black, H. C. 1968. *Law dictionary.* St. Paul, MN: West.

City of Cincinnati Board of Education v. Walter. 58 Ohio St. 2d 368, 390 N.E. 2d 813 (1979), cert. denied, 444 U.S. 1015 (1980).

Commager, H. S. 1978. *The empire of reason: How Europe imagined and America realized the Enlightenment.* Garden City, NY: Anchor/Doubleday.

Dent, N. J. H. 1992. *A Rousseau dictionary.* Oxford, England: Blackwell.

DeRolph v. State of Ohio, Court of Common Pleas, Perry County. 1 July 1994. (See Gongwer News Service, Inc.: Ohio Report. Vol. 63; Report No. 127.)

Dewey, J. [1922] 1994. *The moral writings of John Dewey,* ed. J. Gouinlock. Buffalo, NY: Prometheus.

Durkheim, E. [1925] 1973. *Moral education: A study in the theory and application of the sociology of education.* London: Free Press.

Dworkin, R. M. 1986. *A matter of principle.* Oxford, England: Clarendon.

Edsall, T. B. 1984. *The new politics of inequality.* New York: W. W. Norton.

Fukuyama, F. 1992. *The end of history and the last man.* New York: Avon.

Fuller, L. L. 1979. *The morality of law.* New Haven, CT: Yale University Press.

Galbraith, J. K. 1979. *The nature of mass poverty.* London: Penguin.

Goldsmith, O. [1766] 1961. *The vicar of Wakefield.* New York: New American Library.

Heer, F. 1962. *The medieval world: Europe, 1100–1350,* trans. J. Sondheimer. New York: Mentor.

Hickrod, G. A., and G. Anthony. 1994. *State school finance constituted litigation.* Normal, IL: Center for the Study of Educational Financing, Illinois State University.

Hobbes, T. [1651] 1968. *Leviathan,* ed. C. B. MacPherson. Harmondsworth, England: Penguin.

Hume, D. [1777] 1975. *Enquiries concerning human understanding, and concerning the principles of morals.* 3d ed., ed. L. A. Selby-Bigge, text revision and notes by P. H. Nidditch. Oxford, England: Clarendon.

Hume, D. [1740] 1978. *A treatise of human nature.* 2d ed., ed. L. A. Selby-Bigge, text revision and variant readings by P. H. Nidditch. Oxford, England: Clarendon.

Kant, I. [1797] 1993. *The metaphysics of morals,* trans. M. Gregor. Cambridge, England: Cambridge University Press.

Lawson, J., and H. Silver. 1973. *A social history of education in England.* London: Methuen.

Mann, H. 1847. *The Massachusetts system of common schools: Tenth annual report of the board of education of Massachusetts.* Boston: Dutton & Wentworth.

Montesquieu, C. [1746] 1977. *The spirit of laws,* Book IV, ed. D. W. Carrithers, trans. T. Nugent. Berkeley: University of California Press.

Niebuhr, R. [1932] 1960. *Moral man and immoral society: A study in ethics and politics.* New York: Scribner's.

Rakowski, E. 1991. *Equal justice.* Oxford, England: Clarendon.

Raphael, D. D. 1989. *Problems of political philosophy.* Houndsmill, England: Macmillan.

Rawls, J. 1971. *A theory of justice.* Cambridge, MA: Belknap Press of Harvard University Press.

Rousseau, J-J. [1762, 1754] 1973. *The social contract* and *Discourses,* trans. G. D. H. Cole. London: Dent.

Rousseau, J-J. [1762, 1758] 1978. *On the social contract, with Geneva manuscript,* and *Political economy,* ed. R. D. Masters. New York: St. Martin's Press.

Sullivan, R. J. 1994. *An introduction to Kant's ethics.* Cambridge, England: Cambridge University Press.

Wallerstein, I. 1992. *Geopolitics and geoculture: Essays on the changing world-system.* Cambridge, England: Cambridge University Press.

Wise, A. E. 1983. Educational adequacy: A concept in search of meaning. *Journal of Education Finance* 8(3): 300–315.

World Bank. 1991. *World development report, 1991: The challenge of development.* Oxford, England: Oxford University Press.

CHAPTER ELEVEN

Equity, Adequacy, and Variable Spending in Public Education

RICHARD A. ROSSMILLER

ISSUES CONCERNING FUNDING and fairness in public education have always existed in the United States. They are likely to continue for the foreseeable future as social, economic, demographic, and technological changes continue to alter perceptions of what is right, proper, and just in the allocation and use of the public funds devoted to education. This chapter will briefly describe how views of equity and fairness in the funding of public education have changed over the past 200 years, discuss developments that have influenced the debate during the past 30 years, and suggest ways in which both the fairness and the adequacy of funding for public education might be improved while maintaining substantial parental and community control over education at the local school level.

Although a vast majority of Americans agree that equal educational opportunity is a desirable goal, there is little agreement concerning how equality of educational opportunity should be defined operationally. In his commentary on the concept, Coleman observed that equality of educational opportunity "has had a varied past . . . has changed radically in recent years, and is likely to undergo further change in the future" (Coleman 1968, 7). Given the lack of agreement concerning exactly what equality of educational opportunity implies, it is useful to review some of the interpretations of the term, particularly as they relate to school funding.

Early developments in the New England colonies, particularly Massachusetts, were of great significance for the development of public education in America. The first settlers in New England moved rapidly to establish public schools, in part because of the emphasis they placed on all individuals being able to read and interpret the Bible for themselves. In 1642, the Massachusetts General Court passed an act requiring parents and masters to see to the education of children under their care and control; and in 1647, it required every town of 50 or more families to appoint a teacher to give instruction in reading and writing, and every town of 100 or more families to appoint a schoolmaster to give instruction in Latin grammar. Butts and Cremin identified four principles that characterized the early New England pattern: "The state could require children to be educated; the state could require towns to establish schools; the civil government could supervise and control schools by direct management in the hands of public officials; and public funds could be used for the support of public schools" (Butts and Cremin 1953, 103). Responsibility for the establishment and operation of schools was delegated to each town, and decisions concerning schools were made in the town meeting (not the church), thus establishing the concept of local control of schools and the first evidence of separation of church and state in matters of schooling.

The provisions for public schooling in the early southern colonies much more closely resembled the English system, with little state control of education and greater reliance on the church. The state exercised control only over the education of poor children, illegitimate children, and orphans, and delegated responsibility for enforcement of its requirements to church authorities (Butts and Cremin 1953, 105).

As a result of these early patterns established in the English colonies, at the time of the ratification of the United States Constitution, a tradition of publicly supported, publicly controlled schools that children were required to attend was well established in the New England colonies and had spread westward as settlement proceeded. In the southern colonies, however, no general system of public education existed.

Many influential framers of the Constitution and each of the early presidents viewed universal education as essential to the maintenance of democratic self-government. Madison, for example, writing in 1822, stated:

> A popular Government, without popular information or the means of acquiring it, is but a Prologue to a Farce or a Tragedy; or, perhaps both. Knowledge will forever govern ignorance: And a people who mean to be their own Governors must arm themselves with the power which knowledge gives. (Madison 1910, 103)

Despite this concern for education and its importance to democratic self-government, it is not mentioned in the U.S. Constitution, and the Tenth

Amendment makes it clear that responsibility for public education was to remain with the individual states.

Each state's constitution, including those of the southern states, which had no public school systems, made the legislature responsible for creating and maintaining a system of public schools that were free and open to all children. Indeed, it is these state constitutional provisions that have been the basis for decisions in the cases questioning the fairness of state school finance arrangements for the past quarter-century.

The state constitutional provisions concerning public education were not self-executing; it remained for the state legislature to create the organizational, financial, and administrative procedures through which public schools could be established and maintained. The organizational arrangements adopted by the various states reflected the patterns that existed prior to the American Revolution. In New England and the Middle Atlantic states, legislatures typically delegated authority and responsibility for operating schools to local school districts and their governing boards, thus creating a system of relatively small local units that were independent of other local governmental units. This pattern of independent local school districts is seen today throughout the United States, except for the southeastern states. In the southern states, which did not have a tradition of public education, counties were designated as the organizing unit for school districts—a pattern that persists today throughout the southeastern states. The existence of relatively small school districts tends to exacerbate disparities in local school tax bases and spending patterns found among a state's school districts, particularly when compared with the disparities that exist in states where school districts are organized on county lines and thus tend to be quite large.

EQUAL OPPORTUNITY—HAVING A SCHOOL TO ATTEND

From 1790 until near the end of the nineteenth century, equality of educational opportunity was typically thought of as having access to schooling, that is, having a school to attend. During the first half of the nineteenth century, the struggle was to establish common schools (elementary schools) that were reasonably accessible to all children. Financing public schools was predominantly a local responsibility throughout the nineteenth century, with revenues coming largely from local property taxes levied by each school district. State support, if any, consisted primarily of interest earned from permanent school funds derived from the sale of land grants and small grants distributed on a flat per-pupil or per-teacher basis.

The struggle to establish publicly supported free secondary schools continued until the 1870s, culminating in the Kalamazoo case in Michigan (*Stuart v. School District No. 1*, 1874). In 1874, the Michigan Supreme Court affirmed the legal authority of a school board to levy taxes to support a public high school, and by the turn of the century, most states had authorized tax levies to support high schools and were providing some state aid for high schools.

As the nineteenth century unfolded, policy makers began to note growing disparities in the nature of educational opportunities provided in the schools of the state. For example, the length of the school year varied quite widely, as did the qualifications of teachers. This situation eventually led to the expansion of state financial support, primarily as a means to gain leverage over the decisions of local school authorities. It also led to strengthening the state oversight of local schools to enforce state requirements through procedures such as licensure of teachers and accreditation of schools—in short, the emergence of state school systems.

State aid became a convenient tool for enforcing state mandates. By offering state aid to schools that met certain standards and withholding aid from schools that did not, the states were able to wield both a carrot and a stick. Early state aid took the form of a flat amount of money per pupil or per teacher, with no distinction made between relatively wealthy and relatively poor local school districts. Its primary purpose was to reestablish the authority of the state, not to eliminate disparities in the local tax bases or local spending.

By the turn of the century, the idea of equal educational opportunity was widely accepted. In describing this concept, Coleman stated:

> In the United States, nearly from the beginning, the concept of educational opportunity had a special meaning which focused on equality. This meaning included the following elements:
>
> 1. Providing a *free* education up to a given level which constituted the principal entry point to the labor force;
> 2. Providing a *common curriculum* for all children, regardless of background;
> 3. Partly by design and partly because of low population density, providing that children from diverse backgrounds attend the *same school;*
> 4. Providing equality within a given *locality*, since local taxes provided the source of support for schools (Coleman 1968, 11).

EQUAL OPPORTUNITY—EQUAL SPENDING PER PUPIL

By the beginning of the twentieth century, changing economic and demographic conditions in the United States had widened the disparities
among school districts in their tax bases and expenditures per pupil, and
the state aid that was being distributed did little to reduce these disparities. It was at this time that American public school finance became a
subject of study, with Elwood P. Cubberley completing a doctoral dissertation on the topic at Columbia University (Cubberley 1905). Cubberley's
study revealed that disparities in local tax bases and expenditures per
pupil were mirrored in differences in the quality of teachers, curricula,
facilities, and services provided pupils in local school districts. He recommended that two principles, which are still appropriate today, be considered in the distribution of state aid to local school districts: equalization
of resources and reward for local effort. With regard to equalization, Cubberley expressed his position as follows:

> Theoretically all the children of the state are equally important and are
> entitled to have the same advantages; practically, this can never be quite
> true. The duty of the state is to secure for all as high a minimum of
> good instruction as is possible, but not to reduce all to this minimum;
> to equalize the advantage to all as nearly as can be done with the re-
> sources at hand; to place a premium on those local efforts which will
> enable communities to rise above the legal minimum as far as possible;
> and to encourage communities to extend their educational energies to
> new and desirable undertakings. (Cubberley 1905, 17)

Cubberley emphasized education adequacy—that is, access to an adequate basic educational program for all children—but he did not advocate complete equalization of per-pupil revenues or educational tax rates.
In summarizing Cubberley's contribution to American public school finance, Ward concluded that it was "his conceptualization of a state system of providing aid to local school districts and the justification of that
system. He set the normative foundations for the field in the sense that
the basic values he espoused for school finance . . . have remained the
dominant values in school finance policy" (Ward 1987, 472).

Early in the 1920s proposals were advanced by Updegraff (1919; Updegraff and King 1922) and by Strayer and Haig (1923) that have dominated thinking in the area of state and local funding of education since
that time. Updegraff proposed what is now known as power equalizing;
Strayer and Haig proposed a foundation program.

The foundation program as originally conceived by Strayer and Haig would have gone far toward equalizing spending among the school districts in a state. It consisted of the following elements:

> 1. A local school tax in support of the satisfactory minimum offering would be levied in each district at a rate which would provide the necessary funds for that purpose in the richest district.
> 2. This richest district then might raise all of its school money by means of the local tax, assuming that a satisfactory tax, capable of being locally administered, could be devised.
> 3. Every other district could be permitted to levy a local tax at the same rate and apply the proceeds toward the cost of schools, but—
> 4. Since the rate is uniform, this tax would be sufficient to meet the costs only in the richest districts and the deficiencies would be made up by state subventions (Strayer and Haig 1923, 175–176).

In practice, the foundation program level is rarely, if ever, set at the level of the richest district, as proposed by Strayer and Haig. Rather, it is set at a lower level, for example, near the state average. This tendency, when coupled with an optional local tax levy that is not equalized, makes it impossible to achieve equal spending per pupil.

Updegraff's proposals involved merging the equalization and reward-for-effort principles enunciated by Cubberley, so that school districts levying taxes at the same tax rate would obtain the same level of revenue per pupil through a combination of local tax revenue and state aid. The power-equalization plan first proposed by Updegraff was resurrected with modifications by Coons, Clune, and Sugarman (1970).

It is important to note that Cubberley, Updegraff, and Strayer and Haig all advocated both adequacy and equity. They each stressed the importance of providing an adequate basic educational program for all children and agreed that local districts should be encouraged to go beyond the basic minimum; they did not advocate equal per-pupil expenditure in all districts. The goal of achieving equal spending per pupil throughout the state advocated by some school finance reformers is clearly inconsistent with the positions taken by these seminal thinkers.

The foundation program quickly became the dominant approach used by states to distribute state aid to local school districts, largely through the efforts of Paul Mort and his students at Teachers College, Columbia University. However, states proved unwilling to set the foundation level at the spending level of the richest district because of the very large amounts of state funds that would be required to equalize spending. Consequently, efforts by school finance reformers from 1925 to 1960 focused largely on narrowing the disparities in spending among school districts in a state. Their efforts were aimed at "leveling up" expenditures, that is, raising expenditures per pupil in low-spending districts but not reducing expenditures per pupil in the high-spending districts. Thus they assumed, at least implicitly, that equal opportunity would be achieved if the level of spending per pupil was sufficient to finance an adequate basic education program in each district.

EQUAL OPPORTUNITY—VARIABLE SPENDING APPROPRIATE TO PUPILS' NEEDS

By the 1960s, it had become apparent that children were not equal in their educational needs and that some children would require greater educational expenditures than others if they were to achieve their full potential. The development of special programs for disabled children as early as the 1920s, together with the provision of special state aid for such programs, provides evidence of early recognition of the fact that special education programs for such children were more costly than regular education programs. It was not until the 1960s, however, that special needs other than those associated with physical, mental, or emotional disabilities began to be recognized.

Passage of the Elementary and Secondary Education Act in 1965 signaled recognition that children disadvantaged by their family's economic circumstances often had unique needs that required special educational programs. Special needs may arise from a variety of sources related to the characteristics of the students being served, the characteristics of specific educational programs (e.g., vocational education), and the characteristics of the districts providing educational services (e.g., differences in demography and geography).

Three national studies have established that the cost of educating students with disabilities is at least twice as great as the cost of educating students in regular programs (Kakalik et al. 1981; Moore et al. 1988; Rossmiller et al. 1970). Weightings that reflect the additional cost of educating children with various special needs and the cost of providing comparable education programs in various school districts have become quite common in state school support programs.

EQUAL OPPORTUNITY—EQUAL OUTCOMES

Recent years have witnessed debate about whether equal educational opportunity should be viewed as requiring that students achieve equal outcomes. Our ability to achieve equal educational outcomes hinges on our knowledge of the precise relationship among educational resources and processes, the ability and propensity of students to learn, and the outcomes of education. Clearly, we lack sufficient knowledge of these relationships at the present time. To acquire such knowledge will likely require a commitment of resources and dedication of talent at least as great as was devoted to the development of the space program. Since I see little likelihood that such an investment will be made in the near future, discussions of the merits of using educational funding to guarantee equal student outcomes may provide for interesting disputation but give little direction to policy initiatives.

FAIRNESS IN FUNDING AND THE COURTS

Legal actions contesting the constitutionality of state school finance arrangements that permit wide disparities to exist in per-pupil expenditures and local tax rates have become commonplace since the 1960s. The first two cases, which sought to have funding related to educational needs, were decided by federal district courts under the due-process and equal-protection provisions of the Fourteenth Amendment and were not successful (*Burris v. Wilkerson* 1969; *McInnis v. Shapiro* 1968). In 1973, the U.S. Supreme Court ruled in *San Antonio Independent School District v. Rodriguez* that education is not a "fundamental interest" because it is not mentioned in the U.S. Constitution; and it could find no "suspect class" because low-income children did not live only in property-poor school districts. Consequently, state school finance cases are decided in state courts, with the outcome hinging on how the court interprets the specific provisions for education found in the state constitution.

The question before the courts is whether disparities in expenditure per pupil and in tax bases or tax rates in local school districts are greater than permissible under the state's constitutional provisions for education. Unfortunately, this question is comparable to asking judges to define "how high is up?" No universally accepted standards have been developed to determine how much disparity in school spending is permissible. Although several statistical measures of disparity are available, there is no general agreement on a "correct" number because, as Berne and Stiefel have shown, value judgments are required in interpreting these various statistical measures of equity (Berne and Stiefel 1984).

At the risk of oversimplification, it appears that in the first state school finance cases, the courts placed substantial weight on fiscal neutrality, that is, the extent to which disparities in expenditure were linked to disparities in school district taxable wealth, while in recent years, they have tended to look more closely at the extent to which differences in actual educational opportunities are associated with disparities in spending. They have, for example, considered such variables as depth and breadth of the curriculum provided for students, qualifications of teachers, teacher turnover rates, quality of buildings and other facilities, and the number of pupils per computer. Thus state courts have become more concerned with what educational dollars buy in the way of educational opportunities than with the mere existence of disparities in expenditure. In Kentucky, for example, where the constitution directs the legislature "to provide an efficient system of common schools throughout the commonwealth," the court overturned the entire Kentucky public education system and required the legislature to create an entirely new education structure, not just a new school finance formula (*Rose v. Council for Better Education* 1989).

Although plaintiffs have been successful in approximately half of the state school finance cases, no court has held or implied that a state's constitution requires equal spending per pupil. The courts have been concerned, however, that all students in a state have access to adequate basic educational opportunities. They have also looked with favor on pupil weightings or other provisions designed to reflect differences in the cost of providing appropriate educational programs to students with special needs.

EQUITY VERSUS ADEQUACY IN EDUCATIONAL FUNDING

Program adequacy has recently emerged as a topic of concern in discussions of educational policy. For example, the December 1994 issue of *Educational Policy* is devoted entirely to this subject. There would, of course, be no conflict between equity and adequacy if resources were unlimited and no constraints existed. Unfortunately, resources are not unlimited and taxpayers resist pleas for higher school spending—particularly given the fact that higher levels of spending have not produced significant improvement in student performance. There exists the danger that we will achieve equity in school funding, at least as reflected in little variance in expenditure per pupil throughout a state, but at a level inadequate to provide the programs and services needed if children are to achieve their full potential.

One must recognize that resources are allocated to public schools through the political process, just as they are allocated to other publicly funded activities. The political process favors organized interest groups that are able to articulate clear positions and lobby effectively for their points of view. Taxpayers generally are well-organized. More importantly, taxpayers vote, while school-age children do not. This situation, coupled with the fact that the majority of taxpayers do not have children in the public schools, means that today the interests of schoolchildren are not always well represented in the struggle to obtain adequate funding.

The reluctance of local taxpayers to pay higher taxes has been reflected in recent years in the imposition of taxing or spending limits for schools and in the trend to shift greater responsibility for educational funding to the state and away from local property taxpayers. The result has been a "leveling down" of educational expenditures in states such as California and Oregon, where controls have been placed on local school taxing and spending decisions. Such actions not only interfere with local control of education, they may also result in funding levels that are too low to support adequate basic educational programs in local school districts.

DOES MONEY MAKE A DIFFERENCE?

Any discussion of fairness relative to the funding of public education must ultimately address the question of whether money makes a difference. The research in this area leads one to conclude that money *might* make a difference, but there is no guarantee that it will. Hanushek reviewed 147 educational production function studies—studies that attempted to identify the relationship between school inputs such as expenditure per pupil, class size, teacher experience and training, and so forth, and school outputs as measured by standardized achievement tests. He concluded:

> There exists . . . a consistency to the research findings that does have an immediate application to school policy: Schools differ dramatically in "quality," but not because of the rudimentary factors that many researchers (and policy makers) have looked to for explanation of these differences. For example, differences in quality do not seem to reflect variations in expenditures, class sizes, or other commonly measured attributes of schools and teachers. Instead, they appear to result from differences in teacher "skills" that defy detailed description, but that possibly can be observed directly. (Hanushek 1986, 1141–1142)

Consequently, Hanushek concluded, "there appears to be no strong or systematic relationship between school expenditures and student performance" (Hanushek 1986, 1162).

Hedges, Laine, and Greenwald recently published a reanalysis of the same data used by Hanushek and concluded that resource inputs are related positively to school outcomes (Hedges, Laine, and Greenwald 1994). When they examined per-pupil expenditure and teacher experience, they found positive relationships between student outcomes and these two variables, with no negative relations between them, suggesting that increases in these inputs will be associated with increased student outcomes. With regard to the resource inputs of teacher education, teacher salary, teacher/pupil ratio, administrative inputs, and facilities, they found that with the possible exception of facilities, there was more evidence of positive relations than of negative relations between these resource inputs and student outcomes.

There have been very few studies in which researchers were able to relate instructional expenditures to individual pupils. I tracked the same group of students through three years of elementary school (grades 3, 4, and 5) and gathered a wide array of data concerning student and teacher characteristics, home–school relations, and expenditure per pupil for instruction in reading, language arts, science, and mathematics (Rossmiller 1983b, 1986). No strong relationships were found between expenditure per pupil in each subject-matter area and either the students' standardized test scores or their score gains during the three years of the study. In fact, when students in special programs were included in the analysis, rather high negative correlations between expenditure per pupil and the pupil's performance were noted.

Many studies of "effective schools" have appeared in the educational literature during the past 20 years. These studies typically have attempted to identify why students in some schools consistently demonstrate better academic results than do students in other, very similar schools in the same school district. Conspicuously absent from the list of characteristics of effective schools identified through this research is higher levels of spending per pupil. That is, more effective schools, as measured by student performance, do not spend more money per pupil than schools in which student performance is much lower (Levine and Lezotte 1990; Purkey and Smith 1983).

One may conclude on the basis of the research between expenditure level and student outcomes that money is necessary, but not in itself sufficient, to give assurance of higher student achievement. Rather, it is the way that money is used to acquire other resource inputs—teachers, materials, supplies—and the way these resources are utilized in the school and classrooms that ultimately will determine the impact of money on student outcomes. Hedges, Laine, and Greenwald observed that the pattern of results they obtained "is consistent with the idea that resources matter, but allocation of resources to a specific area (such as reducing class size or improving facilities) may not be helpful in all situations. That is, local circumstances may determine which resource inputs are most effective" (1984, 11). In his response to their analysis, Hanushek conceded that money might matter somewhat but pointed out:

> The past work demonstrates that simply adding resources to districts will not ensure improvement in student performance. Even if some districts can employ resources effectively, as undoubtedly is the case, there is no assurance that overall increases in resources will lead to overall improvements. Indeed, the evidence . . . is consistent with some districts finding effective ways to use resources and others following very ineffective policies. (Hanushek 1994, 8)

WHAT IS FAIR IN FUNDING?

Fairness in funding does not require absolutely equal expenditures per pupil throughout a state. Differences in the physical, mental, emotional, and other characteristics of children will often require educational programs of differing costs if children are to achieve their maximum potential. Differences in the cost of providing comparable programs will differ among school districts for reasons such as differences in cost of living, cost of operation, and demographic and geographic conditions. The court decisions in which existing state school finance provisions have been held unconstitutional have not suggested that equal spending per pupil is required, and often they have explicitly recognized that expenditure differences related to specific educational program requirements are necessary and appropriate. Also, a belief that local control of education is important means that differences in the tastes and preferences of citizens in various local school districts must be respected and may translate into differences in expenditure per pupil.

The question then becomes one of how much disparity in funding per pupil is warranted. The answer requires a value judgment, and one can expect reasonable individuals to differ in their views on this subject. I believe that the most vital element of fairness in funding is assurance that the level of funding in every school district is sufficient to guarantee provision of an adequate basic educational program to every child in the state.

Unfortunately, defining the specific components of such a program is very difficult. Reasonable people of goodwill are likely to differ when confronted with the task of defining exactly what should be included as part of the basic set of educational opportunities provided for all students. For example, questions such as the following are likely to produce disagreement:

- Should new uniforms for the high school marching band be considered part of a basic set of educational opportunities?
- What co-curricular activities should be included as part of the basic set of educational opportunities?
- How many foreign languages should be offered?
- Should instruction in human development be required for every student?

This list could easily be expanded, but it illustrates some of the controversial issues involved in defining exactly what should comprise the basic set of educational opportunities provided for all students.

Strayer and Haig avoided this dilemma by defining their minimum foundation program as permitting any district to have the level of spending found in the wealthiest district in the state if they levied the same tax rate as the wealthiest district (Strayer and Haig 1923). It was their position that local communities should have the discretion to make choices in educational offerings according to local priorities and that sufficient funding should be provided through a combination of local tax revenue and state aid. In practice, however, no state has ever been willing to fund education this generously. Consequently, it is not unusual to find that the foundation program level has been set at or even far below the state average level of spending. And even in states that have established procedures to determine the cost of a basic set of educational opportunities (for example, Texas), the legislature has been unwilling or unable to fund at the specified level.

An alternative approach has been to use statistical measures of disparity to evaluate fairness in funding. Commonly used measures of disparity include the federal range ratio, the coefficient of variation, and the Gini coefficient, although several other disparity measures also are available (Berne and Stiefel 1984, 7–43).

The federal range ratio is the difference between the spending per pupil at the 95th and 5th percentiles of the distribution divided by the value at the 5th percentile. It is an arbitrary measure used in the administration of the federal government's Impact Aid program. While its use by the federal government implies that a 1.25 ratio is equitable, this value is entirely arbitrary and has no statistical validity. I have argued that a federal range ratio of as much as 1.50 is acceptable. A variation of 0.25 should be permitted to allow for the expression of local tastes and preferences, and an additional variation of 0.25 should be allowed to compensate for differences in the cost of providing comparable programs among the various school districts of the state, with adjustments downward if such cost differences are recognized by weightings based on the cost of providing services.

The coefficient of variation is the standard deviation of the distribution divided by its mean and can be expressed in either decimal or percentage form. A coefficient of 0 indicates that expenditures are distributed with exact uniformity. Odden and Picus have suggested that a coefficient of 10 percent (or 0.1) represents a reasonable standard of equity (Odden and Picus 1992, 7–43). The Gini coefficient also measures the extent to which expenditures deviate from an absolutely equal distribution; the smaller the Gini coefficient, the more equal the distribution. Odden and Picus have suggested that a value below 0.1 is desirable (Odden and Picus 1992, 66–68).

The difficulty with each of these measures is that they fail to assess the adequacy of the level of spending per pupil in the lowest-spending districts. Ideally, the state will guarantee a level of spending sufficient to provide children in every district access to an adequate basic set of educational opportunities. Unless this set of opportunities can be reasonably well defined, however, it is impossible to establish reliable estimates of the cost of providing such opportunities.

ACHIEVING FAIRNESS IN FUNDING

While it is a difficult task to determine what level of funding is needed to provide all students access to a basic set of educational opportunities, it is not impossible. Adequacy is best thought of in terms of expected outcomes; that is, what does the student know and what is the student able to do? The first step is to define the level of performance expected of students as a result of their schooling. The goal should be a high minimum standard of performance consistent with the student's potential. There can be little doubt that this first step is the most difficult part of the process.

The second major task is to identify programs that hold promise of enabling students to achieve the desired outcomes and to specify the resources needed for such programs. For example, programs have been developed that have been shown to improve the educational achievement of children from low-income families (Hopfenberg et al. 1993; Madden et al. 1991). If the resource requirements for promising programs can be identified, then the appropriate level of funding can be fixed because the methodology for determining the fiscal requirements to provide such resources is well established (Rossmiller 1983a, 211–230), and the technology for doing so is available (Chambers and Hartman 1983, 193–240). Weightings can be employed to account for differences in the cost of programs meeting the educational needs of diverse categories of students, and adjustments can be made to allow for cost variances among the school districts and schools providing services to students.

EARLY CHILDHOOD DEVELOPMENT AND EQUAL OPPORTUNITY

Rapidly expanding knowledge concerning human development during the period from birth to age 3 underlines the importance of these early years of life to the child's later health and well-being. Although formal public education seldom begins prior to age 3, and more typically at age 5 or 6, a child's educational future may be affected significantly by early experiences. Recent discoveries suggest that the developing brain uses stimuli from the outside world to shape itself and that there are critical periods in which brain cells require specific types of stimulation to develop such powers as vision, language, smell, muscle control, and reasoning.

A report by the Carnegie Task Force on Meeting the Needs of Young Children provides a concise summary of some of the recent research on development during infancy and early childhood, discusses social and economic conditions that impact on the life chances of very young children, and offers recommendations for actions to improve the situation. The task force found that research on human brain development points to five key findings:

> First, the brain development that takes place before age one is more rapid and extensive than we previously realized.
> Second, brain development is much more vulnerable to environmental influence than we ever suspected.
> Third, the influence of early environment on brain development is long-lasting.
> Fourth, the environment affects not only the number of brain cells and number of connections among them, but also the way these connections are "wired."
> And fifth, we have new scientific evidence for the negative impact of early stress on brain function. (Carnegie Task Force 1994, 7–8)

It is evident that the early life experiences of children have a very important bearing on the attitudes, values, and knowledge they bring to the school experience in preschool, kindergarten, or first grade, and that their specific educational needs—indeed, their human potential—are shaped long before they enter school. It is not clear what role schools could or should play during the first three years of a child's life. It is clear, however, that failure to attend to the needs of very young children during these formative years will carry very high social costs in later years, not only in the additional cost of meeting their special needs in school but also in the costs that will be incurred by other public institutions and services. Although the cost of providing support and assistance to very young children and their parents may seem high, they are small compared to the cost of a lifetime of welfare or incarceration.

CONCLUSION

Over the past 200 years, views of what constitutes equal educational opportunity have evolved from providing access to common schools for all children, to providing access to a minimal level of educational opportunities, to providing equal expenditures per pupil, to providing expenditures appropriately differentiated according to the cost of an educational program that will permit each child to achieve his or her full potential.

If high expectations are held for student outcomes, a relatively high level of financial support will be required to provide an adequate basic set of educational opportunities. The specific level of expenditure per pupil required to provide adequate basic educational opportunities will vary from program to program, from school to school, and from district to district depending upon the characteristics of the children being served.

Assuming that a state has established a minimum funding level high enough to provide an adequate set of basic educational opportunities for each child, should individual schools or districts be allowed to spend at a higher level by taxing themselves more heavily? I agree with Cubberley, Updegraff, and Strayer and Haig that local schools should be allowed to go beyond the minimum. Experience over the past two decades makes it clear that schools cannot be improved by edicts from the state or federal government; school improvement occurs at the local school level, and local control is necessary if local needs, tastes, and preferences are to be respected. Since it has not yet been proven that it is possible to spend too much on education, it is reasonable to allow local communities to go beyond the basic educational program funded by the state.

Should states impose constraints or controls on how far beyond the minimum local districts may go? In my view, it is not unreasonable for the state to impose such limitations. First, one would expect to find diminishing marginal returns to investment in education just as one finds them in most areas of human endeavor. Second, other important public needs should not be short-changed, and public resources are limited. Consequently, I believe it reasonable for a state to place limits on local school taxes and/or expenditures, and I suggest that spending should not exceed 175% of the basic funding level—assuming that appropriate adjustments have been made for differences in the cost of providing programs and services to meet the special needs of students.

A large measure of local control can be maintained by permitting individual schools or school districts to spend at higher levels if they choose to supplement the adequate basic set of educational opportunities provided by the state. To ensure a reasonably level playing field, the state should guarantee that a given level of local tax effort would produce equal school revenue in all districts that are at or below a given percentile in local wealth per pupil; I would prefer the 80th percentile or higher. The state should also establish the maximum permissible optional local taxing or spending levels. By "power equalizing" any local tax levy for districts at or below the 80th percentile in wealth and setting maximum spending levels, local citizens would retain the ability to shape fine details of a school or district's educational offerings, while still affording all children in the state an equal opportunity to achieve their full potential.

REFERENCES

Berne, R., and L. Stiefel. 1984. *The measurement of equity in school finance: Conceptual, methodological, and empirical dimensions.* Baltimore: Johns Hopkins University Press.

Burris v. Wilkerson. 1969. 310 F. Supp. 572 Va.

Butts, R. F., and L. A. Cremin. 1953. *A history of education in American culture.* New York: Holt.

Carnegie Task Force on Meeting the Needs of Young Children. 1994. *Starting points: Meeting the needs of our youngest children.* New York: Carnegie Corporation of New York.

Chambers, J. G., and W. T. Hartman. 1983. A resource-cost-based approach to the funding of educational programs: An application to special education. In *Special education policies: Their history, implementation, and finance,* ed. J. G. Chambers and W. T. Hartman. Philadelphia: Temple University Press.

Coleman, J. 1968. The concept of equality of educational opportunity. *Harvard Educational Review,* Winter, 38(1): 7–22.

Coons, J. E., W. H. Clune, and S. D. Sugarman. 1970. *Private wealth and public education.* Cambridge, MA: Harvard University Press.

Cubberley, E. P. 1905. *School funds and their apportionment.* New York: Columbia University Press.

Educational Policy. 1994. December, 8(4): 365–635.

Hanushek, E. A. 1986. The economics of schooling: Production and efficiency in public schools. *Journal of Economic Literature,* September, 24(3): 1141–1177.

Hanushek, E. A. 1994. Money might matter somewhere: A response to Hedges, Laine, and Greenwald. *Educational Researcher,* May, 23(4): 8.

Hedges L. V., R. D. Laine, and R. Greenwald. 1994. Does money matter? A meta-analysis of studies of the effects of differential school inputs on student outcomes. *Educational Researcher,* April, 23(3): 5–14.

Hopfenberg, W. S., H. M. Levin, C. Chaser, S. G. Christensen, M. Moore, P. Soler, I. Brunner, B. Keller, and G. Rodriguez. 1993. *The accelerated schools research guide.* San Francisco: Jossey-Bass.

Kakalik, J. S., W. S. Furry, M. A. Thomas, and M. F. Carney. 1981. *The cost of special education.* Santa Monica, CA: Rand Corporation.

Levine, D. U., and L. W. Lezotte. 1990. *Unusually effective schools: A review and analysis of research and practice.* Madison, WI: National Center for Effective Schools Research and Development.

Madden, N. A., R. E. Slavin, N. L. Karweit, L. Dolan, and B. A. Wasik. 1991. Success for all: Multi-year effects of a schoolwide elementary restructuring program. *Phi Delta Kappan,* April, 72(8): 593–599.

Madison, J. 1900, reprint 1910. Letter to W. T. Barry, Aug. 4, 1822. In *The writings of James Madison comprising his public papers and his private correspondence, including numerous letters and documents now for the first time printed.* Vol. 9, ed. G. Hunt. New York: G. P. Putnam's Sons.

McInnis v. Shapiro. 1968. 293 F. Supp. 327 IL.

Moore, M. T., W. Strang, M. Schwartz, and M. Braddock. 1988. *Patterns in special education service delivery and costs.* Washington, DC: Decision Resources Corporation.

Odden, A. R., and L. O. Picus. 1992. *School finance: A policy perspective.* New York: McGraw-Hill.

Purkey, S. C., and M. S. Smith. 1983. Effective schools: A review. *The Elementary School Journal,* March, 83(4): 427–452.

Rose v. Council for Better Education. 1989. 790 S. W. 2d 186 KY.

Rossmiller, R. A. 1983a. How the cost of the program may be determined. In *The education of minority groups: An enquiry into problems and practices of fifteen countries,* ed. Centre for Educational Research and Innovation. Aldershot, England: Gower.

Rossmiller, R. A. 1983b. Resource allocation and achievement: A classroom analysis. In *School finance and school improvement: Linkages for the 1980s,* ed. A. Odden and D. L. Webb. Cambridge, MA: Ballinger.

Rossmiller, R. A. 1986. *Resource utilization in schools and classrooms.* Madison, WI: Wisconsin Center for Education Research.

Rossmiller, R. A., J. A. Hale, and L. E. Frohreich. 1970. *Educational programs for exceptional children: Resource configurations and costs.* Special study no. 2. Madison, WI: Department of Educational Administration, University of Wisconsin.

San Antonio Independent School District v. Rodriguez. 1973. 411 U.S. 1, 93 S. Ct. 1278, 36 L. Ed.2d 16.

Strayer, G. D., and R. M. Haig. 1923. *The financing of education in the state of New York: A report reviewed and presented by the Educational Finance Inquiry Commission*. New York: Macmillan.

Stuart v. School District No. 1 of Village of Kalamazoo. 1874. 30 Mich. 69.

Updegraff, H. 1919. Application of state funds to the aid of local schools. *University of Pennsylvania, Bulletin 1*. Philadelphia: University of Pennsylvania Press.

Updegraff, H., and L. A. King. 1922. *A survey of the fiscal policies of the state of Pennsylvania in the field of education: A report of the Citizens' Committee on the Finances of Education to the Hon. Gifford Pinchot. Part II: Education*. Harrisburg, PA: Citizens' Committee on the Finances of Pennsylvania.

Ward, J. G. 1987. An inquiry into the normative foundations of American public school finance. *Journal of Education Finance*, Spring, 12(4): 463–477.

An American Primer: A Guide to Democratic School Reform

JOSEPH FEATHERSTONE

My TASK is to sum up a very far-ranging set of discussions on school reform. Trying to respond to the rich themes presented in this volume is a difficult task. Albert Shanker quotes the Russians: "You can make fish soup out of an aquarium, but not the other way around." You will be the judge of whether what follows is more like sense or fish chowder. I have two big ideas to offer, plus polemical elaboration. The first big idea is that "reform" itself is a political process. What you want "reform" to accomplish usually rests on some point of view about the proper direction for the society and maybe the world. It is also important to insist that people's views about education rest on interests and values, and that we should become clearer about the interests and values at stake. The root of a favorite reform word these days, *evaluation*, is, after all, the word *value*.

A corollary to the idea that reform is about values is that people disagree and that reform in a democracy like ours is inevitably political. Therefore, at some fundamental level, reform is a matter of conflict. Values about schooling are not necessarily shared, especially in an era of gridlock and intense political division. Two things that many of us are looking for these days are a way to find some fundamentals about public education on which to agree and some civil ways to agree when we disagree, although so far we are not having much luck.

A less honorific phrase for school reform might be *school wars*. Some of us slip into a habit of speaking as though we are all in agreement about the schools and the society, and as though the issues to tackle are matters of technique and implementation, as they say in the reform business.

I think it is wrong to imagine that we all agree on what needs "re-forming"—hence the occasional quotation marks around the word *reform*. These days, it is often equally misleading to use the word *we*, although achieving good things for students and teachers nearly always involves the hard work of building coalitions. I believe we—if I can presume to speak for many—would have better and more useful debates and more realistic prospects for decent schools if we started declaring our different and common interests, and also if we thought about school reform politi-cally and in terms of building coalitions.

My second big idea is really an appeal for adopting a particular point of view about school reform. I believe that the best foundation for genuine school reform today and in the future is rooted in certain aspects of American educational tradition. I am being selective, to be sure. Ameri-can schools have been profoundly unequal throughout our history, and I would like to abandon that piece of the past. I want to speak on behalf of a branch of our educational tradition that promotes a public vision of classrooms and schools as embryonic democracies—small common-wealths that educate the young for full participation in a democratic soci-ety. My second point, about democracy, links up with my first point, about the essentially political character of school reform. I would express the connection between them by saying that lasting school reform will require the creation of diverse coalitions sharing something like a com-mon vision of public, democratic education for everybody's children. We do not have to agree about everything, but if we are clear about some of the fundamental purposes of public education in a republic, then I think it would be easier for us to move in a common direction. We could learn how to agree to disagree with some civility and goodwill. Conservatives and liberals might, for example, agree that the American tradition of pub-lic, democratic schooling—at risk these days and under assault by free-market and religious radicals—is worth defending and preserving. Maybe we could go even further together. Part of the problem of school "reform" in the last decade or so has been its uncertainty and incoherence in regard to what I see as the chief democratic question: What does it take to prepare all students to participate in work, politics, and culture? The branch of our educational tradition that I draw on demands a full democratic package for everybody's kids.

EDUCATIONAL REFORM IN RETROSPECT: A PERSONAL VIEW

I propose this as a graying veteran of many rounds of school reform. When I was a graduate student in history at Harvard in the early 1960s,

I took part in some of the brilliant curriculum projects inspired and led by Jerome Bruner. As the civil rights movement came north in the 1960s, I was part of movements to make classrooms places where everybody's kids learned and where teachers worked toward a vision of an inclusive, fair, and democratic society. I was a sympathetic critic of some of the early ventures in what was called "community control": efforts to open up schools to the communities they served and shift the balance of power in education to include parents and minority communities. This is unfinished work, in my view. I promoted certain of the classroom and curriculum reforms that were such a creative part of the educational scene in the 1960s and 1970s and made such an impact on both teaching and learning. I even see seeds of some current good practice sprouting from that work.

As an editor for *The New Republic*, which was a very different magazine in those days, I covered education along with politics and culture. It was then that I first began to think of reform in terms of school wars, chronicling the troubles of the civil rights movement as it pushed north and went national, and following the wars over curriculum and pedagogy and politics and culture. Later, as an academic at Harvard, I taught social policy and the history of education—learning that school reform and school wars are, in fact, ancient and highly stylized rituals in American culture. I ran a high school, promoted school reform in Boston and other city schools, and worked at Brown University with Theodore Sizer and the Coalition of Essential Schools. In recent years I have been involved with others in creating a new teacher education program at Michigan State University. Our idea is to remake teacher education through long-term alliances between colleges of education and schools, in an effort to ground teacher education in classroom practice. We are promoting long-term partnerships between classroom teachers and colleges of education, including a year-long internship in schools. While I am gloomy right now about the big picture in American education, and skeptical about much state and national reform, I want to make it clear that I am a wild optimist locally. At Michigan State University (MSU), we are laying down the tracks for visionary teacher education and long-term school development and reform on an unprecedented scale.

Some of these ventures in school reform have been successful, while others have not. Like Deborah Meier, who is one of my heroes, I think of this as steady work for the long haul, involving not just my own lifetime but the work of generations of teachers and activists. Like her, I see myself operating in a democratic tradition which says that the central challenge is helping kids learn what they need to keep learning as citizens and participants in what may some day become a fully democratic culture—how to keep making and remaking knowledge in a context that is always changing.

POINT OF VIEW

One recent project may help us think more intelligently about school "reform." A wonderful teacher named Manuela Jenkins and I have been working on a unit in social studies with ninth graders at Eastern High School in Lansing, tentatively called "How to Talk Back to the Evening News." We are using television news and the local newspaper to help the students become more thoughtful critics of the media. We have tried to get them to see that the news is in a sense "made" by journalists and that the "facts" dealt with in the news always reflect a point of view. How people interpret the news also depends on their point of view—as witness the different interpretations of the O. J. Simpson trial by white and African American viewers. We try to get the students to value truth and objectivity as ideals and to pay attention to the rules of evidence and logic, but we also want them to see that how issues are reported depends on the perspective of the reporter.

We have done some exercises that involve students in looking at the same issue from different points of view, including the issues raised in the last Michigan gubernatorial race. We also talk about how issues are framed: how a problem is defined in the first place, what gets included within the frame, and what gets left out. For example, if you write a headline saying that one-fifth of Lansing schools report some incidents of violence, the information is stated from one perspective. If, on the other hand, the headline announces that four-fifths of the schools report no incidents of violence, then readers will get a much different impression of the situation. We also looked into how television news frames the same story in different ways. A television story on a report concerning juveniles in American prisons "reads" differently if the accompanying "visual" on the TV screen shows the sensitive face of a young boy versus simply a grid with bars resembling an animal cage.

Because stories are told and heard from a point of view, the point of view from which we pick out the "facts," the framing and telling, shapes the story. The democratic challenge is to develop your own voice and your own story but to be able to connect it to a wider narrative. We need to learn to pay attention to the truth, to the rules of logic, evidence, and proof, but we also need to see that people's interpretations of the news derive from values and politics. All this is not so easy to do these confusing days. From our classroom, which includes many dark-skinned, immigrant, and poor kids, we hear echoes of a bitter and divided time: Violence is big news, and race is an enormous fault-line running through the news. The ninth graders, Mrs. Jenkins, and I hear politicians peddling fear and blame, seeking scapegoats for the country's troubles—immigrants and young unmarried mothers, for example. The economy in Michigan is good right now, but people are worried about the future. It seems to many of the ninth graders that a frightened middle class is listening to politicians blaming the poor for being poor. "Why is everyone so angry?" one ninth grader asked me. There's peace in the Middle East and democracy in South Africa. Even in Ireland, old enemies are talking, not just fighting. Why, indeed, are we so vengeful and bitter in this country, where we have relative peace and relative plenty?

One reason, perhaps, was reflected in a topic addressed in the opening panel discussion of the conference: the issue of violence, which troubles the world and the country, not least the schools. There is not just the fact of violence but the issue of violence and how it gets used. My first response to this topic was skepticism. Violence is indeed frightening in many schools, and yet it is the sort of issue that the media cover without really leaving the studio. Violence as a political or educational issue lends itself to simple answers, and a search for scapegoats—evil outsiders we can identify and blame—substitutes for all the communists America lost when the Cold War ended. If you are against violence, does that mean that your opponent is in favor of it? That is the implication, however absurd and lacking in basic civility.

So I was pleasantly surprised when the panel discussion turned out to be thoughtful, with few quick fixes or ready scapegoats. The panelists disagreed mightily, of course. Some stressed looking at violence as a short-term emergency, requiring prompt and decisive action. Others stressed underlying causes, arguing that schools need to become responsible communities, able to teach alternatives to violence. To some, the present situation in schools looks like a decline from a more orderly past. To others, violence in the schools looks like an old story in the history of a remarkably violent society. Different points of view about curriculum and testing and assessment were aired. If students were more engaged in what was taught or if fewer students were failing, the problem of violence in the schools might look different.

The panelists' differences mirror the divides in American politics today, and they are therefore a good starting point for a look at "reform" in education. To conservatives, order itself is the key issue; for liberals, violence is a symptom of a social pathology that also needs dealing with. Because the panelists intelligently represented both points of view, it helped at least one listener to try to frame matters in a refreshingly complex way. I was helped in this by Jerome Bruner's concept of "antinomies." An antinomy, as I understand Bruner, is a tension between two horns of a dilemma that in practice you never really settle. A teacher, for example, can never abolish the tension between the interests of individuals and the interests of a group in a given classroom. You work within this tension, sometimes paying attention to one pole—a troubled kid, perhaps—and sometimes to another, such as the interests and feel of the group as a whole. Similarly with violence: In a school you must deal quickly and decisively with symptoms, but you must also find ways to treat the underlying conditions that create the problem. The other aspect of violence as an ongoing antinomy is the wider social context: Teachers work on violence within the school, but they are also part of a society that teaches many different lessons concerning violence, including the seeming inevitability of guns. Bruner's doctrine of antinomies tells us to prepare for complexity instead of the simplicities that pass for political and educational thinking in the United States today. In education, as opposed to the TV evening news, we are forced to pitch our tent between the horns of the dilemmas; we learn to live with complexity and ambiguity.

ASSESSING A DECADE OF SCHOOL REFORM

From the point of view of educating us about points of view and how we frame issues of school reform, Larry Cuban's fascinating X-ray of the last decade in school reform is brilliant. His anatomy of a national reform movement that is still going strong rings true. It is a movement that has had many impressive policy successes at the state and federal level. Yet the policy successes—measured in legislation and new state policies on testing, curriculum, and so on—have, according to Cuban, failed on two important grounds. First, they have not really affected classroom teaching very much, except perhaps in a largely negative way. Second, the recent decade's reforms have failed to alter the systematic unfairness of education in the United States, what Jonathan Kozol calls our "savage inequalities." Cuban sorted American schools into three tiers: (1) the very successful schools for the affluent, (2) the middling schools for middle- and moderate-income people outside the central cities, and (3) the largely failing schools for the children of the poor, many but by no means all of which are in cities. The rural and small-town poor remain as invisible as ever.

This dismal picture certainly requires some correction. Some state initiatives have spurred interesting adaptations of practice. Not all policies have bypassed or harassed teachers. Some have helped their work in ways that are profoundly suggestive of what real and enduring school reform might look like. Also, school reform in some regions, the South in particular, has meant new funding sources and arrangements for the schools. Cuban's second point may also need qualifying as it becomes apparent that many systems have registered steady, if modest, gains, especially for minority children, in the last two decades. Here again, there may be some lessons for real reform.

Still, Cuban's big map of reform in the last 10 years looks accurate. What, one of my ninth graders might ask, if this reform story were framed differently—by someone with a different point of view? The story might read: Many schools dealing with growing percentages of poor kids have bucked the trend of the times and done a decent job, holding their own in some cases and making real gains in others. In both cases, the aggregate picture might blur important local stories and successes. It is important to note, as David Berliner and Bruce Biddle have argued so eloquently, that the "failure" of American schools (an item of complete faith in many reform circles and an axiom of right-wing politicians in the U.S. Congress and state legislatures) is something that needs careful defining and explaining; it is not a "fact" that we can assume at the outset of every discussion of school reform (Berliner and Biddle 1995).[1]

The other thing we need to do is to keep our eye on the ball. Cuban is talking about the last decade or so of school reform, not the reality of schooling itself. Reform movements and rhetoric are one thing; the daily life of most schools is another. You could even argue that the main achievement of many American schools in the last 10 years or so has been that many successfully resisted ill-advised reform and went about the work of teaching the children. I do not quite believe this; things are not going that well in our ailing schools. But this is the sort of thought that helps us to step back and get some distance from "reform." It reminds us that the royal *we* uttered by school reformers is not always credible. In aggregate, this decade's reform movement stands convicted of Cuban's indictment: School reform has, by and large, bypassed classroom teachers and has not substantially altered the educational possibilities for poor kids.

A skeptic might ask: Why be surprised? Not all who cry "Lord, Lord" will enter the kingdom of heaven, we are told on reliable authority. Similarly, not all who cry "Reform, Reform" belong in the kingdom either. In recent years, a careful scholar would have to scratch hard to locate reform talk that represented the outlook of teachers. Nor have many reformers taken the perspective of poor kids and their families, although some few have. Where was the ardent support for the difficult work of classroom teaching in the last decade? Where was there real sympathy and interest in kids? These rhetorical questions on my part point to inter-esting features of the "reform" landscape of the last decade or so. As a smart ninth grader might put it: What gets left out of the frame is as important as what gets included.

THE IMPORTANCE OF CONTEXT IN EDUCATIONAL REFORM

What is the frame around mainstream school reform? What are the un-stated assumptions? Operating budgets of schools have grown substan-tially, but, given the rising mutinies against tax increases and the militant right-wing rhetoric against government spending, few districts have been willing to spend crucial seed money on reform. The most fundamental trademark of school reform in the 1980s and 1990s has been that it is done on the cheap. The little secret of current school reform is its reluctance to spend money.

I have touched on another big framing context already: Teachers have had astonishingly little voice in most recent school reform. There are important exceptions to this, and I want to take note of them, but the reform era in which we are living may generally be symbolized by the relative absence of working teachers in important reform discussions and documents. Few other nations would dare stage important national dis-cussions of schooling without including classroom practitioners. One rea-son for this may be the hostility between right-wing Republicans and the two major teacher organizations in the United States; but school reform without teachers is, alas, an enduring part of the American style and one of the big obstacles to real reform.

The third interesting context of school reform from the 1980s on is also political. A visiting Martian political economist might have figured out that an important development in the United States in the 1980s was the sense that many aspects of the economy were now tied to world mar-kets, and that a new relationship of the economy and other institutions to the rest of the world was in the making. Yet the Martian would have been surprised to see that there was little debate about corporate respon-sibility either for investing abroad or for downsizing within the United States. In fact, our Martian would note, schools became a scapegoat for wider failures in politics and the economy. There was, and is, much that is wrong with American schools. Also, schools have a real and plausible relation to the changing economy, even though this might not be their only purpose. But education has become the kingdom of shadows where a host of displaced issues find a home. If Americans are deeply worried about jobs and the economic future—and they are, with good reason—why, then, do all eyes turn to the schools rather than to politics or the economy? This was especially handy for the political and business leaders who presided over the hard times and industrial decline in the United States during the 1980s. For a while, teachers were blamed for the failures of the entire society. The more recent reform style, in the better times of the 1990s, has been to attack not so much the teachers as "the system" and to call for "systemic" change, as in: "The system has failed." This all-purpose condemnation legitimizes reform agendas from welfare to education. The line between education and other realms blurs.

This blurring reflects the fourth and related context for educational reform: political gridlock itself. In the current immobility of American politics, education is one of the few realms in which leaders can appear to lead, at least symbolically. No governor of any state today—no legislature worth its salt—is without a bristling array of educational mandates and initiatives. There are urgent and real needs in the schools, to be sure, but the reform agenda in many states is also, in effect, a staged dramatization of "leadership" and policy making in a time of political stalemate. Education is one area in which a politician can at least appear to move forward and make serious public policy despite gridlock, even though, in less solemn and confused times and places, the idea of important educational reform minus either money or teachers might be taken as a joke. Mindless solemnity is reinforced by the new dogma that government spending achieves nothing, and therefore old-style reform (the kind that comes with at least some funds) is discredited. The popularity of incantatory reforms like school "restructuring" derives, in part at least, from the need of the times for symbols and ceremonies that come cheap, which is not to say there are no good reasons to rethink the priorities of schools as organizations.

Thus a cynic would say there is no surprise at all in Mr. Cuban's conclusions. School reform minus teachers and minus money has to be a mainly symbolic affair. What else could it be? There may be a lot to be said for cynicism, but that is not my main point. My main point is that Cuban has given us a window on school reform not only in the recent past, but in the near future, too. A reading of Cuban's account of our last decade of bustling school reform provides us with key questions that relate to one's point of view about "reform" and how "reform" issues get framed, as well as a primer for Americans.

ASKING THE RIGHT QUESTIONS

In my reform primer, we would ask questions like these: Who is reforming whom, and why? Who profits from the proposed "change" in real or symbolic ways? Who are the actors and what are their interests?

Reform ideas and practice do not mean much on their own; they are defined by their political, educational, and social contexts. An idea promoted by one group may have quite another significance when backed by a different group. Thus one needs to pay attention not only to what is being said and done, but also to who is speaking, where, and for whom.

Is reform war or politics by other means? What sort of conflict is going on? In some cases, we should see reform as a tug-of-war involving rival groups, conflicting values and interests, and differing visions of society. Who are the potential winners and losers? The powerful groups and the less powerful groups can both take advantage of reform, although, of course, the advantage is mostly to the powerful ones. But the history of groups such as women and African Americans in relation to reform history is filled with interesting examples of political jujitsu.

Successful reform involves coalition building, accessing the media, and framing issues in certain winning ways; it also requires money, power, and legitimacy. The many triumphs of reformers in the 1980s and 1990s need to be studied by those of us with parallel or rival ideas. But what constitutes success in school reform? By what standards? Who sets the standards? Who writes the stories, and how are they framed and told? Who writes the obituaries for "failed" reforms? Here, then, is a good place to think about point of view and how issues are framed.

What are the uses of reform within education? We need to look at the different uses various groups make of the reform ideas and the way that some groups adapt to the reform climate and its slogans to push in directions they already want to go in. It could be argued, for example, that some big-city systems, schools, and teachers took over many of the characteristic reform slogans of the 1980s and 1990s and used them for their own ends. Often they used them to promote careers, but they also used them to maintain legitimacy and to defend established interests and commitments. When asked what he did in the French Revolution, the statesman Talleyrand is supposed to have answered: "I survived." In a "reform" time, everyone becomes a reformer, although not only for opportunistic reasons. Reform slogans themselves are often vague and abstract enough—think of the word *restructuring*—to lend themselves to a variety of uses. Beyond that, I would argue that many public school figures used the reform movement of the last decade as a way to regain a legitimacy they were starting to lose in the attacks on public education during the Reagan years. Embracing "reform" was a way to stave off the first wave of what might have been a serious assault on the idea of public education itself. Albert Shanker should get a special award for his intellectual integrity and his willingness to criticize public education honestly, but one part of what Shanker has been doing is strategically positioning himself and his union as bona-fide members of the reform community at a time when public education has very shaky standing. We should remind ourselves, additionally, that we have not seen the end of the assault on public education.

In Cuban's words, reforms change schools, but schools also change reforms (Tyack and Cuban 1995). How does this process work? How do new reforms either conflict with or mesh with what Tyack and Cuban call the "grammar of schooling," the common and established practices of "real schools" (Tyack and Cuban 1995)?[2]

Can we reach some long-term perspective on school reform, or must we live from hand to mouth, at the mercy of educational fads, volatile political swings, and mass media that are increasingly dumbed-down? As CNN puts out 12 stories in 13 minutes, are we doomed to live forever under the shadow of the awful American reform pendulum as it swings from one mindless extreme to the other? What is the relationship of reform to real progress in education? Should we equate change and progress? Obviously not (Tyack and Cuban 1995, ch. 1).

What is the relationship of school reform to politics, broadly speaking? To what extent does school reform work within some separate sphere, and to what extent is it best seen as an expression of political values and forces at work in the wider society? In a conservative time, is school reform conservative? Or is that formulation too simple? Are there examples either way—school reform that serves as a direct expression of a political climate, and school reform that sometimes operates in a countervailing fashion to mainstream politics?

Finally, the first of Cuban's two big questions can be asked of any educational reform movement: What are the implications of reform for those the schools traditionally exclude or fail? How are we facing our deepest and most enduring dilemmas? A reform agenda that largely ignores poor children is not only dodging the biggest American educational problem but is, in an important way, a diversion from real reform. It might even be called antireform, or at least fake reform.

If we take Cuban's second big question seriously enough, how does any particular reform look from the point of view of supporting the continuing commitment and participation of classroom practitioners? In a broad sense, teacher education that effectively trains and launches teachers into the profession, and then continues their education as they grow seasoned in the work, ought to be one of the central priorities of school reform. Alas, it seldom is. The old, naive American dream of teacher-proof school reform has never really died. It is resurrected yearly in state legislatures. If we took the goal of teacher growth seriously, what would the clutter of current reforms look like to us? What is the career of different reform ideas and practices in different contexts? History could teach us something here, but so could case studies of reform in different places. If teaching and learning are site-specific and educational practice is rooted in specific contexts, what happens to particular reforms when the contexts change? At what point are reform ideas still recognizable, and at what point do we cease to care? Is the growth and development of teachers measurable? What are the ongoing and cumulative effects of school reform? Can a particular reform mesh with and even promote further growth and development in the schools, or does it, however well intentioned, come to pose a barrier? How do today's reform solutions generate tomorrow's problems and issues? What is the effect of building up layers of reforms over time, like a coral reef? Or, to change the metaphor: California is a good example of a kind of educationally burnt-over district, where crisscrossing layers of burnt and charred school reforms drift over classrooms and district offices (Cohen and Ball 1990).[3] Many school districts these days are becoming living archaeological sites with layer after layer of "reform." What would school reforms look like if they were based less on hand-to-mouth "ideas" and particular gimmicks and more on some principles having to do with the long-term intellectual growth and development of teachers? Should such intellectual growth be the top reform priority? How could we get money and energy for reforms aimed at cultivating teachers and pedagogy at a time when the reformers themselves are discrediting spending money and all educational "programs" suffer from the evil taint of "government"? At the very least, does it not give pause to hear a thoughtful observer like Cuban claim that a decade of busy reform has on the whole not touched life in classrooms, except negatively?

By preparing a primer of questions such as these, perhaps we will be able to break ourselves of the habit of assuming that we are automatically in favor of everything that is called school reform. This habit is lodged in our bones because the American tradition in public education is profoundly reformist. Protestantism is a reform religion, and ours has been the most Protestant of nations. Protestant, nationalist reform is stitched into the deepest layers of our educational consciousness. Public education at its outset was conceived of as a millennial reform movement blending nationalist and religious purposes. It seems natural for us to think of reform as a redemptive drama pitting good against evil. It is hard for Americans to accept the classic view of one of our greatest educational sociologists, Willard Waller, as far back as the 1930s: "Most schemes to alter the schools flounder on the rock of teacher resistance. In our view, much of this resistance is well-founded" (Waller 1932, 38).

PARABLES OF PROGRESS AND DECLINE

The other aspect of our millennial and nationalist reform tradition is the creation of legends of progress or decline. This, too, is part of the habits of mind that our institutions inherit from passionate Protestant divines and their not-so-secular nineteenth-century reform counterparts, such as Horace Mann, as well as turn-of-the-century administrative progressives who advocated "educational science." Tyack and Cuban have an outstanding chapter on the uses and abuses of history in the annals of American reform (Tyack and Cuban 1995, ch. 1). Just as Americans assume that reform is a good, we also have blind faith in either progress or its opposite superstition, decline. Parables of progress and decline are the stock-in-trade of school reform. Proponents of the findings in *A Nation at Risk* as well as our congresspeople are continuing this rhetorical tradition (National Commission on Excellence in Education 1983). It would be good to free ourselves from these old habits of mind and to be able to see clearly those areas where we have made significant gains in education, those where we still have far to go, and even those where we may have lost some ground.

For a wonderful, grandly polemical framing of these issues we should consider Berliner and Biddle's book, *The Manufactured Crisis* (1995). In it, Berliner and Biddle carefully and usefully demolish most of the myths that still abound in current reform debate: Student achievement has drastically declined in recent years; the intellectual abilities of American young people have declined; American schools come up short when measured against other nations' schools; the United States spends more than other nations on education; and spending on education is not related to school performance. They address such issues as whether the productivity of American workers is low because of failures in schooling; whether the United States is producing too few scientists, mathematicians, and engineers; whether American schools are staffed by unqualified teachers; and whether private schools, which are disciplined by the free market, are better than public schools. This grand demolition derby is the main achievement of the book.

Berliner and Biddle also offer an intelligent critique of many current reform proposals: vouchers, lengthening the school day, the use of external reward systems for teachers and students, accountability programs in which schools compete for status or funding, and programs for the "gifted." They perform a profound service for their readers by setting out a series of deep and serious problems that much recent reform rhetoric has systematically obscured and which the mainstream of American reform has largely ignored: the growing extremes of wealth and poverty, the stagnation of the economy, prejudice toward people of color and immigrants, the ghettoization of our cities, violence, drugs, the aging of our population. After reading their work, it is difficult to accept the terms of much of the mainstream reform debate at the state and national levels. Like a Brecht play, *The Manufactured Crisis* distances you from the drama, yet at the same time it reminds you of basic values and enduring issues.

The issues that Berliner and Biddle raise and the questions I derive from Cuban can, taken together, offer guidance for a useful reform primer. If we keep asking these questions, our work as critics and activists is likely to be more intelligent and effective. "Who is reforming whom, and for what purposes?" is always a useful question. It is not self-evident who the good guys are. Change is not always good; it can be bad. In the 1980s and today, good teaching practice is often hamstrung by "reform." At some point, too, we need to cease being surprised when school reform turns out to involve conflict. Conflict is inevitable because when people are arguing about the schools, they are sometimes discussing rival visions of America. Especially today, there are huge disagreements over what kind of a society we want to help the children build in the future—which may be the most basic of all educational issues. One challenge today, as I say, is how to forge coalitions in a diverse and divided society.

THE ONE BEST SYSTEM VERSUS LOCAL DEMOCRATIC TRADITIONS

Those of us raising skeptical questions about the current styles of mainstream school reform today mostly favor hybrid and incremental reform from the inside out, rather than the grand visions imposed on schools from the outside. The One Best System created by the administrative progressives of the Progressive Era may finally be collapsing, as I believe it is, but administrative rationalism, centralized hierarchy, and a naive faith in setting clear, concise goals at the expense of muddled local "hybridizing" wisdom and grassroots experience remain strong features of most American school systems (Tyack and Cuban 1995, epilogue).[4] Still, we skeptics are gaining ground and more of a hearing. Common sense is on our side. Better schooling rarely happens as the result of efforts of people outside the schools, although Berliner and Biddle are surely right that equalizing school funding and allocating money for school reform would vastly change the prospects for real reform in American education. Here is an instance where the political world outside of education decisively shapes the possibilities for real educational progress. Within education, as Tyack and Cuban argue, better schooling will emerge, if it does, from the work of teachers and citizens who actively support and intelligently criticize public education. Teachers do not have a monopoly on educational wisdom, but under any arrangements we are likely to make, they are the ones left dealing with the kids. Helping them to teach better ought to be a top priority of reform.

The One Best System has operated for about a century now on the premise that elite reformers, not classroom teachers and certainly not local community people, would be the central actors in the drama of school reform. The real professionals in education would not be classroom teachers, but rather professors and administrators and reformers. It is a tradition that is in some deep and fundamental way antidemocratic—not only in its disdain for classroom teachers but also in its central conviction that sorting out the human race into gold, silver, and brass ought to be the chief function of schools.

Our patterns of school reform—the deep and enduring structures, the fundamental grammar of school reform, if you will—were developed in the Progressive Era, when a chief function of reform was to take the schools out of the hands of people at the grassroots. Today, as then, there are good arguments for not politicizing education. Indeed, as the free-market and religious ideologies storm today's schools, the virtues of the bureaucratic and distanced One Best System are not negligible. But the mainstream American reform style was fundamentally suspicious of people at the exact place where everything solid and real in education happens: the local school and the classroom. The same era produced the big research universities and established their relation to the One Best System: Top-notch research universities would develop the expertise to guide the system from outside. Experts, not teachers, would decide.

Another of our big shifts in context today is that while the One Best System is dying, we are not exactly sure what to put in its place. As someone running a new field-based teacher education program, I have many ideas about how to build on what we have and how we can draw a new, more vital, and more democratic picture of the relationship of scholars and colleges of education to teachers in the field. But my main point is that the top-down system in which the experts and the superintendents gave commands and wrote reports is not workable now, if it ever was. I do not think it ever was; Willard Waller (1932) was right. Teachers were creative in subverting the One Best System, but they paid a terrible price in so doing. A system organized in contempt of classroom practitioners has always alienated teachers and made them chronically resistant to change. And today, as the "McReforms" are wrapped up and slapped on the counters, teachers have grown more wary of reform than ever. This is another topic understandably overlooked by mainstream reform.

So, in place of the tradition of the One Best System, I would propose a smaller and less well known, but no less traditional, set of ideas. In her wonderful book, *The Power of Their Ideas*, Deborah Meier describes the tradition I have in mind and makes a powerful restatement of its enduring appeal (Meier 1995; Featherstone 1995). This tradition holds that the most fundamental of the educational "basics" to which we need to return is the question of what kind of a society we want in the future and how we can educate students to participate in that society.

In stark contrast to the One Best System, this tradition holds that schools ought to operate as embryonic democratic communities. There is, in fact, no "one best way" to learn, to teach, or to organize a classroom or a school; there are many versions of good practice we need to learn about, share, and develop. Indeed, one of the big differences between the managerial and the democratic views of schooling is that the small-*d* democrats see schools as ongoing, changing communities, and not as fixed outposts of a centralized administration, reform, and practice. The quality of shared experience at the school and classroom level is the touchstone of the whole enterprise and the standard by which everything needs to be measured. This experience has to be a local and site-built affair, which is why the tradition I am describing has a fascination with parent and community participation in schooling, as well as a desire to find workable alternatives to lockstep and factory styles of teaching and learning. The current heirs of this democratic tradition, such as Deborah Meier and James Comer, believe that parents and local communities are the sleeping giants of American education. Jerome Bruner's chapter in this volume outlines brilliantly what might be called the social psychology of a democratic learning community in the school classroom. Although he writes as a contemporary cognitive psychologist with a social bent, he is standing squarely in the democratic tradition, with its profoundly communal and social vision of both learning and democracy. He is also signaling to his colleagues that American psychology took a wrong turn in the generations following William James and John Dewey. Bruner's recent work suggests that it is time to create something new: a psychology that would be directly useful to teachers in the classrooms and to parents.

Much current work in the democratic vein in schools has taken the seemingly simple step of trying to organize teachers and enlist their efforts. In the American context, I want to reiterate that this is a radical and democratic invitation: to welcome teachers into the grand mansion of reform on something like equal terms. There is much to be gained by a style of reform that recruits teachers and helps them to improve learning and become more thoughtful collectively about the work of teaching. Our field-based teacher education program at MSU is an example of how universities can end their distance from the schools and the teachers. We are engaged in helping teachers in schools become partners and colleagues as teacher educators, and there are other examples around the country. Schools have successfully organized to promote the learning and development of veteran teachers. Various projects draw teachers into reform groups and networks—writing projects; the Coalition of Essential Schools; professional alliances and teachers' groups linked to curriculum reform in the humanities, mathematics, and the sciences; the community-based schools in James Comer's projects; Henry Levin's Accelerated Schools; and Deborah Meier's network of public schools in New York City. These are only a few examples that show how teachers can get support to grow as professionals and also take the lead in reform. School reform that is aimed at helping classroom teachers improve teaching and learning is surely a good idea.

This kind of serious professional and subject-matter reform will be more effective if its proponents seek links with the democratic tradition. The democratic reform tradition helps us answer the great unspoken questions in American schools: So what? Why reform? Because, the tradition says, the next generation needs to be educated for full participation in work, culture, and liberty—for life in a vital democracy. Deborah Meier is particularly eloquent in her chapter in restating an old case for paying attention to students' minds—the habits of thought, feeling, and action that complete participation in a democracy requires. She argues for a rigorously intellectual view of democratic learning that requires developing teachers and students who are capable of understanding and articulating powerful ideas.

The goal is participation. In a democratic society, the people are educated to rule. Until now, most democracies have done a first-rate job mainly for the children of the wealthy, but the children of middling folks and particularly of the poor have too often received educational leftovers or worse. Meier's work over the last 20 years is an imaginative vindication of the revolutionary idea that all kids are created equal—that the many can graduate high school with the intellectual competence that history once reserved for the few. She shows that an education ambitious about "the having of wonderful ideas," to use Eleanor Duckworth's (1987) grand phrase, is not a luxury gained at the expense of the Three Rs, but a way of making the Three Rs come alive. The lesson hits home all the more because for some time now, as the center of American educational politics has shifted to the right, Americans have become convinced by education, politics, and the media to expect far less academically of poor and dark-skinned "inner-city" children. Work crews in Congress are busy cutting the remaining social safety nets and ladders as the old war on poverty has turned into a new war against the poor. Few literate Americans today expect a poor Latino student to produce a reasoned view about whether *Hamlet* is a better play than *Macbeth*. Few Americans in a time of civic despair, arising in part from a huge campaign against public education, are prepared to hear that the public schools are the proper sites to nourish the extraordinary but untapped capacity of all our children. Yet Central Park East shows us—and every generation requires fresh testimony—that the big question is not whether democratic and truly public education is possible but whether, as Meier puts it, we want it badly enough.

THE POLITICS OF EDUCATION REFORM

Wanting it badly enough may require revisiting the goals of education and making some fresh vows. In *Tinkering Toward Utopia*, Tyack and Cuban (1995) offer a superb brief for a cautiously optimistic and democratic point of view about the virtues of eclectic, slow, grassroots—"hybridizing"—reform. I, too, have faith in the value of public education in a democracy. Like Tyack and Cuban, I am appalled by the way discussions of education have radically narrowed their terms in recent years. The public policy debate in education has shrunk to arguments over international competition, test scores, and individual choice in schooling. As Tyack and Cuban say, the national conversation about choice has almost forgotten the kinds of choices most vital for civic welfare: collective choices about a common future and choices made through democratic processes about the values and knowledge that citizens want to pass on to the next generation. The biggest choice in education is the choice of what kind of future we want in common. As Deborah Meier puts it, public education may be a useful part of an industrial policy—but it is absolutely essential to the healthy life of a democracy.

Here is a clear instance of where the extreme rightward shift in the political climate has crippled debates on education. It has shaken our grip on the democratic tradition and the reason we have public schools in the first place. The privatization of discourse about the schools has accompanied a radical assault on the public sphere generally, from libraries and city parks to environmental regulations and public schools. Tyack and Cuban warn us that when the purpose of education narrows to economic advantage, and when the main measure of school success is test scores, it becomes all too easy to view schooling as one more consumer good rather than a common good. Hence the popularity of market and voucher schemes, with their appeal to those intent on dismantling public education. The traditional American view of education as a public good has certainly included economic themes, but it has also held out hopes for education that go far beyond individual or national economic gain. "During most of the last century," Tyack and Cuban write, "discussion of the purposes of public education has stressed comprehensive social and political goods more than narrow instrumental ends" (Tyack and Cuban 1995, 141).

I, too, am opposed to market schemes for public education; under market schemes, the rich get richer and the poor get poorer. They represent a terrible model for social services in a diverse and very unequal democracy. Their intellectual cousins, charter schools, have some promise, but only if they do not become prisoners of the religious right. In addition, it is unlikely that they will either reach large numbers of children or promote any serious collective professional development of teachers or pedagogy. Beyond immediate consequences, however, is the loss of vision such schemes would allow—the vision created by Jefferson and Mann and Dewey and generations of citizens and teachers insisting that education has a special role to play in shaping citizens and a polity. In Mann's day, schools were to produce literate, moral citizens who would be able to make the experiment called the American republic work. In times of large-scale immigration, the schools were to "Americanize" newcomers, although there was disagreement over who would define and set the terms of Americanization. Settled groups won some; immigrants won some; and these days, many of us are cheering for the immigrants. Figures such as Dewey countered the elitism of the One Best System and the administrative progressives by insisting on the enduring link between democracy and education. As Tyack and Cuban say, such debates have, at their best, promoted a continuous process of reshaping a democratic institution that, in turn, helped to create a democratic society.

In this tradition, schools are public and common spaces where citizens are educated for complete participation in all our institutions. Schools were called "common" in the past because in theory they drew in everybody's children and educated them to act like citizens together. This civic and small-*r* republican vision of education is still our fundamental commitment. For all the mushrooming inequalities and unfairness, for all the growing social strain and fragmentation in American life, local schools remain the one institution in America where people can still aspire to build a democracy together. But this idea of public education is under attack, as it has been for the past decade; free-market and religious ideologues are on the march. One of the symbolic achievements of school reform in the 1980s and early 1990s has been to legitimize public education at a time when the very notion of public schooling has been under its most serious assault since the time of Horace Mann.

Along with Tyack and Cuban, I would insist that the aspiration for equality, however elusive and however increasingly honored in the breach, is a central feature of our tradition. You do not hear much about equality in these neo-Darwinian days. Buried underneath today's abstract, greedy, and economistic rationales for public policy and mainstream reform in education is the public and small-*r* republican vision that Abraham Lincoln articulated in the Gettysburg Address: the dream of a nation conceived in liberty and dedicated to the proposition that all men and women are created equal. If it could happen, Lincoln implied, a fusion ticket of liberty and equality would create "government of the people, by the people, and for the people." Many who read Lincoln also saw something beyond government: an inclusive world of democratic experience in which each person would participate and have a voice and grow to full height. Walt Whitman dreamed this dream; he celebrated the mystery of individual personality and spoke of the United States as a nation of nations. Schools were the little republics and small commonwealths in which the next generation would learn their version of the dream in common. Without equality, as Lincoln already foresaw, liberty could turn American life into a jungle. Without education, our sense of community with other citizens would weaken radically. The purpose of schooling in a democracy is linked to a version of the purposes of art in a democracy. Dewey often spoke of shared experience (Dewey 1916). In arguing for public support of the arts, critic Robert Hughes speaks of the creation of mutuality and the passage from feeling into shared meaning (Hughes 1996, 34). These are lost ideas in need of being recaptured.

THE ROOTS OF DEMOCRATIC EDUCATION

The roots of a democratic approach to education go back a long way, and there have been several major landmarks. The political revolutions of the eighteenth century made life, liberty, and the pursuit of happiness everybody's birthright. The changes in family life and the growing equality of relations between men and women in the nineteenth century greatly influenced democratic education. The rich celebration of childhood, growth, and learning has profoundly shaped Anglo-American culture, thought, and literature since the infancy of Wordsworth.

Activists, reformers, and poets such as Keats and Whitman saw the connection between democracy and the idea of growth. They dared to imagine a society in which, for the first time in history, everyone would be allowed to grow to the fullest extent possible. For the first time in history, schools would take in everybody's children. Emerson and Whitman believed that democratic forms of government would require a democratic culture and even a new democratic personality to come to a full flowering, and that such a culture, if it ever came about, would overthrow older hierarchies of experience to make a rainbow culture for the nation of nations.

Democratic education is also rooted in the work of well-known figures such as John Dewey and W. E. B. Du Bois, as well as less well-known educators such as Margaret Haley, of the Chicago Federation of Teachers at the turn of the last century; Leonard Covello, the principal in the 1930s and 1940s of Benjamin Franklin High School in New York City; and the many others who worked to make the growth of everybody's children a staple of the schools. The democratic dream of a society in which each would grow to full potential through participating in school communities led many such practitioners into the schools and into the political movements of the day. They connected their classroom work to abolitionism, to the struggle for women's rights, to the movements on behalf of African Americans and immigrants, and to the struggle for the rights of working people. The thread linking practice in the schools to democratic movements outside the schools was the idea of a classroom as a democratic learning community involved in the work of creating a wider democracy. At its best in the past and in current reform practice, the tradition works simultaneously on Cuban's two reform challenges: pedagogy and the children of the poor.

This is, of course, a dissenting, minority tradition of thought, politics, and practice in the United States. As such, it is often marginalized or defeated. On the other hand, in a time of much misguided and rootless reform, low morale in the schools, confusion in politics, and amnesia in the wider culture, it is useful to remind ourselves that in each generation there have been hundreds and even thousands of teachers and principals and community people working on the agenda of democracy. The complete history of education in schools and classrooms at the local level has never really been written. The history we get tends to be the history of official policy, not the story of the lives of the teachers, families, and children who are making the real policy—teaching and learning at the street level.

Perhaps I am especially conscious of the forgotten educational work in the United States of Amnesia because my grandmother was such a figure. She was the teaching principal of a mainly immigrant school in the coal-mining country of northeastern Pennsylvania. She was also an activist in the campaign against child labor, a passionate partisan of the union movement, and one of the first women to sit on the state Democratic Committee in Pennsylvania. She linked the work of teaching to the work of building a democratic society. You graduated from her school knowing how to read a Browning poem and how to brush your teeth, and somehow both of these accomplishments were linked with the common goal of the betterment of all the people. My grandmother did not teach just to raise the test scores, but rather to raise humanity. Like many urban progressives and radicals of the day, she blended her Irish Catholic faith with her hopes for democracy and a more pluralistic society. Her work as a teaching principal would not necessarily be included in some simple catalogue of typical "progressive" pedagogical reforms—she was a classroom tyrant, in fact—but in the depth of her aspiration she was, as my grandfather might have put it, more democratic and progressive than the pope. There are problems with writing a history of educational reform that only looks narrowly at education.

It is important for us today to hear these stories and voices at the street level. They give us perspective and a second wind for real school reform. For a fictitious imagining of this history in one Ohio city—"Turin"—one should look at Herbert Kohl's wonderful essay, "The Good Old Days" (Kohl 1995, 125–172). Kohl traces three generations of teachers in one family, showing how each one, as a classroom practitioner, responds to the times and works to create a version of democratic education that meets the needs of a new generation. Kohl's fictional tableau of school reform over time shows us a tradition at work in the lives of teachers. He shows us how democratic ideas stretch like a lifeline linking the generations together. He also reminds us that the work of people such as Deborah Meier makes something new happen for a novel age, while they are also building on the work of the past.

We do not have good measuring devices for the success or failure of education reform. Cuban and Tyack are eloquent on this point. Still, I would offer the conjecture that the reform practice that occurred in the eras I have mentioned went further than more recent efforts have gone, precisely because it was linked to wider causes and movements and because working teachers found a way to connect the daily practice of teaching to Lincoln's "unfinished work"—turning the United States into a real, not just a paper, democracy. The two agendas—the development of teachers and pedagogy, and the education of the poor—intertwined in this tradition in a way that gives us a standard by which to measure contemporary reform. It also provides an example to spur us on to the creation of something fresh on today's reform landscape.

Many of the teachers with whom I am now working have similar democratic ideas in mind. This vision is what helps them get to school on a cold morning. But in a time when the democratic side is in disarray, it is hard to make the connection—to let the tradition rise up and speak in a new voice. Maybe, then, we should ask what the democratic issues are for us, both in school and out of school. Berliner and Biddle have their list. What is ours? Where are the places to strike a blow for democracy—in supporting the rights of immigrants? African-American families? working people and the union movement? women? Where are the possible coalitions? The "Stand for Children" movement of the Children's Defense Fund looks like a good example to me. Where do these wider concerns link to the smaller world of the classroom? What about a classroom where all the children are encouraged to find their voices? What about schools where teachers work on the challenge of helping all children to develop powerful ideas and where imagination and creativity are every child's birthright? When we have some idea of the values we are working for, as well as some idea about how they have played out in the past, we will be more grounded. We will be less apt to be victims of shifting political fashion and reform fads and more likely to work from a long-term perspective. I think that most teachers share the belief of Tyack and Cuban in small, eclectic, and incremental changes that come together in a hybrid way. I also think that it makes a difference when these small changes are linked to a wider and ongoing sense of democratic possibility. As teachers, we "vote" for democracy not only at the ballot box but also with a piece of chalk and a chalkboard.

I do not have a five-point program to offer. Like many people, I am not certain about where to go next in education and in politics. Still, it is an advantage to work within a tradition, and the one I am describing is surely no monolith, although it has a big idea: Those of us who teach in or for public schools labor so that everybody's kids will be able to participate as fully as possible in the economy, in the culture, and in liberty. Education for full participation is the mark of a democratic tradition. For that same reason, reform that—finally—includes teachers is a terrific idea. Likewise, forming coalitions to defend and promote the idea of public, democratic education seems essential, too. Work, culture, and liberty both for ourselves and our students is the package that W. E. B. Du Bois and John Dewey insisted on. So should we.

If we are not to repeat the history of reform during the last 10 years, with its fear-mongering and scapegoating, its indifference and hostility to teachers, and its neglect of poor children, we will need more democratic movements outside the classroom. We will also need a more imaginative sense of how small steps within the classroom can link to larger democratic possibilities. We will need coalitions both inside and outside education, but the coalitions will live or die by their spark and spirit. In the end, true educational reform is more like a religious or political movement than anything else—like all good teaching, it is a matter of faith and passion. In this, as in so much else, Emily Dickinson is our prophet: "Imagination lights the slow fuse of possibility."

NOTES

1. Berliner and Biddle are so vehement in their denunciation of reform myths that a reader may dismiss their book as a simple polemic. It is a polemic, but it is also a wonderful and learned demonstration of the intelligent uses and abuses of quantitative data. It is also a gold mine of information on the American educational reform scene. It is strongest on the neglected social issues in reform, while weaker in its grasp of the need for real intellectual and professional development. At some points, a cursory reader might get the impression that teaching and learning in American schools are fine and that our biggest professional problems would disappear if only all those irritating reformers would just get out of the way.

2. Tyack and Cuban's book is the indispensable skeptic's guide to current and past school reform, one from which I have learned a great deal. The footnotes alone are worth the price of purchase.

3. Cohen and Ball here and elsewhere argue for a style of reform and teacher professional development that takes into account both the situated character of teaching on-site and the need for teachers to explore subject matter in relation to their own teaching.

4. Tyack and Cuban have scattered useful arguments in favor of eclectic and "hybrid" reform at the school level throughout their book, but note the epilogue in particular.

REFERENCES

Berliner, D.C., and B. J. Biddle. 1995. *The manufactured crisis: Myths, fraud, and the attack on America's public schools.* Reading, MA: Addison-Wesley.

Cohen, D. K., and D. L. Ball. 1990. Relations between policy and practice: A commentary. In *Educational Evaluation and Policy Analysis*, Fall, 12(3): 249–256.

Dewey, J. 1916. *Democracy and education: An introduction to the philosophy of education.* New York: Macmillan.

Duckworth, E. 1987. *The having of wonderful ideas and other essays.* New York: Teachers College Press.

Featherstone, J. 1995. Review of Meier: *The power of their ideas: Lessons for America from a small school in Harlem. The Nation*, 12 June, 260(24): 890.

Hughes, R. 1996. The case for elitist do-gooders. *The New Yorker,* 27 May, 72(13): 32–34.

Kohl, H. 1995. *Should we burn Babar? Essays on children's literature and the power of stories.* New York: New Press.

Meier, D. 1995. *The power of their ideas: Lessons for America from a small school in Harlem.* Boston: Beacon.

National Commission on Excellence in Education. 1983. *A nation at risk: The imperative for educational reform.* Washington, DC: U.S. Department of Education.

Tyack, D., and L. Cuban. 1995. *Tinkering toward utopia: A century of public school reform.* Cambridge, MA: Harvard University Press.

Waller, W. 1932. *The sociology of teaching.* New York: Wiley.

ABOUT THE EDITOR AND
THE CONTRIBUTORS

Barry S. Kogan is Clarence and Robert Efroymson Professor of Philosophy and Jewish Religious Thought at Hebrew Union College–Jewish Institute of Religion in Cincinnati, Ohio and former Director, HUC–UC Ethics Center and Starkoff Institute of Ethics. He is the author of *Averroes and the Metaphysics of Causation* and editor of *A Time to Be Born and a Time to Die: The Ethics of Choice, The Corporation and the Community: Mutual Antagonism and Mutual Responsibility,* and *Spinoza: A Tercentenary Perspective.*

•

Kern Alexander is President of Murray State University, Murray, Kentucky; former University Distinguished Professor, Virginia Tech; former President, Western Kentucky University; former Education Policy Coordinator, state of Florida; and national and international consultant on education finance and equity in education funding. He is the author or editor of numerous books—including *Public School Finance in the United States, Reforming Education in a Changing World: International Perspectives,* and *American Public School Law*—as well as executive editor of *Journal of Education Finance.*

John L. Anderson is President of the New American Schools Development Corporation; former Director of Governmental Programs–Education for IBM, Washington, D.C.; coordinator of the Business Roundtable's Initiative for Primary and Secondary Education; and member, Presidential Transition Team, Department of Education.

Jerome Bruner is Research Professor of Psychology and Senior Research Fellow in Law, New York University; former Professor of Psychology at Harvard University and Watts Professor at Oxford University; former member, President's Science Advisory Commission; member, Board of Directors of the National Academy of Education; and leader of the constructivist movement in the human sciences. He is the author of *The Process of*

Education, On Knowing: Essays for the Left Hand, Actual Minds, Possible Worlds, and *Acts of Meaning.*

Larry Cuban is Professor of Education, Stanford University; former high school teacher; District Superintendent of Schools, Arlington Public Schools, Arlington, Virginia; and Director, Staff Development, District of Columbia Public Schools. He is the author of *To Make a Difference: Teaching in the Inner City, How Teachers Taught,* and *The Managerial Imperative: The Practice of Leadership in Schools,* as well as the co-author of *Tinkering Toward Utopia.*

Joseph Featherstone is Professor of Education and Director of the Experimental Teacher Education Program, Michigan State University, and former Visiting Professor of Education, Harvard University. He is the author of *Schools Where Children Learn* and *What Schools Can Do* as well as numerous articles on educational issues for the *New York Times, Atlantic Monthly, New Republic,* and *Harvard Educational Review.*

Edward T. Joyner is Director, Comer Project for Change in Education, Yale University Child Study Center; educational consultant on developing collaborative public schools; and former high school and college instructor, high school assistant principal, and middle school principal. He is the author of *The Comer Model: School Improvement for Students At-Risk* and *Mobilizing Resources Within the Schools to Better Serve Children At-Risk* as well as articles and training manuals on child development and school change.

Deborah Meier is Co-Director of the Central Park East Secondary School; founder and Teacher–Director within the network of public alternative elementary schools in East Harlem; and President of the Center for Collaborative Education of New York, an affiliate of the Coalition of Essential Schools led by Ted Sizer of Brown University. She is the author of *The Power of Their Ideas: Lessons for America from a Small School in Harlem* and numerous articles on educational issues in *The Nation* and *The Harvard Education Letter.*

Nel Noddings is the Lee I. Jacks Professor of Child Education and former Acting Dean of the School of Education, Stanford University; former elementary, junior high, and high school teacher; former assistant principal and curriculum supervisor (K–12); former Director of Pre-Collegiate Education, University of Chicago; and past President of the National Philosophy of Education Society. She is the author of *Caring: A Feminine Approach* *to Ethics and Moral Education, The Challenge to Care in Schools,* and *Educating for Intelligent Belief or Unbelief.*

Richard A. Rossmiller is Emeritus Professor of Education Administration, University of Wisconsin, Madison; Director, National Center for Effective Schools Research and Development, University of Wisconsin, Madison; former President, American Education Finance Association; and national and international consultant and expert witness on school administration and finance issues. He is the author of or contributor to numerous books and monographs, including *The Effective Schools Process,* "Financing Schools" in the *Encyclopedia of Educational Research,* and "School Finance Reform Through Litigation: Expressway or Cul-de-Sac?" in *School Law Update, 1986.*

Albert Shanker was President of the American Federation of Teachers (a post he had held for 22 years); a national and international leader in the movement for education reform; the first teacher elected to the AFL-CIO Executive Board; and founding President of Education International, a federation of 20 million teachers from democratic countries. He authored "Where We Stand," a regular column on educational issues that appeared in the Sunday *New York Times.* Albert Shanker passed away on February 22, 1997.

Lee S. Shulman is the Charles E. Ducommun Professor of Education, Stanford University; Director of the Carnegie Corporation project to design and field-test new strategies to assess teaching at the elementary and secondary levels; past President of the American Educational Research Association; and immediate past President of the National Academy of Education. He is the author of numerous articles appearing in *Journal of Curriculum Studies, Educational Leadership,* and *Journal of Staff Development.*

Robert L. Wehling is Senior Vice President for Public Affairs, Procter & Gamble Worldwide, The Procter & Gamble Company; Co-Chair of the Ohio Education Improvement Consortium; member, Executive Committee, Cincinnati Youth Collaborative; Director of the Education Excellence Partnership; Trustee of the Ohio School Development Corporation; member, Governor's Education Management Council; and Director of the Advertising Council's "Education," "Healthy Start," and "Breaking the Cycle of Disadvantage" campaigns.

Index

Abbott, Jim, 87
Academic mastery, 7, 8, 117–118
Accelerated Schools, 201
Accountability, 14–15, 18, 127, 128–129
Achievement of students, 109–117, 125–126, 197
  comparative approach to, 111–119
  diversity and, 113–115
  elitism and, 112–113
  in private versus public schools, 110–111
  standards and, 115–117
  teacher training and, 117–119
  tests and, 109–110, 113
  writing, 110
Adequacy of programs, 174–175
Advanced Placement (AP) courses, 18, 112
Affirmative action, 65
African Americans, at Central Park East Elementary School, 66
Alexander, Kern, 2, 10, 139–165, 140
Alternative schools, 24
America 2000, 129
American College Test (ACT), 113
American Federation of Teachers (AFT), 112
Americanization, 203
Anderson, E., 21
Anderson, John L., 2, 8–9, 123–131
Annenberg Foundation, 44
Annenberg Institute for School Reform, 125
Anthony, G., 140
Antinomies, 4–5, 33–36, 190
Applebee, A. N., 110
Apprenticeship programs, 113
Ash, D., 102
Ashkinaze, C., 20–21
Assessment
  of school reform, 190–191
  student testing and, 7–8
  of teachers, 8, 118
At-risk students, 36–38, 76–79, 151–152

Audrey Cohen College System of Education, 129, 131
Authentic Teaching, Learning, and Assessment for All Students (ATLAS), 129–130

Baby boom, 1
Ball, Deborah L., 7, 19, 95–99, 196
Barlow, J., 144, 159
Barnett, W. S., 39
Barry, B. M., 145, 151
Bateson, Mary Catherine, 54–55
Batlistich, V., 79
Battle, Lynwood L., 2
Bellah, R. N., 55
Bennett, William J., 2
Benson, P., 110
Bentham, Jeremy, 145, 146
Berlin, I., 153, 155
Berliner, David C., 12, 191, 197–198, 207
Berne, R., 173, 178
Biddle, Bruce J., 12, 191, 197–198, 207
Bilingual education, 44
Black, H. C., 162
Blended school reform, 3–4, 16, 19, 21, 22, 28
Bloom, B. S., 37
Bohr, Niels, 33
Bosk, Charles L., 105
Bourdieu, Pierre, 41
Boyer, E., 45
Braddock, M., 172
Bradley, A., 18
Brenzel, B., 20–21
Brown, Ann L., 26, 27, 40, 100, 102
Brown v. Board of Education, 38
Bruner, Jerome S., 2, 4–5, 11, 33–48, 37, 38, 51, 90–91, 98, 99, 100, 187, 190, 200
Brunner, I., 179
Bryk, A., 21
Buber, Martin, 5, 53

Burris v. Wilkerson, 173
Bush, George, 129, 164
Business-education partnerships, 3, 9–10, 132–138
  Cincinnati Youth Collaborative (CYC), 9, 134–135
  Ohio Education Improvement Consortium, 9, 135–137
  problems of, 133–134
Butts, R. F., 167

California, 21, 175
  Oakland Head Start project, 39–41, 44
Calvin, W. H., 36
Campbell, E., 14, 20
Campione, J., 102
Capper, C. A., 18
Carnegie Endowment for the Advancement of Teaching, 45
Carnegie Forum on Education and the Economy, 23
Carnegie Task Force on Meeting the Needs of Young Children, 77, 180–181
Carney, M. F., 172
Censorship, 148
Center for Collaborative Education, 64
Center for Education Statistics, 111
Central Park East Elementary School (New York City), 66–69
Central Park East Secondary School (New York City), 5–6, 12, 61–64, 67, 70, 90, 104
Chambers, J. G., 180
Charlottesville goals, 43, 44, 46n
Charter schools, 203
Chaser, C., 179
Chicago, Illinois, 21
Children's Defense Fund, 77, 207
China, 8, 116, 148
Christensen, S. G., 179
Cincinnati Youth Collaborative (CYC), 9, 134–135
City of Cincinnati Board of Education v. Walter, 140
Civil rights, 23, 147–148
Civil War, 26
Clark, R., 21
Clarke-Stewart, A., 39
Class. *See* Social class
Clinton, Bill, 16, 129

Clune, W. H., 21, 171
Coalition of Essential Schools, 44, 64, 90, 104, 187, 201
Cohen, David K., 17, 19, 23, 117–118, 196
Cole, M., 38
Coleman, J., 14, 20, 166, 169
Collaborative approach
  among teachers, 8, 116–117
  building culture for, 42–46
  between business and schools, 132–138
  in classroom, 4–5, 34–35
  Comer Process and, 79–83
  in Head Start program, 40–42
  in learning process, 101
  between universities and schools, 187
Comenius, 147
Comer, James P., 6, 27, 76, 78–84, 200, 201
Comer Process, 79–83
  critical operations of, 82–83
  developmental pathways in, 80–82
  guiding principles of, 83
  structures in, 82
Comer Project for a Change in Education, 12, 90
Commager, H. S., 147
Committee of Ten, 24
Community, 200
  at Central Park East schools, 65–66, 69
  influence on values, 74–76, 78, 84–86
mathematics, 96
  process of building, 65–66
  school ties to, 124–125
Community control, 24, 157–163, 167, 182, 187, 198–202
Community of learners, 99, 101–104
Community support networks, 3, 6
Compensatory education, 24
Conant, James, 24
Co-NECT Schools, 130, 131
Constitution, U.S., 146–147, 167–168, 173
Continuing education, 8
Cooley, C., 78
Coons, J. E., 171
Cooperative learning, 26
Covello, Leonard, 205
Cremin, L. A., 24, 167
Cuban, Larry, 2, 3–4, 11, 14–32, 15, 17, 23, 25–26, 27, 57, 90, 95, 190, 193, 195–198, 202, 203, 205, 206
Cubberley, Ellwood P., 11, 170, 181

Cultural deprivation, 38
Curriculum
  educational reform and changes in,
    23–25
mathematics, 50, 58
  spiral, 51, 56, 98
  voluntary national, 17–18

Darling-Hammond, L., 19
Decentralization, of governance, 23
Decision-making, 22–23
  Effective Schools movement and, 14–15,
    23, 137, 176–177
Deep understanding, 7, 95–99, 103–104
Deficit models, 87
Dell, William, 147
Democratic education, 185–208
  essential components of, 5–6
  habits of mind in, 5–6, 60–71
Dent, N. J. H., 143–144, 159
Department of Education, U.S., 111
Deprivation hypothesis, 36–38, 151–152
DeRolph v. State of Ohio, 10, 140, 141
Derrida, J., 35
Desegregation, 24, 64–65
Developmental Studies Center, 77–86
Dewey, John, 50, 66, 100, 143, 200, 203–205,
    207
Dickinson, Emily, 208
Diversity, 113–115
Dolan, L., 179
Dossey, J. A., 110
Dropouts, 18, 21
Du Bois, W. E. B., 205, 207
Duckworth, E., 201
Durkheim, E., 143
Dworkin, R. M., 150

Early childhood development, 37–38,
    180–181
Edelman, M. W., 77
Edmonds, Ron, 27
Edsall, T. B., 163
Education
  function of, 4, 34
  goals of, 1–2
Educationally deprived students, 36–38,
    151–152
Educational reform. See also Democratic
  education

blended approach to, 3–4, 16, 19, 21,
    22, 28
challenges to assumptions of, 7–8
context in, 192–193, 202–204
curriculum and, 23–25
deficit models of, 87
goals of education and, 1–2
governance and, 19, 22–23
historical context for, 3–4, 14–29, 186–
    188, 190–193
interaction between teachers and stu-
    dents in, 6–7, 89–105
learning by teachers and, 6–7, 89–105
limits of, 20–22
as mandate, 64–66
One Best System and, 198–202
organizational-effectiveness approach to,
    3–4, 16–18, 20–22, 26–27, 28, 125–126
pedagogical approach to, 3–4, 16, 18–19,
    22, 27, 28, 90, 125–126
point of view and, 188–190, 191
politics of, 202–204
progress versus decline and, 197–198
questions in, 193–196
school wars and, 185–186, 187
skepticism toward assumptions in, 7–8,
    107–119
teaching practices in, 3–4, 25–26
value of traditional approach to, 119–120
Education Commission of the States (ECS),
    125
Effective Schools movement, 14–15, 23, 137,
    176–177
Elementary and Secondary Education Act
    (ESEA), 129, 172
Eliot, Charles, 24
Elitism, 112–113
Elmore, Richard F., 17, 19, 21, 23, 27
Emotions, in learning process, 101
Empathy, habits of mind and, 5–6, 63–64
End of History and the Last Man, The (Fuku-
    yama), 157–158
England, 8, 112, 113, 147, 163
Equality of educational opportunity,
    168–173
  access to school and, 168–169
  adequacy and, 174–175
  deviating from strict, 155–156, 172
  early childhood development and,
    180–181

Equality of educational opportunity
  (*continued*)
    early developments, 146–148, 166–167
    equal outcomes and, 172–173
    equity in funding and, 10–11, 149–150,
      166, 168–173, 180–181
    ethical primacy of, 153–154
    fairness and, 177–180
    legal actions and, 140–141, 144, 173–174
    liberty and, 157–161
    local control and, 157–163, 167, 182,
      198–202
    per-pupil spending and, 170–172,
      175–180
    types of inequality and, 150–153
Equilibrium of poverty (Galbraith), 163
Equity in funding, 139–164, 166–182
    access to school and, 168–169
    adequacy versus, 174–175
    deviating from strict, 155–156, 172
    early childhood development and,
      180–181
    equality of educational opportunity and,
      10–11, 149–150, 166, 168–173,
      180–181
    equal outcomes and, 172–173
    ethics and, 143–146, 153–155
    fairness and, 177–180
  fundamentality of education and, 146–149
    historical analysis of, 10–11, 146–149,
      166–172
    importance of, 10
    law of reciprocity and, 145–146
    legal challenges and, 140–141, 144,
      173–174
    liberty and, 157–161
    local control and, 157–163, 167, 182,
      198–202
    per-pupil expenditures, 170–172, 175–180
    republican government and, 141–144,
      167–168
    types of inequality, 150–153
    value of money and, 156–157
Essays on the Mind II (Helvetius), 145
Ethics, 54
    and children at risk, 36–38, 76–79,
      151–152
    equity in funding and, 143–146, 153–155
    moral influence of adults on, 74–76
Existential meaning, 52–58

Expeditionary Learning/Outward Bound,
  130, 131

Family, 3, 6
  characteristics of, 43, 45–46
    conferences between teachers and, 68
    influence on values, 78
Featherstone, Joseph, 2, 11–12, 185–209, 200
Feminism, 35, 44
Fine, M., 21
Finn, C., 24
Flexible scheduling, 24
Foertsch, M. A., 110
Forgive and Remember (Bosk), 105
France, 8, 112, 113–114
Free schools, 24
Frohreich, L. E., 172
Fuhrman, S., 21
Fukuyama, F., 157–158
Fullan, M., 27
Fuller, L. L., 146, 147
Furry, W. S., 172

Galbraith, J. K., 163
Gandhi, Mahatma, 81
Gardner, Howard, 19, 27, 44, 56
Geertz, C., 35, 36
General Accounting Office, U.S., 20
General Equivalency Diploma (GED), 18
Gentile, C. A., 110
Germany, 8, 112, 113, 114, 115, 116, 117–118
Goals 2000 legislation, 17, 18
Goals of education, 1–2
Goldsmith, O., 139, 163
Goodlad, J. L., 26
Gopnik, A., 35, 38
Gordon, A., 102
Governance, 19, 22–23
Green, A., 113
Greenwald, R., 175–176

Habits of mind, 1–2
    empathy and, 5–6, 63–64
    list of, 61
    progress versus decline and, 197–198
    skepticism and, 5–6, 62–63
Haig, R. M., 11, 170–171, 178, 181
Hale, J. A., 172
Haley, Margaret, 205
Hansot, E., 22–24

Hanuschek, E. A., 175, 177
Harp, L., 18
Harrington, Jean Patrice, 2
Hartman, W. T., 180
Hawkins, David, 7, 91
Haynes, N. M., 87
Head Start program, 36–42
collaborative community in, 40–42
    deprivation hypothesis and, 36–38
    impact of, 38–39, 40
    IQ gains and, 38–39
    in Oakland project, 39–41, 44
    praxis and, 41–42
Hedges, L. V., 175–176
Heer, F., 147
Helvetius, 145
Henderson, Theresa, 2
Hernandez, D. J., 43
Hernandez, Josie, 70
Herrnstein, R. J., 35, 38
Hickrod, G. A., 140
Higher education
    remediation and, 7–8, 111
    teacher training in, 116–119
    and top tier of schools, 20
university-school partnerships, 187
Hillel, 91
Hispanic Americans, at Central Park East
    Elementary School, 66
Hobbes, Thomas, 145, 151
Hobson, C., 14, 20
Hopfenberg, W. S., 179
Horace's Compromise (Sizer), 67
Hughes, R., 204
Hugo, Victor, 80
Hume, David, 145, 146
Hunt, J., 36

Immigration, 1, 24, 41, 43, 114
Incidental learning, 52, 53
Indiana, 2
Individual experience, in learning, 4, 35–
    36, 50, 92, 104–105
Industrialization, 1
Infants, learning by, 37–38
IQ, Head Start program and, 38–39

Jackson, P. W., 25, 52
Jacquet, L., 77
James, William, 78, 200

Jamison, M. T., 18
Japan, 8, 111–112, 113, 115, 116
Jefferson, Thomas, 147–148, 203
Jencks, C., 14
Jenkins, L., 110
Jensen, A. R., 38
Jones, L. R., 110
Joyner, Edward T., 2, 6, 64, 74–88
Judge, H. G., 45

Kakalik, J. S., 172
Kalnins, I., 37
Kant, Immanuel, 145–146, 159–160
Kantor, H., 20–21
Karweit, N. L., 179
Kearns, David T., 123
Keats, John, 204–205
Keislar, E. R., 91
Keller, B., 179
Keller, Helen, 87
Kelley, C., 18
Kennedy High School (New York City), 70
Kentucky, 2, 21, 174
Kindergarten, 25–26
Kindness, 75
King, L. A., 170
King, Martin Luther, Jr., 81
Kirst, M., 18
Kliebard, H. M., 24
Kogan, Barry S., 1–13
Kohl, Herbert, 206
Kozol, Jonathan, 20–22, 25, 190
Kranz, J., 19
Krug, E., 24

Laine, R. D., 175–176
Langers, J., 110
Latz, E., 37
Law of reciprocity, 145–146
Lawson, J., 147
Learning by Discovery (Shulman and
    Keislar), 91
Learning process
    activity in, 99–100
    collaboration in, 101
    community in, 101–104
    deep understanding in, 7, 95–99, 103–104
    emotional and affective component, 101
    existential meaning and, 52–58
    incidental learning in, 52, 53

Learning process (*continued*)
    individual experience in, 35–36, 50, 92,
        104–105
    nature of, 4, 34–35
    principles of, 99–103
    reciprocal teaching in, 100–101
    reflection in, 100
    in teacher learning, 6–7, 8, 91–105, 112
    wait-time in, 7, 93–95
    "whole-hog" approach to, 52–53
Levin, Henry M., 27, 179, 201
Levine, D. U., 176
Lewis, C., 83
Lezotte, L. W., 176
Lincoln, Abraham, 204, 206
Local control, 24, 157–163, 167, 182,
    198–202
Local knowledge (Geertz), 35
Locke, John, 159, 160

MacIntyre, Alasdair, 54, 55
Mackworth, N. H., 37
Madden, N. A., 179
Madison, J., 167
Magnet schools, 24
Malen, B. R., 19
Mann, Horace, 147–149, 154–155, 197, 203
Manufactured Crisis, The (Berliner and
    Biddle), 197–198
Massachusetts, 147, 166–167
Massell, D., 21
Mastery, 7, 8, 117–118
Mathematics, 19, 26, 110
    community in, 96
    curricula for, 50, 58
    for deep understanding, 7, 95–99
    learning of, 51–52
    real-world problems in, 50
    wait-time and, 7, 93–95
Mathews, J., 21
McInnis v. Shapiro, 173
McLaughlin, Milbrey W., 19, 27, 103
McPartland, J., 14, 20
Mead, G. H., 78
Meier, Deborah, 2, 5–6, 11, 27, 60–73, 93,
    104, 118–119, 187, 200–202, 206
Meiering, Judith A., 2
Meltzoff, A. N., 35, 38
Metacognition, 100
Metaphysics of Morals, The (Kant), 159

Michigan, 169
Michigan State University (MSU), 187
Middle schools, 24
Mill, John Stuart, 160
Minority groups, 43
    at Central Park East Elementary
        School, 66
    test scores and, 18
Mirel, J., 23
Modern Red Schoolhouse, The, 130, 131
Montesquieu, C., 142–143
Mood, A., 14, 20
Moore, M. T., 172, 179
Mort, Paul, 171
Motivation to learn, 5, 49–58
Mullis, I. V. S., 110
Multi-age grouping, 124
Multiculturalism, 44
Murphy, J., 16, 18, 23, 25
Murray, C., 35
Mussen, P. H., 37

Nakagawa, K., 102
National Alliance for Restructuring Educa-
    tion, The, 130, 131
National Assessment of Chapter 1 Indepen-
    dent Review Panel, 20
National Assessment of Educational Prog-
    ress (NAEP), 18, 109–110
National Center for Health Statistics, 77
National Center for Improving Science Edu-
    cation (NCISE), 112
National Commission on Excellence in Edu-
    cation, 15–16, 197
National Council of Teachers of Mathemat-
    ics (NCTM), 19
National Education Goals Panel, 44, 46n
National Education Summit, 129
National Science Foundation, 24
Nation at Risk, A, 15–16, 45, 197
Nature-nurture controversy, 35
New American Schools (NAS), 8–9,
    123–131
    design teams in, 124–125, 129–131
    emergence of, 123–124
    lessons of, 128–129
    strategy of, 125–126
    supportive operating environment and,
        127–128

Newark, New Jersey, mathematics curriculum, 58
New Jersey, 21, 58
New York (state), 21
New York City
  Central Park East Elementary School, 66–69
  Central Park East Secondary School, 5–6, 12, 61–64, 67, 70, 90, 104
  mathematics curriculum, 58
  secondary school attendance rates, 68–69
Niebuhr, R., 139, 145, 149
Noddings, Nel, 2–3, 5, 49–59, 57
Norms, 6, 76
Norway, 41

Oakland (California) Head Start project, 39–41, 44
O'Day, J., 16, 17, 21
Odden, A. R., 179
Ogawa, R., 19
Ohio, 2, 140–141, 144, 164
Ohio Education Improvement Consortium, 9, 135–137
Ohio's BEST (Building Excellent Schools for Today and the 21st Century), 136–137
Olson, L., 21
Open classrooms, 24
Oregon, 175
Orfield, G., 20–21
Organizational-effectiveness school reform, 3–4, 16–18, 20–22, 26–27, 28, 125–126
"Other," concept of, 63, 66
Outward Bound, 130, 131

Paley, V. G., 41
Palincsar, A. S., 40, 100
Papousek, H., 37
"Pedagogical amnesia" (Shulman), 92, 98
Pedagogical school reform, 3–4, 16, 18–19, 22, 27, 28, 90, 125–126
Peterson, P., 19, 23
Petty, William, 147
Picus, L. O., 179
Pilgrims, 147
Point of view, 188–190, 191
Power of Their Ideas, The (Meier), 200
Praxis, in Head Start, 41–42
Pregnancy, teenage, 21
Principal, original conception of, 70

Private education
  achievement and, 110–111
  Catholic schools, 110–111
  public education versus, 63–64
Process of Education Reconsidered (Bruner), 51
Professional development, 6–7, 8, 91–105, 117–119, 124, 127, 128–129, 203
Progressive school reform, 23, 24, 198–199, 206
Project-based units, 124
Public education
  historical assumptions regarding, 17
  increased access to, 1
  private education versus, 63–64
Purkey, S. C., 176
Putnam, J., 19

Racial segregation, 1
Raftery, J. R., 23
Rakowski, E., 153–154, 156, 157
Raphael, D. D., 160
Ravitch, D., 23, 24
Rawls, J., 150–151, 155–156
Reading achievement, 110
Reading tests, 18
Reagan, Ronald, 164, 194
Reciprocal teaching, 100–101
Reflective approach, 100
Reineke, J., 19
Remediation, by higher education institutions, 7–8, 111
Republican government, 141–143
Restructuring, 130, 131, 193, 194
Ribble, M. A., 36
Rist, R. C., 21
Rodriguez, G., 179
Rogers, D., 25
Rollow, S., 21
Roots and Wings, 130, 131
Rose v. Council for Better Education, 174
Rossmiller, Richard A., 2, 10–11, 166–184, 172, 176, 180
Rothman, R., 18
Rousseau, Jean-Jacques, 143, 150, 159, 160
Rowe, Mary Budd, 7, 93–95, 99
Rudolph, Wilma, 87
Russell Sage Foundation, 43
Russia, 112
Rutherford, K., 102

Salapatek, P., 37
Salmon, R. G., 140
San Antonio Independent School District v. Rodriguez, 173
SAT (Scholastic Assessment Test), 18
Savage Inequalities (Kozol), 190
Scaffolding, 100–101
Scaife, M., 37
Schaps, Eric, 6, 27, 78–79, 83, 86
Scholastic Assessment Test (SAT), 113
School lunches, 65
Schools, 3, 6
    function of, 4, 34
    goals for, 83, 84
Schwab-Stone, M., 77
Schwartz, M., 172
Schweinhart, L. J., 39
Science, 24, 26, 112
Second Treatise of Civil Government (Locke), 159
Sexual activity, 77
Shanker, Albert, 3, 7–8, 93, 107–122, 108, 185, 194–195
Shulman, Lee S., 3, 6–7, 89–106, 90, 91
Silver, H., 147
Site-based management, 19
Sizer, Theodore, 5–6, 27, 44, 64, 67, 78, 187
Skepticism
    habits of mind and, 5–6, 62–63
    toward educational reform, 7–8, 107–119
Slavin, Robert E., 27, 179
Smith, M., 16, 17, 21
Smith, M. S., 176
Social class
    and public versus private school, 63–64
    separate populations based on, 43
Social Contract, The (Rousseau), 159
Social system of schooling, 20–22
    first tier, 20
    second tier, 20
    third tier, 20–22
Soler, P., 179
Solomon, D., 79
Spillane, J., 17
Spindler, G. D., 21
Spiral curriculum (Bruner), 51, 56, 98
Standardized tests, 7–8, 18, 20, 108, 109–110, 112, 113
Standards, 21, 115–117, 124, 127
Stechler, G., 37

Steedman, H., 113
Stevenson, H. W., 41, 116
Stiefel, L., 173, 178
Stigler, J. W., 41, 116
Strang, W., 172
Strayer, G. D., 11, 170–171, 178, 181
Stuart v. School District No. 1, 169
Student(s)
    achievement of. *See* Achievement of students
    at-risk, 36–38, 76–79, 151–152
    dilemma of, 53–58
    educationally deprived, 36–38, 151–152
    interaction between teachers and, 6–7, 89–105
    motivation of, 5, 53–58
Student-centered instruction, 16, 18–19, 25–26, 28, 83, 84
Success for All, 137
Sugerman, S. D., 171
Sullivan, R. J., 145
Sullivan, W. M., 55
Supreme Court, U.S., 173
Swidler, A., 55
Systemic reform. *See* Organizational-effectiveness school reform

Taft High School (Cincinnati), 135
Talbert, J. E., 103
Taxes, 152–153, 158–159, 162–163, 170–172, 173, 175
Teacher(s)
    assessment of, 8, 118
    centrality of, 7
    collaboration among, 8, 116–117
    conferences between family and, 68
    interaction between students and, 6–7, 89–105
    isolation of, 117, 118
    mastery of subject by, 8, 117–118
    professional development and, 6–7, 8, 91–105, 117–119, 124, 127, 128–129, 203
    wait-time and, 7, 93–95
Teacher-centered instruction, 16, 25–26, 28
Teacher training, 116–119
Teaching
    and motivation to learn, 5, 49–58
    and student-centered approach, 16, 18–19, 25–26, 28, 83, 84

and teacher-centered approach, 16, 25–26, 28
Technical schools, 113, 115
Tests, 7–8, 18, 20, 108, 109–110, 112, 113
Texas, 21, 109, 178
Textbooks, international comparison of, 111–112, 116
Thematic-based units, 124
Thomas, M. A., 172
Tinkering Toward Utopia (Tyack and Cuban), 202–203
Tipton, S., 55
Tomain, Joseph P., 3
Total inclusion, 108
Tracking, 65, 115
Tyack, D., 22–24, 27, 195, 197, 198, 202, 203, 206
Tyree, A. K., Jr., 20

United Kingdom, 112
University-school partnerships, 187
Untaught lessons (Jackson), 52, 53
Updegraff, H., 11, 170, 171, 181
Urbanization, 1

Valentine, J., 39
Values, 1–2, 6, 76, 185
    community influence on, 74–76, 78, 84–86
    family influence on, 78
Violence, 77, 189–190
Virginia, 14–15, 43
Voice, 188–190, 192

Voluntary national curriculum, 17–18
Voucher systems, 66
Vredevoogd, J., 19

Wait-time, 7, 93–95
Wales, 112, 113
Waller, Willard, 196, 199
Wallerstein, I., 162
Ward, J. G., 170
Wasik, B. A., 179
Watson, M., 83
Weber, Max, 55
Wehling, Robert L., 3, 9–10, 132–138
Weikart, D. P., 39
Weinfeld, F., 14, 20
Whitman, Walt, 204–205
Whole child approach, 6
    child-centered process and, 83, 84
    Comer Process and, 79–83
Willis, Paul, 54
Wisdom of practice (Hawkins), 7, 13, 91, 92, 94
Wise, A. E., 20, 157
Wonder, Stevie, 87
World Bank, 163
World War I, 24
World War II, 1
Writing achievement, 110

York, R., 14, 20
You Can't Say You Can't Play (Paley), 41

Zigler, E., 39
Zilversmit, A., 26